Outwitting Dogs

Outwitting Dogs

Terry Ryan
and
Kirsten Mortensen

Series Concept Created by Bill Adler, Jr.

THE LYONS PRESS
Guilford, Connecticut
An imprint of The Globe Pequot Press

The Lyons Press is an imprint of The Globe Pequot Press.

10 9 8 7 6 5 4 3 2

Printed in the United States of America

Designed by Stephanie Doyle

ISBN 1-59228-243-1

Library of Congress Cataloging-in-Publication Data is available on file.

To all the dogs we've loved—
those we've outwitted, and those who have outwitted us.

Table of Contents

Introduction   **xi**

1   Outwitting Dogs: It Really Is Possible   **1**

For Anyone Thinking of Getting a Dog . . . ✦ Preparation
Step 1: Picking the Right Dog ✦ Preparation Step 2: Getting
the Right Stuff ✦ Preparation Step 3: Think About Timing ✦
Preparation Step 4: Getting Ready to Train

2   Sizing Up the Challenge:
Why It's Actually Possible to Outwit Dogs   **17**

Who's Training Whom? ✦ An Ounce of Prevention

3   Sooooo Cute—And Such a Pain in the Neck!
Outwitting Puppies   **25**

A Puppy's Developmental Stages ✦ Socialization ✦ The
Older Puppy ✦ A Bit More on Puppies and Training ✦ Fun
and Games

4   Housetraining: Outwitting the Dog Who Needs to Go   **41**

An Outwitting Strategy for Housetraining ✦ Forming Good
Pottying Habits ✦ Your Number One Tool: The Crate ✦
Tethering: Another Option ✦ Use Honey, Not Vinegar ✦
Housetraining Made Easy ✦ When Accidents Happen ✦
Excited Urination ✦ Submissive Urination ✦ Cleaning Up ✦
Using Your Noggin

5   My Shoe! My Shoe! Outwitting the Dog Who Loves to Chew   61
Chewing and Puppies ✦ Training the Chewing Puppy ✦
Boredom, Stress, and Chewing ✦ Bad Habits ✦ Self-Rewarding
Behaviors ✦ Directing Chewing Behavior ✦ Reinforcing
Positive Chewing ✦ Last But Not Least: It's Just Stuff

6   Please Fence Me In!
Guidelines for Making Your Dog's Yard Time Safe   75
Before the Recall, Start with Management ✦ Fences ✦
Tie-Outs ✦ Leashes ✦ The Lure of an Open Door ✦
Training Door Manners

7   Hey—Get Back Here! Outwitting the Dog Who Won't Come   85
The Foundation of a Recall ✦ Introducing the Word *Come* ✦
Practice, Practice, Practice

8   Down! Stop It! Don't Do That!
Outwitting the Dog Who Has Baaaad Manners   99
Setting the Right Expectations ✦ Management ✦ Calm Is
Good ✦ Basic Behaviors That Help with Manners: Sit,
Down, Stay ✦ Sit ✦ Adding the Cue ✦ Down ✦ Stay ✦
Resource Guarding: Prevention Is Best ✦ When You Need
a Little Space ✦ Self-Control

9   Strain, Cough, Lunge:
Outwitting the Dog Who Pulls on Leash Walks   119
What's *Walking Nicely* Mean, Anyway? ✦ The Walk from
a Dog's Perspective ✦ Rewarding a Loose Leash ✦ Special
Tools for Leash Training ✦ Puppies and Leash Walking ✦
Training to Heel

10 Please Don't Leave Me!
Outwitting the Dog Who Hates Being Left Alone   137
Know Your Dog ✦ Preventing Future Problems ✦ Other
Ideas for Your Home-Alone Training ✦ When Separation
Is a Serious Problem . . . ✦ A Question of Degree ✦

Management ✦ Desensitization ✦ Beware the Unintentional
Reward ✦ Other Ideas to Help with Separation Problems ✦
And Finally, A Word About Leaving Dogs Alone

11 BARKBARKBARKBARK:
Outwitting the Dog Who Barks Too Much   **155**

Hey, Hey, Hey! ✦ Why Bark? Why Now? ✦ The Big Picture ✦
Helping the Anxious or Frightened Barker ✦ Desensitization
for Barkers ✦ Last But Not Least: Relax

12 Best-Friend-in-Training:
Outwitting the Dog Who Isn't Nice to Other People   **173**

Understanding Your Dog's Reactions ✦ Socialization: The
First Step ✦ But Even If You Start Late . . . ✦ How's Your
Dog Doing Today? ✦ Easy Does it ✦ Associating People with
Good Things ✦ Desensitizing Trips to the Vet ✦ A Little
Help from Your Friends ✦ Avoid Creating a Dog Who Bites ✦
If Your Dog Has Already Bitten

13 Why Can't You Be Friends?
Outwitting the Dog Who Isn't Nice to Other Dogs   **191**

The Dark Side—Or Is It? ✦ In Dog Terms (Or as Close as
We Can Get) ✦ Observing Your Dog ✦ Training: Help for
the Reactive Dog ✦ Offensive vs. Defensive ✦ Why Pay
Attention? ✦ Communication Between Dog and Dog ✦
Talking to Your Dog ✦ They Don't Necessarily Want to
Fight ✦ So What Can We Do?

14 Now for a Real Challenge:
Outwitting Kids and Dogs at the Same Time   **207**

A Boy and His Dog ✦ Supervision, Supervision, Supervision
✦ Resource Guarding: Special Hot Spot ✦ Management ✦
Hey, Kids: No Misbehavin' ✦ Manners ✦ Happy Practice ✦
Bringing Home Baby ✦ Toddlers ✦ Older Children ✦ Kids
and Dogs: Not Impossible After All

15 There Goes the Neighborhood:
   When the Problem Is Next Door   229
   I Just Love Your Dog, But . . . ✦ Managing Unwanted
   Behaviors: Barking, Toileting, and Loose Dogs ✦ Training
   Someone Else's Dog ✦ Dogs with Bad Manners ✦ Close
   Encounters with Loose Dogs ✦ Know the Law ✦ When Your
   Dog Is Leashed—and the Other Dog Isn't

16 Tools, Tricks, and Something Different:
   When Basic Outwitting Strategies Seem Too Easy   241
   Just a Bit of Theory ✦ Clicker Training ✦ Capturing Behaviors
   ✦ Shaping: When a Behavior Is Only Close ✦ Adding the Cue
   ✦ Behavior Chains ✦ A Few More Tips for Effective Clicker
   Training ✦ Tricks for Treats

17 Outwitting Dog Trainers (And You Thought
   This Book Wouldn't Help You Outwit Other People)   259
   What You See Is What You'll Get ✦ Old Theory Isn't
   Always Good Theory ✦ Puppy Classes ✦ Stand Up for
   What You Believe ✦ So Where'd You Go to School? ✦ Do
   You Need a Behaviorist?

Appendix   267

Index   271

Introduction

Dogs. How we love them. How cute they can look. Those big brown eyes. Those soft ears. Innocent as angels. Only one thing: Looks can deceive. Oh, can they deceive. Those little angels—our sweet little angels—can cause all kinds of trouble. Big trouble. The truth is, those "little angels" can have the upper hand before you can say "Golden Retriever."

What kind of trouble, you ask? Well, it depends on the dog. Some have been known to claim entire houses as their personal toilets. Others specialize in eating furniture. Or knocking people over just to say hello. Or chasing visitors away, including some who are supposed to be there, like mail deliverers. Or repair people. Or your in-laws.

The fact is, dogs are animals. When you think about it, that may be the reason we like them so much. They're like us, but they're also very different. They see the world differently than we do. They solve certain problems differently than we do. They communicate differently than we do.

We like them, even love them. But sometimes we get into trouble because after we invite them into our homes, they turn around and behave—like animals.

A National Obsession?

According to the American Pet Products Manufacturers Association, 40 million American households include at least one dog. That's 39 percent of households. The APPMA also reports that, on average, if you own any pet, it will cost you $460 per year. The biggest chunk of that will be veterinary care, followed by food, then other supplies.

One big difference between dogs and humans is language. Yes, dogs can learn to associate certain human words with certain behaviors or opportunities. Your dog may well learn what "Want to take a walk?" means. Hopefully, your dog will also learn that when you say "sit" or "down" or "give," you expect the dog to respond in certain ways.

But dogs don't learn language the way people do. We have to teach them to associate words with particular behaviors. And this takes a bit of technique—plus repetition, practice, and consistency. And even under the best circumstances, there's always a chance your dog will get something wrong. There are plenty of dogs out there who think "Come! Come!" really means "Run! Run!"

To make matters even more complicated, dogs can be very, very tricky. When they want something, they can be awfully clever about getting it. Their problem-solving skills can be amazing. And they can learn the difference between breaking a rule and getting caught breaking a rule. You can call it sneaky if you like, but in reality, it's doggy smarts.

The good news is that, fortunately, most humans are smarter than most dogs. Just by virtue of your having begun to read this book, you're proving that you're pretty far up the intelligence scale. (Ever catch your dog reading a book?) Your brain is many times larger than a dog's. You're capable of certain kinds of thinking, like abstraction and rational analysis, that dogs are not.

In other words, you have what it takes to outwit a dog.

Chapter 1

OUTWITTING DOGS:
IT REALLY IS POSSIBLE

A Canadian psychologist is selling a video that teaches you how to test your dog's IQ. Here's how it works: If you spend $12.99 for the video, your dog is smarter than you.

—Jay Leno

If you're going to get a dog, there's something you need to face: Some amount of accommodation is inevitable. You're going to have to give something up. Maybe lots of things.

Now, it may be that you already realize this, because you already have a dog. At this point, the first thing to do is take a deep breath and relax. Your life has changed. Well, half the battle is your mental attitude. You can get through this.

But what if you don't have a dog yet? Maybe you're only *thinking* about it at this point. Maybe the kids are begging you for a dog and you're about to give in. Or maybe you're a "cat person" who's just proposed marriage to a "dog person" and you want to know what you're up against. Or maybe you had a dog as a kid, and now that you're an adult you'd like to get one again. Your parents did all the training the first time; now you want an idea of how to go about it yourself before you take the plunge.

Whatever the situation is, you have your routine, your living space, your stuff. You probably have a job or will at some point in the next 10 or 15 years. You may have other pets, who may, incidentally, look like food or toys to a dog.

So let's take a look at how bringing a dog into your life is going to change it.

For Anyone Thinking of Getting a Dog . . .

Dogs are dependent. They have physical needs that crop up every few hours, regardless of your mood or your schedule. They're social animals. They aren't happy if left alone for long periods of time. They're active animals. They can't be confined for too long, and if you don't give them things to do they'll make up their own fun. In other words, they're demanding.

Dogs also have their little quirks. They love to chew, for example. Chewing, to a dog, is as fun as watching television or reading a book is to a human. It's great recreation. It's a way to relax. It's what dogs like to do when there's nothing else going on. What's more, dogs aren't born knowing the difference between a $2 piece of rawhide and a $2,000 leather chair. They both chew real good, to a dog.

Another quirk about dogs: They aren't very good with flush toilets. To them, the ground is a toilet. And from a dog's perspective, the ground includes the floors inside your house—unless you teach your dog the difference.

So what does that mean to you? It means that, before you get that dog, you need to prepare yourself mentally. From now on, your routine is going to revolve, to some extent, around your dog. You're going to have to adjust your life to make sure your dog gets enough exercise, potty breaks, training, and attention. Every day. And while you're at it, you should prepare yourself mentally for the possibility of seeing some of your stuff get damaged, especially if your new friend is coming as a puppy.

There are some extreme steps you can take to minimize your risks. You could, for example, buy a house that is completely tiled inside, with drain holes in the floor of each room, kind of like the shower room at the local health club. That way, if you run into a little trouble house-training your dog, no problem—just hose things down.

You may also think about selling any furniture that's worth any money or storing any that has sentimental value. Replace it with junk you pick up on the curb on garbage day and presto: No more worrying about a dog gnawing on a chair leg.

Outside, you could consider replacing your flower beds and lawn with gravel. Then if your dog wants to dig, who cares? Just rake the stones once a week or so to level things out, and you're done. (No more mowing, either!)

Okay, so these options sound a bit extreme. Plus, if you have any other humans living with you, they might object.

So what's a more reasonable way to prepare?

The first step, odd as it may sound, is to pick the right dog. Get this step right, and you solve a whole bunch of problems—by avoiding them in the first place.

Preparation Step 1: Picking the Right Dog

To pick the right dog, you need to understand what type of dog will best fit you, your family, and your lifestyle. Suppose you're shopping for a purebred dog. And suppose you're a couch potato who thinks opening the refrigerator door qualifies as an aerobic workout. You'd be crazy to adopt a dog bred for physical work. Dogs bred to hunt (like Weimaraners or coon hounds) or herd (like Border Collies or Australian Shepherds) are often high-energy animals who need hours of exercise a day. If they don't get that exercise, they might find other ways to burn off their energy, like eating your walls—while you're trying to catch a nap.

If, on the other hand, you jog 12 miles a day and think power-climbing mountains is a great way to spend your weekends, don't pick a little lapdog who was bred to sit quietly and warm the legs of royal courtiers. The little guy will struggle to keep up with you. Unless you plan on carrying him while you scale your peaks.

Part of what we're talking about here is what dog people call temperament. Think of it as a dog's basic personality. Dogs can be lively and high-energy, or laid-back. They can be outgoing or introverted. Some welcome new experiences. Others take a wait-and-see attitude about new things.

For those of us who want to bring dogs into our homes as companions, temperament is perhaps the most important consideration.

So how do you go about finding a dog with the right temperament for you?

You can start by researching breeds. Look for books on dog breeds—there are many.

Then, as you narrow your search, talk to reputable breeders with experience in the breeds that interest you. A reputable breeder is one who deliberately breeds animals for particular traits. These traits may include looks, if the breeder breeds primarily to produce show dogs. It may be the dogs' ability to do a certain type of work. For example, some Labrador Retriever breeders select their breeding stock for retrieving ability.

Other breeders breed purebred dogs specifically as pets. These breeders are less concerned with how a dog looks, and more concerned with whether their dogs will make good companion animals.

A person is not considered a reputable breeder if he has a couple of purebred dogs and figures puppies are a good way to make a little extra money.

Why does this matter? Because temperament is partly the result of breeding—genetics. And conscientious breeders pay attention to temperament. They don't just throw any old male and female dog together to make puppies. They consider the dogs' temperaments—and the temperaments of their parents and grandparents—and how it will affect the puppies.

This is true even when breeders breed for show. Each breed's American Kennel Club (AKC) standard describes what that breed's temperament should be, right along with descriptions of the dog's coat, head shape, and other physical characteristics. Fox Terriers are supposed to be "gay, lively and active." A Puli should be "affectionate, intelligent and . . . sensibly suspicious." A Newfoundland should exhibit "sweetness of temperament."

Because their show dogs have to exhibit the right temperament, show breeders need to know their breed's ideal temperament. And they need to develop animals who have that temperament. So these breeders have a wealth of information about the temperament of their chosen breeds.

Another important resource for learning about breed temperament is rescue organizations. These are not-for-profit, volunteer, breed-specific groups that foster and place dogs who need homes. In many cases, their dogs have ended up in rescue because they were a poor match for their original homes. So rescue groups have lots of information about what can go wrong with their breeds. After all, they don't want your future dog to end up with them.

If you have Internet access, you can find online mailing lists that are breed-specific. Find them by doing a search or visiting a service, like Yahoo!, that hosts online groups. The members of these lists share common interests in particular breeds. Many have owned a particular breed of dog for some time, and will share information about the breed's temperament. One word of caution, however, when consulting this type of source. Anyone can give advice. But their information may or may not be valid. Some of it may be based on data, but some may be anecdotal. Take any information you glean from this type of source with a degree of skepticism.

You can also find books and Web site questionnaires that will help you match your lifestyle and other preferences to particular breeds of dog. These resources are helpful, but can't replace talking to people who have actually owned the breed.

Of course, temperament is only one factor you should consider. The size of the dog also matters. If you live in a studio apartment, a Saint Bernard may make things a bit crowded. If your home is a sprawling Montana ranch, a bigger dog would fit nicely. (Of course, size can take a backseat to temperament on this count as well: A small dog with a lively temperament can take up more space than a laid-back larger dog.)

Particular breeds of dogs also may have little quirks. As one example, there are herding dogs, like Welsh Corgis and Australian Cattle Dogs, who were originally bred for cattle droving. These dogs were supposed to help move cows from place to place, and they did it by nipping at the cows' heels. This is fine if you need to move cattle. But it's trouble when these dogs nip at the heels of running children. Kids don't like it very much, and you probably won't, either. You can minimize this tendency through training, but it isn't easy. So if you have kids, and you're not up for the hassle, pick another type of dog.

Some breeds of dog tend to be more vocal than others.

Grooming needs are another consideration. Long-haired dogs require frequent, if not daily, brushing. Some breeds, like Poodles, have hair that grows continually. It needs to be trimmed periodically or it will grow out of control. Other dogs never need their coats trimmed—because they shed all the time.

These characteristics all refer to purebreds. But suppose you plan to get a mixed breed? Sometimes you can guesstimate a dog's characteristics by what breed (or breeds) he most closely resembles. If the dog has a German Shepherd coat and upright ears, for example, he may have a Shepherd's temperament and exercise needs. If the dog has a Pit Bull's head, it may have a Pit Bull's drive and tenacity. And so on. If you're adopting from an animal shelter, ask the staff what the dog's lineage might be. If you're adopting from a neighbor or your cousin on the farm, ask about the dog's parents. Take some time to consider what the dog's breed heritage might be.

Considering a breed's general characteristics is, however, only a start. Within any breed there will be individual variations in temperament. Border Collies are known to be high-energy dogs, but that doesn't mean there isn't a Border Collie out there, somewhere, who would prefer to sleep 23 hours a day. Golden Retrievers are usually thought of as mellow, friendly love muffins, but there is probably a Golden somewhere who is fearful and high-strung.

Thinking Outside the Breed

Learning about breed characteristics is helpful. But it can also tempt us to draw conclusions about dogs that don't always match reality.

When our son Kyle was eight years old, we had a young English Cocker who was great at scent tracking. She was so good, in fact, that she easily earned her American Kennel Club "Tracking Dog Excellent" title.

After a while, word got out with the county sheriff's department that an ace tracking dog lived at our house. So one night the sheriff called to see if I'd go out on a search for an escaped felon. When Kyle—who had helped me train the dog by laying out track for her to practice on—learned that I'd refused, he was mortified. "Mom, it would be way cool if she found the bad guy!"

"But Kyle," I said, "the sheriff probably thinks we still have German Shepherds. He'd laugh himself silly if I showed up with a little English Cocker."

Kyle wasn't dissuaded. "Mom, she could be an undercover police dog!"

And you know, Kyle had a point. When we think of police dogs, we think of German Shepherds, or perhaps other large breeds like Rottweilers or Doberman Pinschers. But sometimes it helps to question our assumptions about breeds—otherwise we might overlook a dog's true talents.

T. R.

In fact, any given individual dog may tend to be confident or fearful, aggressive or laid-back, spirited or quiet, open to new experiences or happier with the tried and true. Some dogs are naturally receptive to making new friends. Others are, by nature, wary of strangers. To a certain extent, you can modify these tendencies through training. But it's far wiser to select an individual dog born with traits you need in a pet. If you teach piano lessons in your home, for example, and you get a dog who tends to mistrust strangers, you've put tremendous pressure on yourself as a dog owner. It's a big enough challenge to train the basics, like where to potty and when to sit. Don't add an extra burden by picking a dog who comes with special training needs.

So how do you figure out whether that individual dog you're considering has the right temperament for you? Unless you're experienced with dogs, the best thing to do is ask someone who has seen a lot of them. If you're adopting a dog from a shelter, be honest with the staff about your tolerance for certain characteristics. Tell them if you think a hyper, barky dog will drive you bonkers or is just what you're looking for to liven up your life. Then let them guide you to a dog they have observed to have the temperament you want.

Do the same if you're adopting from a breeder.

One thing you should try to avoid is to adopt a "puppy mill" dog from a pet store. The goal of puppy mills is to turn out large numbers of puppies for a profit. As a result, the puppies' socialization, health, and other needs may be neglected.

And this can have negative consequences for you later. As one example, consider housetraining. One of the biggest advantages you have when it's time to housetrain a puppy is that most puppies try not to soil their beds (we'll explain more about this in chapter 4). When puppies are first born, their mother keeps their bed clean by eating their feces. She herself leaves the bed when she needs to potty. Then, when the puppies get older, they will leave the bed to potty as well. This appears to be instinctive behavior: Dogs naturally want to keep their sleeping area clean.

Now, suppose you have a situation where the mother dog and her puppies can't leave their bed. This is often true at puppy mills, where dogs are kept in small cages or crates. In this case, the puppy will be living in a dirty bed. The puppy will be sleeping and playing in his feces and the feces of his mother and littermates. As a result, the natural tendency of the puppy to keep his den clean may be lost. So when that puppy, months later, goes home to live with a human, housetraining becomes much more difficult.

Dogs bred in puppy mills may also have missed out on important socialization. Ideally, puppies should be exposed to a variety of experiences before 16 weeks of age. For example, they should be introduced to normal household activities and sounds, like vacuuming, doorbells, and television noise. When puppies have these kinds of experiences from the start, they tend to be more flexible and tolerant later on.

In fact, conscientious breeders will deliberately expose their puppies to all kinds of experiences. This makes your job easier, because you're less likely to end up with a dog who freaks out when you open an umbrella or slam the car door.

This doesn't mean you shouldn't ask questions, even if you buy from a small breeder. For example, did the puppies live in the breeder's home, or were they kept in a barn or kennel? If the puppies were isolated from normal household routines and human contact, you should strongly consider going elsewhere to pick your dog.

If you're looking in an animal shelter, there may be no way to know the history of the dog. In that case, pay attention to how the dog behaves and reacts to the environment. Spend time with the dog before you make a final decision. Observe her closely. What does she do if she sees something unusual? Flinch and run away? Or run up to sniff it? When you talk and try to play, does the dog pay attention or ignore you? Does she seem nervous and jumpy or relaxed? To some extent, the answer to these questions will depend on the environment. A dog in a shelter may, for example, be overwhelmed or anxious. Try taking the dog out for a walk around the shelter grounds to observe her away from the noisy kennels. Another factor is the dog's age. Sometimes dogs calm down a bit as they get older. Allow for these variables as you look for clues to the dog's temperament.

Preparation Step 2: Getting the Right Stuff

Once you've picked your dog, the next step is to prepare your home. Here's the basic stuff you'll need to be ready for your dog:

+ Food.

+ Food and water dishes.

+ Treats.

+ Chew toys.

+ Collar.

+ Leash.

+ Crate.

FOOD

There are numerous choices for feeding your dog. There's the dry and canned stuff you can pick up at your local supermarket. There are premium brands of commercial dog food carried by dealers and pet supply stores. There are special formulations of commercial dog foods for puppies, overweight dogs, seniors, and dogs with particular health problems.

The majority of commercial dog food brands are made of a combination of grain by-products and meat by-products from rendering plants. Some specialty brands use only food-grade ingredients; these tend to be expensive because the ingredients cost more. Some dog owners skip the store-bought stuff entirely and feed their dogs homemade meals. A subcategory of this is raw diets, which include uncooked meat and bone.

Because switching diets can cause diarrhea, if you decide to feed your dog a different diet than was provided by the breeder, shelter, or previous owner, make the switch gradually. For example, if you're switching the dog from one brand of commercial dog food to another, for the first week, feed three-quarters of the dog's old food mixed with one-quarter of the new food. The second week, make a 50–50 mix. The third week, feed a quarter of the old food mixed with three-quarters of the new. By the fourth week, your switch will be complete.

If you're switching from commercial dog food to a raw diet, follow the recommendations of someone who has some experience with the transition.

A common mistake many novice dog owners make is to overfeed. Just because your dog acts like he's starving doesn't mean you're not feeding enough. Most dogs act hungry all the time. (As we'll see later, however, this is actually a good thing.) So watch your dog's weight. Ask a vet how to tell if your dog is too fat or too thin and adjust your feedings accordingly.

DISHES

Ceramic or stainless-steel dishes are a good choice for dog food dishes. If you select ceramic, however, make sure it's food-grade ceramic.

Some dishes come with rubberized bottoms so that they don't slide as easily when a dog is eating.

Plastic is okay, but watch if you have a puppy or a devoted chewer. The dish could end up in pieces. In addition, some dogs seem to be allergic to plastic.

Dogs need a constant supply of fresh water. Make sure you pick a water dish that is properly sized to your dog.

TREATS

One of the primary things that motivates dogs is food. Therefore, if you plan to outwit your dog, you'll need to have a good supply of treats on hand. (We'll go into more detail on training with treats in chapter 7.)

Prepackaged treats are an option for special occasions, but not for everyday training: They can be too big, too high-calorie, and too expensive.

Another option is to use your dog's regular dinner food as treats. If you feed kibble, for example, you can reserve some or all of your dog's normal daily diet for training, and use pieces of kibble as training treats.

Some people use "people food," such as bits of cheese or hot dog, for training treats. This is fine if your dog's digestion can tolerate it—and if you keep in mind that your dog needs to eat a balanced diet. It's probably a good idea to keep these kinds of treats to less than 10 percent of your dog's total diet.

Check with your vet if you have any questions about what you should or shouldn't use as treats for your dog.

CHEW TOYS

Dogs love to chew. Puppies love to chew even more. So one of your biggest challenges, as a dog owner, is to make sure your dog chews toys, not your valuable stuff. Don't wait until you've brought your dog home. Stock up on chew toys.

The best chew toys are hard rubber toys that won't come apart. If you give a dog cloth or soft rubber toys, make sure you pay attention. Once they start shredding, take them away or your dog may swallow pieces. (For more on chewing and chew toys, see chapter 5.)

COLLAR

Flat buckle collars are the best choice for puppies. Don't spend a mint on a puppy's collar, however, because your puppy is going to outgrow it in a matter of months. Once your dog is full grown, you may want to invest in a more expensive collar. Rolled leather collars are preferred by some owners because they're gentler on a dog's neck hair. (For more on training collars, see chapter 9.)

LEASH

The basic leash model is leather or woven nylon. Leashes come in various lengths. If you have a small dog, you need a longer leash, because it's farther from your hand to the dog's neck.

It's a good idea to purchase a simple, 6-foot nylon leash for training purposes. Some dog owners also like retractable leashes. These have a release button so you can give your dog extra leash length during walks, if appropriate.

CRATE

A crate serves double duty as both your dog's den and a training tool. It also makes a great, safe way to transport dogs. For these reasons, you'll want to have one on hand when it's time to bring your dog home. For a complete discussion of crates, go to chapter 4.

Preparation Step 3: Think About Timing

Another issue you should consider as you prepare to bring a dog into your life is what your schedule will be like—particularly for the first few days. As you'll see later in this book, a key part of training is learning how to read your dog's behavior. For instance, will he feel comfortable about being left alone, or will it make him feel anxious? You won't have answers to questions like this until you've spent some time with him.

Ideally, you should plan to begin your new life together during a period when you'll be able to spend quite a bit of time with your dog. If you work, for instance, try to arrange to take some vacation days. If you're planning to go out of town, postpone bringing your new dog or puppy home until the trip is over.

The key is to give you and your dog some time together to get to know each other and start some basic training. Chances are, you'll enjoy that time immensely. And you may also find that it gives you a chance to identify potential behavior problems. That's important, because sometimes it's easier to fix behavior problems if you catch them early.

Preparation Step 4: Getting Ready to Train

Now that you've picked what kind of dog you want, and have your shopping list all ready for food, dishes, and the other stuff you'll need, there's one more area you need to consider: training.

So what is dog training, exactly? At first glance, it may seem that training a dog means teaching the dog what certain human words mean. *Sit* means "sit." *Come* means "run up to me." *Drop it* means "let go of that television remote, it's not your toy!"

It's true that associating certain human words with certain dog behaviors is part of training. But in fact, training encompasses much more. Remember, you're bringing an animal into your house. Dogs are active. They don't live in cages like hamsters; they have the run of the place.

Think about what that means. All day long, your dog will be with you, with your human friends and family, around your stuff. How do you want your dog to behave? There's no single answer to this question. It depends on you, your home situation, and what you can tolerate. Most people will be pretty sure they don't want their dogs to get in the habit of pottying indoors. But for other behaviors, you need to figure out how you want your dog to behave.

Here are some things to consider (we'll cover all of these in more detail later).

GREETINGS

How do you want your dog to greet people? Will it be okay if she jumps up on them? Bear in mind that this is a black-and-white question. It's not fair for you to say, "Sometimes it will be okay, but not when my grandmother comes. Or when I'm wearing nylons." If there's a chance Grandma can be knocked over, you'll need to teach your dog to greet people by sitting—all the time.

LEASH MANNERS

What do you want leash walks to be like? If you live in a city or suburb, and you'll be exercising your dog with walks, you need to consider this question. Will it be okay for your dog to pull? Or will you go crazy unless he walks near you so the leash hangs loose?

KIDS

Do you have kids? If so, how do you want your dog to behave with them? Unfortunately, lots can go wrong when you mix dogs and kids, and that's not counting bites. For example, a kid walking around with food looks like a vending machine to a dog.

AND MORE

How do you want your dog to behave when you're catching some downtime? When the phone rings? When you're eating a meal?

When you open the back door, do you want your dog to push out past you or wait until you've gone outside first?

✦ ✦ ✦

These are only a few examples. You can certainly think of more as you reflect on your lifestyle and routine. If you do yoga on the living room rug, for example, maybe you'd rather have a dog who knows to lie down quietly until you're finished, instead of coming up and nosing your ear just when you're about to experience nirvana. If you dislike door-to-door solicitors, you may not want a dog who sleeps when the doorbell rings. And so on.

What these examples should suggest is that training dogs is more than teaching them to respond to a handful of verbal cues like *sit, down,* and *come.* When we bring dogs into our lives, they affect our lives continually, all day, every day. The trick is to shape our dogs' behaviors in ways that will help them fit into our lives successfully.

The good news is that you have what it takes to do this: your brains.

So let's take a closer look at how you, the human, can use your wits to help your dog or puppy become a wonderful companion.

Chapter 2

SIZING UP THE CHALLENGE: WHY IT'S ACTUALLY POSSIBLE TO OUTWIT DOGS

If dogs could talk, it would take a lot of the fun out of owning one.
—Andrew A. Rooney

Before you get started on your dog training program, it's helpful to review how you measure up against your dog. Humans have advantages over dogs. But make no mistake, dogs have advantages over humans, too.

Dogs are canines. Long ago, their ancestors killed animals for food. A lot has changed since then. Thanks to tens of thousands of years of selective breeding, humans have created a more mellow version of these wild animals. Today the domestic dog's instinct to chase and kill other animals is significantly modified. It is "softened."

But that doesn't mean the urge to chase and catch is gone entirely. The mildest little lapdog will still perk up excitedly if a squirrel jumps onto the windowsill. And certain activities can stimulate a dog's chase-and-grab behavior. Throwing a Frisbee is one example. When dogs race around with running kids, that can also stimulate chasing and grabbing.

Should you be afraid of these behaviors? In most cases, no. In most cases, a dog catching Frisbees or romping with children is just being

playful. At the same time, don't kid yourself. Dogs aren't cartoon characters. They aren't people who happen to have four legs and big noses.
They're dogs. They have the quick reflexes and sharp teeth that kept them alive when they were wild animals. Larger dogs are also strong. And just about any dog who's not sick or injured can run faster than a human.

For you, the dog owner, this means two things. First, if you plan to control your dog by being quick and fleet-footed, forget it. You're going to lose, if not every time, then often enough to undermine your training success. Second, if your dog grabs, it will hurt.

Bites Happen . . .

It's unfortunate, but true: Hundreds of thousands of people have to seek medical care for dog bites every year.* Even more people are probably bitten but don't seek treatment.

One lesson from these statistics is that we need to pay attention to how we raise, train, and manage our dogs. We need to find ways to minimize the chances that our dogs will bite. Here's where training technique comes in. See chapter 12 for more information about what you can do to minimize the chances your dog will bite.

* Sacks JJ, Kresnow M, Houston B. Dog bites: how big a problem? *Injury Prevention* 2 (1996), 52–54; http://www.cdc.gov/ncipc/duip/dog4.pdf. Annually in the United States 4.7 million people are bitten by dogs. Of these, approximately 800,000 people require medical attention. That is, each year 1.8 percent of the U.S. population is bitten by a dog, and 0.3 percent seeks medical care for a bite.

Quick reflexes and sharp teeth are two big advantages a dog has. But they aren't all. Dogs are also terrific problem solvers. Say you hate it when your dog strews kitchen garbage all over the floor. So one of your rules is *Stay out of the kitchen wastebasket.* When you see your dog sticking her nose into the wastebasket, you yell and chase her away. Now, to your dog, this is a problem, because to a dog, the kitchen wastebasket is one of the most wonderful, fragrant, intriguing, alluring, intoxicating objects in the whole house (the only exceptions being the kitty litter box and the sandwich your kids left on the coffee table).

So now your dog has a problem. On the one hand, there's this wonderful wastebasket. On the other hand is you, the human who goes nuts when she tries to explore the wastebasket.

So your dog solves the problem. How? She now investigates the kitchen wastebasket only when you're not around. She waits until you're relaxed in the living room, watching television. Then, during a commercial break, you head for the kitchen just in time to see your dog exiting by another door. And of course, there's garbage strewn all over the floor—except the bits your dog decided were edible, of course.

To your dog, the problem is solved. She's had 10 minutes of fun with the kitchen garbage without being yelled at. To you, your dog is being sneaky. Call it what you want. The point is, dogs can, and do, figure out how to get around human rules. It's a talent they've got, and they *will* use it.

So now that we've established that you are physically inferior, and can even be outsmarted by dogs, let's take a look at your strengths.

YOU CONTROL THE GOODIES

There are certain things that dogs really, really want. Food is high on this list. And guess what? You control your dog's access to food. You're the one who fills your dog's dish. You're the one who doles out treats.

You're also the one with the opposable thumbs. You can open doors. When your dog is on a leash, you're the one who decides whether to move or stand still. You're the one who decides how much leash to give your dog—whether to keep him at your side or let him sniff around that tree trunk.

You decide whether to pay attention to your dog or ignore him. You decide when to throw a toy or put it away. You can also reach the itchy places that need scratching.

So if you control the goodies, what does this gain you?

As it turns out, it gains you a lot. In fact, it gets back to one of your dog's strengths—his problem-solving ability. It's a hassle when he wants to get into the kitchen garbage. But you can turn it to your advantage when you want to outwit him.

Take food. If you set it up right, you can present your dog with the perfect problem: how to get you to turn over some food. After all, who says you should be feeding your dog for free? Make him work. In fact, play it right, and you can get your dog to do just about anything you want him to do—by showing him that, if he does the right thing, he'll get food.

You can do this because you have another human advantage.

YOU CAN PLAN FUTURE CONSEQUENCES

Dogs learn primarily by trial and error. Take a dog who learns a clever trick all by herself, like how to open a kitchen cupboard door.

She could never explain the physics involved. She can't tell you that the door is held fast by a magnet or mechanical latch of some kind. And although she probably observed you opening that door, she didn't think to herself, *Hmm. My human uses a hand to open that door. I don't have a hand, but maybe I could try exerting a similar force using my mouth.*

It's far more likely that there's something rewarding, for this particular dog, about opening the cupboard door. Maybe that's where the doggy snacks are stored. Or the kitchen garbage can. Or something else that smells interesting. If that's the case, the dog might see the cupboard door as a problem to be solved.

Or maybe opening the door excites the household humans, which gives the dog a nice little rush in return. Or maybe the dog is simply an active, inquisitive sort, and opening the cupboard door is inherently fun.

Or maybe it's a combination of factors.

Whatever the motivation, what happens next is that the dog starts to experiment with the door. Maybe she paws at it. Or noses it. Or bites at the latch. Sooner or later the door opens. Success! The dog grabs a mouthful of treats, or dumps the garbage can over and snatches a chicken bone. Or runs away from an excited human in a wonderful game of Chase Me. Reward!

Now it's just a matter of replication. It takes some dogs only one or two successes to learn a new "trick" like this one.

But notice how the dog, this very clever dog, learned. It wasn't through theory, or planning, or analysis. It was through attacking the problem head-on and just trying something.

Yes, the dog may use an approach she's learned elsewhere. If a dog can paw open a kitchen cupboard door, she may next try to paw a screen door to the porch, or a crate door, or bedroom door.

But the basis is still straightforward, just-do-it experimentation. The reward flowed naturally out of the experiment's success. The dog didn't place the box of treats in the cupboard so that, if she opened the door successfully, she'd be rewarded. She didn't arrange, ahead of time, for the Chase Me game. Those things just happened.

Humans, on the other hand, can arrange for consequences. We can think ahead. We can arrange outcomes.

The simplest example is to use a food reward when a dog does something you like. You say "sit." Your dog sits. You give your dog a food reward. This doesn't occur in nature. There isn't a "sit bush" out on the savanna somewhere that automatically dispenses pieces of cheese if a dog sits nearby.

You, the human, arranged it. You did so because you're able to think ahead in time. You can imagine your dog actually sitting when you say "sit," and you can plan to have a treat ready before you say "sit," and you can figure out that by rewarding your dog, you'll make it more likely she'll sit the next time you say "sit."

Who's Training Whom?

Which brings up a strange point. If you give your dog a treat for sitting, it's almost like your dog is training you. In fact, you may notice that your dog starts sitting even when you haven't said "sit," in the hope that you'll hand out a treat. You'll be minding your own business, stir-frying your tofu or grilling a hamburger, and suddenly realize your dog is next to you, in a perfect tucked sit, gazing up at you with happy, expectant eyes. And it occurs to you—*My dog has me trained to give out treats when she sits! Yikes!*

Well, you have two choices. You can worry about it. Or you can realize that you have a dog who is going out of her way to please you, because she knows that when she does, nice things happen.

Now, maybe you don't like the idea of giving your dog rewards. Maybe you think *My dog should sit just because she's a dog and I'm the human, anytime I say "sit."* Hey, you're entitled to your opinion. And in many cases, you can completely intimidate a dog until she shrinks into a sit every time you say "sit." But then what do you have? You have a dog who's terrified of you. Your dog doesn't understand why you do what you do. Only that you're scary.

Plus, using intimidation can—and does—backfire with some dogs. Some dogs shut down. They lose their spark. Their spirits are broken. Others become aggressive.

Using rewards, not intimidation, doesn't always come naturally to everyone. It can take a little practice. But it works, and it works beautifully. Many of the top professional animal trainers in the world use rewards, including food rewards. Dolphin trainers, trainers who prepare animals for movie roles, and many leading dog obedience trainers use rewards to shape animals' behaviors.

So when you choose to train this way, you're in excellent company. You're in the company of some of the most successful, most experienced, smartest trainers out there. Please give yourself a treat!

An Ounce of Prevention

Planning consequences isn't just a matter of rewards. It's also important to use your human ingenuity in other ways. The key is that, in every area of your dog's life, you need to set him up for success, not failure.

Training professionals often call this "management." The basic idea is that you can arrange things so that your dog doesn't develop bad habits in the first place. When you do, you make everything else much, much easier.

In fact, that's what outwitting your dog is all about. When you use your brains, you'll be happier. Your dog will be happier. You'll be able to enjoy each other's company. And isn't that what having a dog is all about?

Know Thy Dog

Part of good management is knowing how well your dog can handle certain types of temptation—or stress. You need to observe your dog and set realistic expectations. Sometimes that means being totally honest with yourself about your dog's needs and temperament.

I learned this lesson the hard way. When I was in college, I adopted a high-energy Doberman mix. We developed a close bond from the day I brought her home—and since I didn't know a thing about teaching her to handle being separated from me, that ended up causing us problems.

One day while I was home on break, I borrowed my mom's car to go visit some friends. I took Brett along. I knew she'd be in the car, alone, for a while. But if it worried me, I ignored the warning bells.

Boy, did I live to regret that. When I returned to the car and got in, I couldn't see the windshield. That was because strips of fabric from the car ceiling were hanging down in front of my face. My dog had shredded the interior of my mom's new Oldsmobile Cutlass Salon.

Needless to say, over 20 years later, I still haven't heard the end of it.

The moral of the story: If you suspect your dog might not have the temperament or self-control to deal with a situation, find a way to avoid that situation altogether. In my case, I should have left my dog with my folks. Or crated her in the car with a selection of engrossing chew toys. Instead I set up my dog—and me, as her trainer—for a dismal failure.

K. M.

Chapter 3

SOOOOO CUTE—AND SUCH A PAIN IN THE NECK! OUTWITTING PUPPIES

Well, yes, the puppies dug holes sometimes, and sometimes they rolled on a few plants. But what of it? When hail beats the garden flat, we accept it as an act of God. Well, puppies are an act of God, and one of his very pleasantest. I believe in a balanced universe: some poppies and some puppies. To miss the joy is to miss all.
> —Bertha Damon, "Ruffled Paws"

Oh! Puppies!

Those big, happy eyes. Those oversized paws. Those floppy little bodies. They're irresistible. Even a puppy's breath smells good.

Well, here's a secret. You know why puppies are so darn cute? Because if they weren't absolutely adorable, nobody with any sense at all would ever, in a million years, get anywhere *near* them.

Puppies, besides being cute, are high-energy little creatures, with insatiable curiosity. Sure, they sleep a lot. But when they're not asleep, they seem to spend just about every waking minute making trouble.

Puppies also want attention. A lot of attention. From the minute a puppy is born, she's with her mother and littermates 24 hours a day. Then all of a sudden, she's taken away from her dog family and finds herself left alone sometimes. When puppies are left alone, they're unhappy. And when they're unhappy, they do things humans don't like very much. Like yelp and whimper. And chew on things.

If all this isn't bad enough, puppies are also learning all the time. You can use that to your advantage, of course. You can start training a puppy practically from birth, as a matter of fact. But it can also backfire. The things your puppy learns today may be tomorrow's bad habits.

Take jumping up. It's very cute to have an itty-bitty little eight-week-old Labrador puppy greet everyone by rearing up on her hind legs and pawing. But that itty-bitty Lab is going to grow up into a 75-pound hunk of muscle. And when that happens, jumping up to paw people won't be so cute. It will knock people over. It will ruin their clothes and possibly even cause injury.

Can you train a 75-pound adult dog to stop jumping up on people? Yes, it's possible. But it's a lot easier if you don't let your dog form bad habits in the first place.

A Puppy's Developmental Stages

Have you ever sat down for a conversation with a preschool-aged child? If so, you probably realized two things. First, human children are, in many ways, miniature adults. And second, human children are, in many ways, so different from adults that they could be from another planet. Children see the world differently than adults. They make decisions differently. They distinguish between reality and fantasy differently.

So it should come as no surprise that puppies are more than miniature adult dogs. Yes, they are quite like adult dogs in many ways. But like human children, they have special needs and unique ways of interacting with the world.

Researchers have identified specific developmental stages that puppies go through. Understanding these stages can help us raise puppies that become well-adjusted adult dogs.

THE FIRST TWO WEEKS

Puppies are born blind, deaf, and totally dependent on their mothers. They can smell and taste, but they need their mother and their litter-mates to keep warm. Have you ever watched a litter of newly born pup-pies? When they're hungry, they swim and squirm to their mothers to nurse. When they're sleepy, they sleep in a big pile.

Researchers believe that for the first two weeks or so, most puppy behavior is simply reflexive—an involuntary response to stimuli.

There isn't much humans need to do for puppies at this age. Some studies suggest that exposing very young puppies to slightly stressful ex-periences will help them handle stress better when they're adults. No-body knows for certain if this works. And in any case, most of us won't be meeting such young puppies.

WEEKS THREE AND FOUR

Around the third week or so, puppies' ears and eyes open completely. They start to see. If you move an object in front of them, they'll move their eyes and turn their heads to watch it.

The puppies' baby teeth start to show, and they begin to experiment with lapping and chewing.

It's at this stage that puppies start to show some bladder and bowel control. Newborn puppies depend on their mothers to relieve them-selves. By licking her puppies, the mother dog stimulates them to uri-nate and defecate. But by week three or four, puppies begin to potty by themselves.

Young puppies seem to make an effort to potty away from their sleeping spot. They seem to have a natural tendency to stay clean. It's also believed that, if puppies are prevented from doing this, they can lose this tendency. This can have consequences later: As we discussed in the last chapter, the puppies may be harder to housetrain.

Puppies at this age also appear to begin to interact socially. They may nudge or paw at their littermates. Their human caretakers may also begin introducing them to new experiences, such as radio or television noise. However, puppies at this age are still very dependent on their mother and littermates for their development.

WEEKS FOUR THROUGH EIGHT

At around the third and fourth week of a puppy's life, he enters a period in which socialization becomes critical. The socialization period is a developmental period that begins around the end of the first month in a puppy's life and ends around the 16th week. During this period, the puppy begins to sort out when experiences are okay and when things may be threatening.

Ideally, the puppy's caretaker (which may be you, if you adopt a six- to eight-week-old puppy) will use this time to expose him to a rich variety of experiences. It's critical, however, that this happen in a way that is nonthreatening to the puppy.

For example, one thing that can seem threatening to some puppies is the noise of a vacuum cleaner. So a good exercise during the puppy's socialization period would be to expose the puppy to vacuum cleaner noise.

The key is to make sure that, as you do this, the puppy never appears anxious or frightened. If necessary, you may need to keep the vacuum cleaner a long way away from the puppy, or muffle its motor with blankets. You'll know you're okay if your puppy either ignores the sound entirely or walks up to the vacuum confidently to investigate. Then, as the puppy becomes used to the muffled and/or distant vacuum cleaner noise, you can try running the motor without the blankets and/or moving it closer. As long as the experience never becomes too intense, too fast, your puppy will learn that vacuum cleaners are okay.

To succeed at this, it's important to learn to read your puppy for signs of anxiety. See chapter 10 for more information on how to do that.

Of course, life for a dog involves more than the sound of vacuum cleaners. A puppy's socialization period should be enriched with a wide variety of experiences, from exposure to household noises and the sound of thunderstorms, to being around different dogs—again, with the caveat that this be done in a way that doesn't frighten the puppy or make him anxious.

One of the most basic experiences a puppy needs is exposure to people. Research suggests that puppies form attachments to people most easily when they are between six and eight weeks of age. For this reason, it's important that puppies of this age are handled daily by people. Conscientious breeders will make sure their puppies get some time in their homes as well, so they start getting used to human noises and activities.

BITE INHIBITION

During the second month, puppies also learn another important lesson: how much pressure to exert when they playbite.

Playbiting and mouthing are natural for puppies. As they play with each other, however, sometimes a puppy bites too hard. The bite-ee responds, naturally, with a loud and startling yelp. If the biter persists, the puppy being bitten will quit the game and go away.

The bite-ee's reaction helps train the biter. The biter learns that gentle playing is rewarded with more play. Hard biting has a different consequence—startling noises or even the end of the game.

This is one reason why it's important for young puppies to be left with their littermates. Puppies teach each other bite inhibition. Later, these early lessons will help the puppy play more gently with humans.

(See chapter 5 for more on chewing and on improving bite inhibition, if your puppy mouths too hard during play.)

EARLY COMMUNICATION SKILLS

The second month is also a time when puppies begin developing more complex social behaviors. At this age some puppies seem to begin showing submissive behaviors. Others seem to show pushy behaviors. This suggests that they are beginning to use body language to communicate with each other. However, puppies at this age also appear to trade roles with one another. For example, one puppy might chew another's ears for a while, then lie down and let another puppy chew hers.

Socialization

So how old should your puppy be before you bring him home?

Puppies learn a lot about life from their littermates. These skills will help the puppy form appropriate relationships with other dogs later. At the same time, leaving a puppy with his litter for too long may make it harder for him to form relationships with people—especially if he doesn't have much contact with people. So if you're shopping for a puppy, it's best to find one 8 to 12 weeks old. This gives you the best chance of proactively socializing your new companion.

Although your puppy's littermates (and, hopefully, former human caretaker) got the socialization ball rolling, there's still a lot to do.

In fact, giving your puppy a rich variety of positive life experiences during his socialization period is arguably the most important type of training you can do at this point. There's a window, during your puppy's development, during which these types of experiences have their greatest effect. They literally influence the way your puppy's brain develops. Miss this opportunity, and it may be difficult to make it up later. Right now, your puppy is a little sponge, soaking up information about what is normal and what is not. Later it becomes much harder to teach a dog that something that appears odd isn't unusual at all.

One of the ways you can take advantage of this window is to handle your puppy in gentle, nonthreatening ways. Use these games to expose your puppy to the types of experiences that she'll encounter for the rest of her life, like being picked up, having her teeth checked and nails clipped, and being bathed.

Here are some handling exercises to work on with your puppy:

+ **Picking her up.** Pick up your puppy, making sure to support her body. The one rule of this exercise: Never put her down *unless* she's being still. If you put her down while she's kicking and wiggling, she may learn that *kicking and wriggling gets me put down*. What you want her to learn is that *being still is rewarded by being put down*.

✦ **Touching her mouth.** Dampen a square of gauze with water. Hold your puppy in your lap and use the gauze to massage her gums. Touch her teeth and mouth with your fingers. This gets your puppy used to the sort of handling she'll later experience during vet visits.

✦ **Handling her collar.** Handle your puppy's collar frequently. Pretend to check to see if it is too loose or too tight.

✦ **Touching all over.** Touch your puppy on the legs, backside, belly, and other parts of her body.

✦ **Touching her feet.** Because your puppy will need to have her toenails trimmed regularly for the rest of her life, be sure to get her used to having her feet handled. Hold her in your lap and touch her toes. If she reacts calmly to that, try holding her feet and manipulating her toes. If she doesn't like that, stop and go back to just touching them.

✦ **Bathing.** Put just a little water in a sink, and put your puppy "uphill" from the water, so she stays dry. Pretend-bathe her with a warm, damp cloth. Splash in the water so it makes splashy noises. Let her sniff some puppy shampoo.

As you do these kinds of exercises, make sure you're protecting your puppy from being frightened or overwhelmed. It's a fine line, but an important one: Puppies who are exposed to experiences in a nonthreatening way are more likely to become resilient and confident. But puppies who are exposed to experiences that frighten them may become fearful, timid, wary, or "reactive" (meaning they show an exaggerated reaction) to those types of experiences in the future.

The key is to expose them to lots of experiences—but don't expose them to experiences that cause them to cross the line and become anxious or afraid. Become a careful observer of your puppy's reactions. As you expose your puppy to new experiences—whether it's handling her feet, riding in a car, or walking down a crowded street and seeing and smelling different animals—watch her body language for signs that she's becoming uncomfortable. (See chapter 10 for a description of behaviors that suggest discomfort or anxiety.) If you detect that your puppy is becoming uncomfortable, stop. Remove her. Then find a way to expose her to that experience more gradually.

For example, does your puppy seem uncomfortable around crowds of people? Start by approaching one or two strangers at a time. As your puppy builds up confidence, try visiting a park where there are lots of people—only don't get too close to them.

It's also important to give your puppy the leeway to adjust the space between himself and strangers. If he wants to back away from someone, let him. Don't restrain him on a leash, or hold him up to people—you want him to feel he has some control over how close he gets.

Later—if your puppy is comfortable with it—you can move closer to larger groups of people, and so on. Simply match your socialization schedule to your puppy's reactions.

As you work on socialization, don't forget to expose your puppy to people with different appearances. Examples include men with beards, people wearing hats or carrying umbrellas, people of different ethnic backgrounds, and people in wheelchairs. See chapter 12 for more on how to help your puppy get along with all kinds of people.

It's also important to expose your pup to children of all ages, including babies and toddlers. Still, this part of socialization has unique challenges. You need to make sure the children treat your puppy appropriately, for one thing. See chapter 14 for more on outwitting kids and dogs at the same time.

As you get to know your puppy, you may notice that her reactions change. Sometimes puppies go through periods when they seem more fearful. Don't assume that just because your puppy was comfortable in a situation once, she will be tomorrow or next week. Keep your eye on her. Be ready to back off if she shows signs of anxiety.

Another question that puppy owners often ask is whether it's safe to take puppies on outings before they are fully immunized against diseases like distemper. It's best to ask your veterinarian. In some cases, vets will suggest you carry your puppy in your arms for the first few weeks. Just be aware that proper socialization, during this period of your puppy's development, is critically important.

THAT FIRST VET VISIT

Speaking of veterinarians, as you socialize your puppy, don't forget vet trips.

Visiting a vet can be downright traumatic to dogs. For starters, the vet is often the place where dogs are immunized—and shots can hurt. Other things vets do may also be unpleasant to dogs. Vets handle dogs' feet. They hold mouths open. They look in ears.

The risk is that your puppy will decide that vet offices are terrible places. The puppy may even decide that vets are terrible people. Every vet has stories of dogs who try to bite them—chances are, they're dealing with dogs who believe veterinarians are threatening or scary. Sadly, once a dog has reached this point, the vet may require the dog to be muzzled or even sedated.

Fear and Trembling

My first dog, Brett, developed a terrible anxiety about vet visits. As soon as we got out of the car, she would start to shake and put her tail between her legs. In the waiting room, she would strain on her leash toward the door. Once the visit was over, she would practically drag me outside.

So when I got a new puppy, I decided I would make vet visits fun. Whenever we went to the vet for a checkup, I would load up on treats.

I'd feed my puppy constantly throughout the visit. As a result, I now have a dog who thinks vet visits are wonderful social outings—complete with hors d'oeuvres!

K. M.

OTHER DOGS

Helping your puppy become comfortable with all kinds of people is important. But it's also important to help your puppy become comfortable around other dogs.

During puppies' first few weeks, they begin to develop rudimentary dog communication skills. It takes more than a few weeks' practice, however, for dogs to become fluent in these skills.

So how will he learn? Practice, practice, practice. But just as you need to be careful about socializing your pup in other situations, control this learning experience as well. If your puppy gets bullied, you might end up with a dog who's afraid of other dogs. You also don't want your puppy to become a bully.

A great way to manage the situation is to pick a well-mannered adult dog as a playmate for your puppy. This type of dog will teach your puppy what behaviors are acceptable.

But What Does Bullying Look Like?

When dogs play with each other, they don't break out a deck of cards or start a game of catch. They chase each other. They knock each other down. They playbite. If you haven't been around dogs a lot, this can look pretty rough—even disturbing. Rest assured. Most of the time, to the dogs, it's pure fun.

On the other hand, sometimes bullying looks a lot like innocent playing. It can be hard to tell when a game of chase or a wrestling match has turned ugly.

So how do you tell the difference?

A good way to do this is to watch both dogs' reactions. Consider a game of chase. Did the dog who is being chased initiate the game? Did she approach the other dog, maybe playbow (forequarters to the ground, hindquarters up, tail wagging), then leap toward the other dog in a pretend jab and dart away? If this was how the game started, the fun is probably mutual.

Next, how does the chase-ee behave while being chased? What is her body language? Does she look happy, or frightened? If her tail is between her legs, if she runs to her human for protection or otherwise seems scared or anxious, then the game has crossed the line into bullying. It's time for people to intervene and break it up, perhaps by putting the chaser on a leash for a while until everybody calms down.

The Older Puppy

Once a puppy has reached the 16-week mark, he's probably made some important conclusions about the world. He has a good idea about what's normal and what's strange. At this point, technically, he's passed out of his socialization period. But don't stop exposing him to positive experiences. Your puppy is still learning. If you stop giving him these experiences, he may lose his newfound confidence.

You may also find some new challenges arise in the coming months. Dogs hit sexual maturity as early as six months. But from a behavior standpoint, they may not mature until they are one or two years old (owners of more exuberant breeds might amend this to four, six, or ten years old).

Some dogs seem to go through periods that are not unlike human adolescence. For example, young puppies are natural followers. But as they mature, they may become more independent and self-reliant. The outside world becomes more interesting. You may find it harder to get your pup's attention—especially when there are new things to explore.

It may also seem, at times, like early training lessons are suddenly forgotten. The puppy who always comes when called suddenly runs the other way. You say "sit" and your half-grown dog looks at you like you're nuts—like she's never heard the word before.

Some people call this "the seven-month crazies," but the reality is that not all dogs go through this stage at the same time. The key is to be ready for it, if—and when—it happens. If you spot some teenager-ish shenanigans, keep your cool and remain consistent. Most important, don't let your dog's new experiments become tomorrow's bad habits. If you notice your dog backsliding on training, pretend you're starting over from scratch. Pretend you never worked on the sit and start teaching it all over again. The good news is, you'll find the learning comes quicker the second time.

And one other, related point. Training your dog is an ongoing process. It's not realistic to think you can work on training for the first 6 months, or 12 months, or 36 months of her life, and then you're done.

Instead, you should plan to work with your dog for the whole of her life. Sure, there will probably be a time when she becomes wonderfully fluent at the behaviors you've trained. But she'll still need to practice them from time to time.

A Bit More on Puppies and Training

Back in the olden days, "the experts" sometimes advised dog owners to not bother training puppies. That's advice that's no longer given. Puppies, like human children, learn very quickly. And early training can establish good, solid habits that will last a dog's lifetime.

Some of the behaviors you may want to work on are those that will make your puppy a compatible member of your family. Teaching these behaviors does two things. It helps your puppy begin to learn self-control. And it ensures that you have some ability to control your puppy if you need to. Some examples might be:

+ Sit.

+ Down.

+ Come (recall).

+ Leave it (leave an object alone).

You'll find tips for training these behaviors later in the book.

You should also begin working on housetraining as soon as your puppy comes home (see chapter 4).

Puppyhood is also the right time to introduce a different kind of training: training that can help prevent problems from cropping up later. One of the most important is preventing resource guarding, a behavior in which dogs or puppies snatch, growl, bare their teeth, or even bite to protect something they have claimed as theirs—such as food, dinner dishes, toys, beds or sleeping spots, or even "their" people.

One way to help prevent this kind of behavior is training exercises that help your puppy get used to letting you take things away. You also want to avoid games that teach your dog to withhold objects from you.

1. **Never play Keep Away.** If your puppy has a toy and is playing Keep Away—running away from you or dodging you to try to get you to chase—don't play. Ignore the pup. Turn away—and promise yourself you'll begin the next two exercises later in the day.

2. **Your on and off button.** This exercise teaches your puppy that giving up a toy means "playtime!" To do it, you need a long tug toy or a ball on a rope. You can make a suitable training toy by tying a ball into the toe of a short length of nylon stocking or an old sock. The ball should be small enough to grab, but large enough to avoid choking your pup. The nylon or sock should be long enough so that a 5- or 6-inch "handle" will dangle outside the pup's mouth when she holds the ball.

   First, let your puppy have the ball end of the toy. She may tug a bit; that's okay. Then, when you are ready to get the toy back, simply hold tight to the handle and stop moving your arm. Say nothing. If she doesn't let go, slowly work your hand up to the toy's handle until you are holding your hand right against her mouth. At the same time:

✦ Keep your arms right against your body, and

✦ Freeze so that no tug action can take place.

Continue to say nothing. Since this is no fun for the puppy, eventually she'll let go. Wait her out. She may try harder to get a tug going before she gives up—that's okay. Be patient. Sooner or later, she'll begin to let go. Immediately say "my turn" and take the toy. Hold the toy for a second or two, then begin to play again.

The nice thing about this exercise is that your puppy will think she's training you. *Hey, look, if I want to get my human to play, all I need to do is let go of the toy.*

Of course, we all know who's outwitting whom!

3. **Give and Take.** This is a separate exercise, not to be done during playtime. Put some goodies in your pocket and sit on the floor with your puppy. (If he's rambunctious, it might be helpful to keep him on a leash.) Invite him to take your special tug toy in his mouth. Don't throw it; just let him take it. While the toy is in his mouth, offer him a treat. He'll probably spit the toy in order to be able to eat the treat. As soon as he starts to release the toy, say "my turn," take the toy, and give him the treat.

With practice, you'll get to the point where your puppy will give and take quickly, 80 to 90 percent of the time. When that happens, you can start saying "my turn" without showing the food. Take the food out of hiding only when you get the toy back.

When your puppy masters this, you can start making him "play the lottery." Don't give him a treat every time you take the toy. Vary it. For example, make him give the toy twice in a row before you reward him. Then, the next time, make it three times in a row. The time after that, only once. Doing this helps keep the game exciting for him.

Fun and Games

As we saw in the above exercise, training puppies is an awful lot like playing with them. Puppies love to play. And that gives us humans a tremendous advantage. We can set up games that our puppies will love—and at the same time build a foundation for future training.

Here are some other "games" you can play with your puppy:

✦ **Hand-feeding.** Instead of putting your puppy's food in a bowl and walking away, make mealtimes a time for fun, positive interactions. Hold the dinner dish and hand your puppy her food, a bit at a time. You and your puppy will enjoy it. It also shows your puppy that your hands give food, instead of taking it away.

✦ **Hide-and-Seek.** Have a helper hold your puppy by the collar or leash. Make a big deal of leaving—"Good-bye! See ya later!"— while you go out of sight to hide behind a chair, under the bed, or in an open closet. Your puppy is then turned loose to find you. You can add some extra fun by taking your puppy's dinner bowl with you, or perhaps the joyful reunion can end with a nice puppy massage.

✦ **Foraging.** Have your helper hold your puppy while you hide her dinner bowl or some treats. When your puppy is turned loose, she'll have a ball finding the hidden food.

Play these games anytime you have some time to spend with your puppy, and you'll be on your way to a great training foundation.

Chapter 4

HOUSETRAINING: OUTWITTING THE DOG WHO NEEDS TO GO

He's got his dog trained so that it only does it on newspapers. The trouble is it does it when he's reading the blasted things.
—Honoré de Balzac, *The Country Doctor*

Still think owning a dog is for you? Try this:

One calm, balmy afternoon, leave work 15 minutes early—so you'll be home before your neighbors. Pour yourself a refreshing glass of lemonade. Then step out back, pull up a lawn chair, and listen.

Hear that shrieking? That's the sound of your neighbors—the ones who have a dog. They've just walked in the door—and stepped in a big soft pile of doggy surprise.

It's one of the things you can't quite appreciate unless you've had an unhousetrained dog. Practically the whole world makes a fine potty spot. Including floors, rugs . . . and furniture. All furniture. Possibly including your bed.

It also happens that potty training problems are one of the main reasons dogs end up in animal shelters. When you think about it, that's not surprising. We humans have funny ideas about this subject. We confine our own business to the toilet for the most part. And before our kids

learn to use the toilet, we keep them wrapped tightly in highly ab-
sorbent materials.

Dogs, on the other hand, are much more freewheeling. (Also, they
look silly in Pampers.) For example: Dogs don't mind stinky smells. In
fact, they like stinky smells. When a dog sees another dog's poo deposit,
instead of wrinkling his furry face in disgust, he rushes over to get a
good close sniff.

That doesn't mean dogs don't have limits. They do. In fact, as we
mentioned in chapter 1, most dogs would rather not soil their beds. This
appears to be instinctive behavior: They naturally want to keep their
sleeping area clean. Which, as it happens, gives us humans a great tool
for housetraining our dogs.

An Outwitting Strategy for Housetraining

When it comes to housetraining your dog, you have two things in your
favor.

First, dogs can learn to hold it. Bear in mind, however, that puppies
can't hold for as long as adult dogs—particularly during the day, when a
puppy is eating, drinking, and playing. A six-week-old puppy has to go
far more frequently than an 18-month-old adolescent dog. So don't expect too much too soon, or you'll set your pup up to disappoint you.

And second, in most cases elimination behavior is a matter of habit.
And you, as the human, have what it takes to pick and strengthen the
pottying habits you like.

Let's take a closer look at how establishing the right habits can help
you housetrain your dog.

Poo on Cue

As you housetrain your dog, you can incorporate a verbal cue,
such as *go potty* or *do it*. Simply speak your chosen cue as your dog

begins to eliminate. Use a cheerful voice and be consistent. Over time, your dog will associate the cue with the need to go. Saying it will actually stimulate the dog to do her business. It's a handy way to outwit your dog when you're in a hurry.

Some people use separate cues for number one and number two.

I have a friend who hums a little tune—a great idea if you have nearby neighbors. How about a bit of "Singin' in the Rain" for pee and the opening bars of Beethoven's Fifth for poo?

T. R.

Forming Good Pottying Habits

Dogs form habits. They don't know they form habits. But we do. The trick, when it comes to housetraining (not to mention everything else), is to get your dog to form habits that you like.

So what pottying habits would you like your dog to have?

Most people start by figuring out where they'd like their dogs to do their business. But don't rush to decide this question too quickly. For example, if your only requirement is "outside, of course!"—well, that's a good start. But it's only a start. Where outside? For example, is there a specific spot on your property that would work as a designated potty spot?

Here's why you need to think this over. Say you decide you don't really care where outside your dog does her business. In fact, you decide what you'll do is put your dog on a leash and take her for a walk two or three times a day, and you figure she'll get things taken care of at some point on the walk. Then, when she's emptied herself out, so to speak, you'll turn around and head for home.

What you might end up with is a dog who has a particular habit: doing her business on her walk.

But that's not all. Suppose, for your dog, walks are one of the highlights of her day. She may figure out that when she potties too soon, the walk ends too soon. So why should she be in a rush to do her thing?

Then one day you are in a hurry, and it's pouring down rain, and your dog is standing by the front door with that expectant look on her face.

Guess what. You're going for a walk. In the rain. And you'll be out there until your dog (who may just happen to love the rain) is good and ready to come back indoors.

Now let's imagine a different scenario. What happens if, from day one, you take your dog out, lead her to a designated potty spot, and wait for her to do her business? And what if you don't start her walk until she's finished?

Now your dog is on her way to a different habit: If she eliminates, right away, in a prechosen spot, she'll get something nice—a walk.

This habit has a big advantage for you, the human of the duo. Your dog will be likely to go as soon as she gets to her spot, because she learns that the sooner she goes, the sooner the walk begins. You may not take her on that walk every time, of course. Maybe not in the pouring-down rain. But as long as you usually follow potty time with a walk, the habit will stick.

One more thing about habits: They cut both ways. If you let your dog get into the habit of using your living room rug, you've just made your housetraining job a whole lot harder.

In other words, when it comes to housetraining, you also need to think about preventing bad habits. Dog trainers often call this "management." What's nice about that term is that it puts the responsibility right where it belongs: with you, the manager.

Your Dog's Manager

Leading trainers today often advocate management when it comes to training dogs. But what's that mean?

Managing dogs is much like managing people. Like a people manager, you need to start by deciding what behavior you want, then figuring out how to get it. For example, as a manager, you set goals for your dog. Then you design incentives to inspire your dog to meet those goals, in the same way that people managers use incentives like bonuses to motivate their staff.

Managers also keep a sharp eye out for potential problems, and find ways to head them off before they cause significant damage. Suppose you also have a cat, and you don't want your dog eating the cat's food. If you put the cat's dish up out of the dog's reach, you've solved the problem using management.

And finally, managers accept responsibility for how their staff performs. When your dog succeeds, you can take the credit. But if your dog fails, sorry, you need to take credit for that, too. Just don't be too hard on yourself. Mistakes happen. It's up to you to keep perfecting your training until it works.

Your Number One Tool: The Crate

Crates are a great management tool, and not just for housetraining. Crates let you create a little room for your dog—a place where he can go to curl up and be alone for a while. They also help you prevent other behavior issues, like destructive chewing. For example, if you're stepping out to run some errands, you can put your dog in his crate with a nice chew toy, instead of giving him the run of the house while you're gone. This is especially helpful for puppies and young dogs, who can find countless ways to get into mischief when you're not right there to stop it.

But best of all, crates are an invaluable tool for housetraining. Why? Because they let you confine a dog to his bed. Remember that in the vast majority of cases, dogs won't soil their beds. So a dog in a crate will do his best to hold it. This works to your advantage in two ways. First, it helps puppies develop the physical skills needed to control elimination. And second, it prevents accidents.

If you're totally new to dogs, and you've never seen a crate, stop by a pet supply store and take a look. There are three basic kinds: plastic, wire, and nylon mesh.

+ **Wire crates** are collapsible for easy storage when not in use. They provide the most ventilation. They're easy to see out of.

+ **Plastic crates are sturdier.** They are built to double as airline carriers and are the safest for car travel, too. They provide more privacy for dogs and are less drafty than wire crates.

+ **Nylon mesh crates** are very light and collapsible. They aren't as secure as plastic crates, however. And of course, some dogs will happily chew their way out of anything as flimsy as nylon.

Crates also come in many different sizes. So what size do you need for your dog? Here's where things get a little tricky. The crate should be big enough for your dog to lie down in, turn around in, and sit in—when she's fully grown. If your dog is already grown up, sizing a crate is easy. But if your dog is a puppy, you need to start with a smaller crate. Or you could find a way to block off part of a larger crate, so that your puppy is confined to a bed-sized area inside.

Once you have a crate, make sure you train your dog to be comfortable going into it. Associate the crate with good things. Usually this means food and really fun chew toys.

Feed your dog in the crate. Toss treats in from time to time, so your dog starts thinking of the crate as a kind of doggy vending machine. When you do shut your dog in, leave a chew toy. Then, when you let your dog out of the crate, pick up the toy and put it away. This also helps show your dog that the crate is a special place.

What if your dog whines and scratches and fusses? Well, it depends. Remember, you're trying to outwit the furry little guy. Do you want him to learn that, if he makes a big enough scene, you'll let him out? No? Then it's best to stay away from the crate while he's making a fuss. Don't let him out. That would reward him for fussing. Instead, wait until he's quiet. Then walk over and let him out.

And when you let him out, don't make a big deal about it. Don't praise him or give him a treat. You want to associate treats with being in the crate, not with being let out.

The crate is also a great place for dogs—and especially puppies—to sleep. Once your dog is reliably toilet trained, you can leave the crate door open at night. But with puppies, the crate door prevents midnight wandering—and midnight elimination habits you don't want your pup to form.

CRATETRAINING PUPPIES

Puppies need frequent potty breaks. Very young puppies may need to go as often as every hour. For this reason, the only time you can be absolutely sure your young puppy *doesn't* need to go is for 30 minutes or so after her last potty break.

Remember that preventing bad habits from getting established is half the battle. And there are two ways to prevent a puppy from having an accident. One is to keep a close watch on her to look for signs that she's ready to go. What signs? It will depend on your dog. Most puppies act a bit restless. They may leave off playing and suddenly start walking around and sniffing at the floor. Some puppies circle. As you get to know your puppy, you may find you develop a sixth sense and can just tell when she's ready to go.

Getting to Know Your Dog

Learning your puppy's cues can take a little time, even if you've had a dog before.

My last dog was a Doberman mix, slim and leggy. When she squatted to pee, the posture was unmistakable: Her haunches dropped a good 6 or 8 inches.

My current dog is a Pembroke Welsh Corgi. Her belly barely clears the ground. So imagine my surprise the day I brought her home and she peed right in front of my eyes—and I didn't know she was doing it until I saw the puddle. With those short little legs, her squat looked the same, to me, as her standing up.

K. M.

The other way to prevent puppy accidents is to use the crate. This doesn't mean your puppy should be in his crate 24 hours a day. Far from it. You want your puppy to learn what behavior you expect when he's out of the crate, too. Instead, use your crate selectively, something like this:

1. Take the puppy outside. When the pup finishes peeing and pooping, praise him and give him a treat.

2. Now you know your dog is good for at least 30 minutes with relatively little supervision (at least as far as housetraining is concerned).

3. After 30 minutes, start monitoring the puppy more closely.

4. When you notice signs that your puppy needs to go, whisk him out to his spot. If he goes, praise and treat.

5. If he doesn't go after four or five minutes, come back inside and put him in his crate for 30 minutes. Then repeat from step 1.

You can also use your crate for overnight housetraining:

1. Pick up food and water dishes in early evening.

2. Take the puppy outdoors right before you turn in.

3. The first night, set your alarm clock to go off several hours before you normally get up, and take the puppy outside to do his business.

4. On subsequent nights, slowly advance the time you get up, training your puppy to wait longer and longer, until he's able to hold until your normal waking time.

CRATETRAINING OLDER DOGS

If you adopt an older dog who's not already housetrained, you can use your crate in much the same way. .

However, sometimes older dogs don't take to crates as quickly as puppies. *Don't force a reluctant dog to accept a crate.* Take your time: Use baby steps. First, get your dog used to stepping inside the crate to take a treat. Then get her used to staying inside while you close the door for a minute. If you proceed gradually, and show her that only good things happen when she's in her crate, with time she'll start to feel completely comfortable.

When Dogs Soil Their Crates

If your dog does go in her crate, use the following list to determine the cause:

✓ **Medical problem.** Anytime a dog has a sudden change in her elimination behavior, your first stop is the vet. A number of physical problems, including urinary tract infections, can cause a dog who was able to hold it to suddenly start soiling her crate. Some dogs are also sensitive to dietary changes. The resulting intestinal upset can cause housetraining problems.

✓ **Dog too young.** Puppies just can't hold it as long as adult dogs. Take the age of your dog in months and add one. This is how many hours your dog should be able to hold during the night. (Example: A three-month old pup should be able to wait four hours.) This varies by individual, however. Also, if your puppy slurps up a whole bowlful of water right before bedtime, don't be surprised if she doesn't make it to midnight. So be sensitive to when you feed and water your puppy, and how much, and coordinate your potty schedule accordingly. And if you have to leave your puppy crated for more than four or five hours (say, while you're at work), try to arrange for a petsitter or neighbor to give your pup regular potty breaks.

✓ **Crate too large.** If there's enough room in the crate for your dog to soil one end and sleep in another, you need a smaller crate. Another possibility is to block part of the crate with a box to make the available space smaller.

✓ **Dog history of soiled bedding.** Puppies forced to sleep in soiled beds may lose their natural instinct to keep their sleeping space clean. Consult a professional trainer for help.

✓ **Other behavioral problems.** Once you've ruled out the other causes, seek a professional trainer or behavior specialist for help. (See chapter 17 for information on how to select qualified professional help.)

Tethering: Another Option

Another way to manage a dog during housetraining is tethering.

With this approach, you use a leash or rope to confine your dog. You can either tie the dog to you, so that he can't wander off and pick an out-of-the-way spot to eliminate. Or you can tether him to a doorknob or heavy piece of furniture. If the rope is short enough, this will have the same effect as the crate: It will confine him to his bed so he is encouraged to hold.

Don't use this type of restraint unless you're supervising your dog, however. Most dogs are savvy enough to chew through a rope or leash in, say, about 30 seconds. (And before you reach for a chain instead, bear in mind that many dogs are also quick-witted enough to crack a tooth on a chain—and dental work is more expensive than nylon leashes.)

In addition, an unsupervised dog or puppy could become entangled in a tether.

Use Honey, Not Vinegar

Crates are a great tool for preventing bad housetraining habits. But the other half of the equation is establishing good housetraining habits.

To do this, you need to really use your wits.

First, some background. Throughout this book, we advocate using reward-based techniques. One compelling reason for this is *it's almost always easier to train dogs with rewards than with punishment.* Housetraining is great for helping us understand why this is so.

Consider this: To a dog, something that happened in the distant past—that is, four or five minutes ago—may have *no connection* to what happened just now. Let's use a hypothetical housetraining example to show this principle in action:

1. Dog pees on carpet and goes away.

2. Human walks in five minutes later and sees pee spot.

3. Human yells and sets off in search of dog.

4. Human finds dog in kitchen sniffing for crumbs under the table. Human hits dog with newspaper.

5. Dog learns that humans go berserk when she sniffs for crumbs under the kitchen table.

Notice what is missing here. The dog has no idea that the human is upset about the pee on the carpet. The act of relieving herself, as far as the dog is concerned, is completely removed from the consequence.

A variation on this sequence is to drag the dog back to the pee spot and then whack her with a newspaper (or rub her nose in it, or whatever).

But this is also doomed to failure, because being dragged up to the pee spot by a human has nothing to do with the act of peeing, as far as many dogs are concerned. What the dog may learn, in this case, is something like *If my human grabs me by the collar and drags me toward the living room, I'm about to get yelled at and whacked with a newspaper.*

A smart, strong dog might take this one step further. She might decide that, the next time someone grabs her collar and starts dragging her somewhere, she should show her teeth or even nip. After all, something bad is about to happen to her, right? So why not see if she can stop it?

In this case, you've not only failed to outwit your dog, you've begun training her to be aggressive toward you. Not a good outcome.

Reward-based training, on the other hand, can help pet owners get around the timing problem, because generally you reward a dog right after she does what you want her to do:

1. You take dog outdoors.

2. Dog pees.

3. You praise dog and give her a treat.

In this case, you're watching for the behavior you want. And, since you follow the desired behavior with a treat, your dog is likely to associate the praise and treat with the peeing.

Furthermore, even if she doesn't catch the connection, it's better to give your dog a treat she doesn't understand than harsh punishment that she doesn't understand.

You're outwitting your dog.

Now, suppose you catch your dog in the act. Should you punish him?

While punishing a dog during the act is better than punishing after the fact, it still makes you into something threatening or scary. So you still risk causing your dog to think he needs to protect himself from you.

In addition, using punishment alone to housetrain your dog has a significant flaw. Again, this comes back to how dogs perceive the world. We humans are pretty good at understanding rules and how to apply them. Take speed limits, for example. If you're driving along and see a sign that reads SPEED LIMIT 35, you know that this rule applies until you see another sign that gives you different instructions.

But suppose you thought the 35 mph speed limit only applied while the sign was visible. Suppose you thought there was no speed limit as soon as you'd passed the sign. You'd be thinking more like a dog. Your insurance rates would also go up, owing to your many speeding tickets.

(This, plus the fact that they would constantly be driving over lawns in pursuit of squirrels, are the main reasons dogs aren't allowed to drive.)

So how does this apply to housetraining? Think of it this way: If you're going to train your dog by stopping him from doing something wrong, you're going to have to watch him constantly, and catch him every single time—every time he makes a mistake.

That's fine if you don't have anything else to do. But chances are you do. And that's why many people run into trouble with housetraining. They catch their dog peeing in the kitchen—but a week later, they're busy with something else when he pees in the spare bedroom. What's this dog going to learn? One major possibility: that peeing in the kitchen gets him in trouble, but peeing in the bedroom is okay.

So think about it. Isn't it easier to work on just 1 thing (*go here, in this spot*) than 100 things (*don't go here, or here, or here, or here, or here . . .*)?

Combine this with management, and you set up yourself, and your dog, to succeed.

Outwitted!

When we humans fail to appreciate how dogs perceive cause and effect, the results can be peculiar.

For example, an acquaintance got a new dog and began to housetrain him using punishment. The first day, the dog pooed in the kitchen, and was punished. The dog learned right away that he shouldn't go in the kitchen.

So the next day, he pooed in the living room. Again, he was punished. Now he'd learned he shouldn't go in the living room.

The third day, he went in the hallway. He was punished for that. Okay, so the hallway is off-limits, too.

Hmm. Finally, the dog thinks he's got it. He's been punished three times, each time for pooing on the floor.

So on the fourth day, he climbed up on the coffee table and pooed there.

T. R.

Housetraining Made Easy

Using reward-based housetraining is smart, because it's effective. And it's also easy. Here's all you need to do:

1. **Catch your dog in the act.** This means that, especially at first, you need to be there when your dog does her business. Tempting as it is to open the door and let your dog out by herself, you're better off putting her on a leash and walking her out to her spot, especially when she is a puppy.

2. **Reward your dog for getting it right.** Your dog can't read this page. She doesn't understand how much you paid for your living room carpet. But she does know she likes getting a treat. And when she does something that results in a treat, she's more likely to do that same thing again.

Just Don't Reward Too Soon

A word of caution about rewarding during housetraining: Make sure your dog is completely finished before you dispense the treat.

A woman I know made this mistake, rewarding her puppy right after he started to potty—instead of waiting for him to finish.

So guess what—she trained the pup to stop midstream. Then, since the puppy wasn't finished eliminating, he had accidents inside later.

T. R.

When Accidents Happen

If you do an absolutely, 100 percent perfect job of managing your dog, accidents will never be a issue. And believe it or not, we've heard rumors that some people do raise puppies without a single accident. Or so they claim. We're not sure they're being completely honest with us, if you really want to know.

Most of us mere mortal pet owners will lapse once or twice. We'll get involved in a phone call or television show or family crisis. We'll fail to notice that our dog is waiting anxiously by the door. And next thing you know, the poor dog has messed up, so to speak.

So what do you do if this happens to you?

The answer is: It depends on the dog and the situation.

If you actually see your dog preparing to let go, you may want to make a sudden loud noise to interrupt him. Try slapping your hand against a wall, clapping, or saying "ugh!" or "ahh!" The idea is not to punish the dog, but to make him stop midstream. Quickly hustle him outdoors to finish. Then reward him with praise and a treat. Hey, he may have had a little help, but he still got it half right.

This technique makes use of something behaviorists call the orienting reflex. To understand what the orienting reflex is, imagine you're working on your computer. Or reading a book.

Suddenly, a door slams.

You instantly look up from whatever you're working on. All your senses are focused on the slamming noise. This is the orienting reflex.

Using the orienting reflex to interrupt behavior is a useful training tool. It won't necessarily prevent the mistake from ever happening again. But it does give you a chance to redirect the behavior in a way you want—and then reward your dog for it.

You need to tailor this technique to your dog. If he's sound-sensitive or tends to be fearful, you may want to use a softer noise or simply approach him, pick him up, or take his collar.

And remember, if you find your dog's mistake after the fact, sorry—you've been outwitted. Resolve to do a better job managing him in the future. Then clean up.

Excited Urination

Sometimes a young, high-energy dog will dribble urine while doing something that excites her, like greeting people. Typically, she'll dance around and wiggle her greeting, all the while depositing little drops of urine all over the floor. She doesn't seem to notice she's doing it, however. She may pause briefly to urinate, but that's just an interlude—she's mostly paying attention to saying hi.

For this type of housetraining problem, start by getting the dog a checkup at the vet to rule out any health problems.

As your dog matures, she may outgrow this behavior. In the meantime, here are some things to try:

✦ Before guests arrive, take the dog out to relieve herself.

✦ You can keep a large, washable piece of carpet near the door so that your dog's peeing won't make you quite so crazy.

✦ Minimize the excitement of greetings. Avoid petting your dog or making eye contact. Instead, turn away, facing the wall. Talk to her only after things have settled down. If this helps, you can gradually increase the amount of attention you give your dog during greetings. For example, start by just glancing at her. If this doesn't stimulate the overexcited behavior, you can add saying a word or two.

✦ Train her to sit to greet you and visitors to your home. (See chapter 8 for how to train a sit.)

Submissive Urination

Young or inexperienced dogs sometimes urinate to show deference to a canine or human leader. If your dog does this, the urination will be accompanied by subordinate body posture. He may lie down on his side, roll over on his back, avoid eye contact, or lick his lips.

With this type of housetraining problem, it's important to help your dog feel comfortable and confident. Avoid towering over him, standing directly in front of him, staring at him, or reaching over his head or shoulders. Never punish him; don't even speak sharply to him. Doing so will make him less confident, and could make the problem even worse.

Instead relax around him, or even act bored. Breathe deeply, lower your eyes, yawn.

Keep greetings calm. As with the excited urinator, stop petting or making eye contact with him during greetings. When you pat him, stoop low and to his side. Pat him under the chin or on his chest.

If you find he can handle this low-key contact without urinating, you can add slightly more intense greetings. But do so gradually. Make sure he can handle each stage before you move on.

Cleaning Up

And cleaning up is important. Very important. Because if your dog smells past mistakes on your floor, or rug, or coffee table, she may think that it's now her potty spot.

The first trick is to clean the accident up as soon as possible.

Don't let your dog watch you do it. Believe it or not, some particularly quick-witted dogs are born instigators. Once they figure out how much fun it is to make their humans clean up messes, they might try it again for the entertainment value alone.

Block the spot with a chair or other object until it dries.

You should also purchase a product designed for cleaning up pet odors. These products use enzymes to break down residual soiling. As a result, they do a good job of completely eliminating the smells of your dog's mistakes. You can find these products in pet supply stores, department stores, and even supermarkets.

Using Your Noggin

Every dog is unique. At the same time, all dogs tend to follow the same general laws of behavior. For example, if something is rewarding, they tend to do it more. If something is not rewarding, they tend to do it less.

So ultimately, housetraining your dog, like all the other training challenges you're taking on, is a matter of understanding your dog and figuring out why he chooses certain behaviors over others.

Sometimes you might feel stumped. A puppy just doesn't seem to get it. A dog who seemed housetrained suddenly starts having accidents. A dog catches on when it comes to poo but acts clueless about where to pee.

Yes, it's weird. But you've got what it takes to figure things out. Use your head. Observe your dog. Take notes, if you have to. Reread this chapter to see if you've overlooked anything.

And before you know it, you'll have a housetrained dog.

The Great Poop Deck Mystery

We were doing so well housetraining our English Cocker Spaniel puppy. Lacey would sit by the door, wait for someone to let her out, and do her business at the far end of the backyard, which we'd picked for her toilet area.

But on cold, snowy days, instead of walking off the deck into the yard to toilet, she would potty right on the deck.

The family began to call it the Poop Deck. What could be going wrong? Nothing like this had ever happened with our other dogs. "Should have gotten a real dog," said a not-so-helpful family friend who prefers German Shepherds. "No, I wanted something small and sporting," I replied. "Should have gotten a Corvette," he retorted. "She's being wimpy," my son volunteered. "She's not as smart as my Golden, Mom," my daughter offered. "She's cold," my husband suggested. "You shouldn't take so much fur off when you groom her. We'd better buy her a coat."

Personal pride and love of this puppy (she's much cuddlier than a sports car) urged me to get to the bottom of the problem. She was okay unless it was really snowy. This was a good clue, but how could I use that information to solve the problem?

I observed her and the environment carefully. Then I noticed something: When it was snowy, the deck was completely covered with snow . . . just like the backyard. But when it warmed up, the snow melted off the deck. And when there was no snow on the deck, Lacey would step down into the yard like a good girl.

It occurred to me that, during the backyard training sessions, she was invariably rewarded for toileting in the snow—because there was snow everywhere.

And so it hit me. We'd trained Lacey to go on snow. In her mind, that was what we expected of her.

Sure enough, when spring came, Lacey went farther and farther into the shady parts of the yard to find some snow. Then finally, the last bit of snow melted away—and she figured out that grass was okay, too.

T. R.

Chapter 5

MY SHOE! MY SHOE! OUTWITTING THE DOG WHO LOVES TO CHEW

Of course he chewed boots and worried our stockings and swallowed our garters. The moment we took off our stockings he would dart away with one, we after him.

—D. H. Lawrence, "Rex"

Dogs love to chew.

Of course, it's impossible to actually experience chewing from a dog's perspective. But many people believe chewing is relaxing to dogs. It may relieve tension, or stress, or alleviate boredom. Regular chewing may also help keep dogs' jaw muscles in tip-top condition—very important for a born carnivore.

Where dogs get into trouble is when we try to share space with them. Because the funny thing about dogs is, they aren't too particular about what they chew. It could be a chew toy. Or it could be your brand-new pair of Italian dress shoes or that $750 limited-edition Beanie Baby. Dogs have also been known to chew things that aren't particularly chewy—like rocks. Which might seem easier on your pocketbook, until you realize what your veterinarian charges for doggy dental work or emergency surgery.

Chewing and Puppies

The most notorious chewers are puppies. By the time they're eight weeks old, most puppies chew as if it were their full-time job. They also treat everything and everyone like a chew toy. A puppy, left on his own in the house or yard, will wander around chewing anything and everything he bumps into: from rugs and sticks to phone jacks and leashes. Ever watched a human baby who crawls around, putting everything she can pick up into her mouth? Puppies act pretty much the same way. Everything they can reach has to be sniffed, tasted, and subjected to a little chew. Or, if you're not around to intervene, maybe a nice long chew.

A related puppy problem isn't chewing, exactly, but mouthing. Puppies like to play, and their mouths are like a child's hands. They use their mouths to explore the world and to play. If you're the playmate, that can mean sharp little puppy teeth clamping down on your skin.

This kind of behavior is not teething, by the way. It isn't something you should ignore, hoping your puppy will outgrow it.

Jaws!

He looked so cute. A gentlemanly Boston Terrier with a grizzled muzzle, sitting politely on a leash next to his elderly owner one afternoon at the park. "Does he like strangers?" I asked after the woman and I made eye contact. "Oh, yes," she answered, so I approached happily and knelt to pet her dog.

And then the mauling began. Oh, he liked strangers, all right—the way other dogs like rawhide. Over and over, that little guy grabbed my hands in his mouth and chomped. It wasn't aggressive—he was wriggling all over with happiness. It was mouthing—this distinguished old fellow was mouthing me just like he had mouthed people years ago when he was a puppy.

I made a quick excuse and backed away. There were welts on my hands where the Boston's teeth had raked my skin. But what struck me most was that the woman didn't warn me. I could only assume that she'd accepted her dog's mouthing long ago. To her, it wasn't a problem. But for her dog, it was a real shame. He'd just lost a new friend, and I'm sure it wasn't the first time.

K. M.

If you have a puppy or young dog who mouths inappropriately, there are several things you can try to modify that behavior:

1. Yelp! In chapter 3, we described how puppies teach their litter-mates bite inhibition—the ability to control how much pressure the puppy uses when mouthing in play. When a puppy bites down too hard, the bite-ee yelps, startling the biter and inter-rupting play. You can communicate the same way. Say *"At!"* in a sharp, high-pitched tone.

2. In many cases, your puppy will respond by letting go and looking up. This is what behaviorists call the orienting reflex (introduced in chapter 4). He may even back up a bit to look at you. Then, when he starts to play again, he may start to use his mouth more gently. If he does, great—continue the play. If not . . .

3. . . . walk away. If just yelping doesn't cause your puppy to play more gently, end the play. Look away and fold your arms, or even walk away from your puppy—far enough that he can see you don't want to play anymore. Like yelping, this imitates how puppies communicate with one another. When a biter doesn't get the message that a bite hurts, the bite-ee breaks off play. If you do this consistently, you will teach your puppy that biting too hard ends the fun—a powerful lesson.

4. Redirect the mouthing. Sometimes, the easiest thing to do is to substitute a toy for your skin. Give your puppy a chew toy. The goal here is to help prevent a bad habit from getting started.

Training the Chewing Puppy

Since all puppies chew, one of your jobs is to help your puppy learn to chew the right things. This helps establish good habits right away—before bad habits can get started.

Here's a training exercise that helps teach a puppy the difference between good toys—objects that it's okay to chew—and bad or illegal toys, including objects you want your puppy to leave alone.

Here's how it works. Start by putting three puppy toys on the floor, along with an object you don't want your puppy to chew, like a book, shoe, or child's toy. If your puppy starts to investigate one of the chew toys, praise her and immediately start a play or retrieve session with her and her toy.

If she investigates the illegal object, first just ignore her. You may find that withdrawing your attention is enough—she'll leave the illegal toy and come to you. At this point, you can start the game again. Be consistent. Always ignore her if she becomes interested in the illegal toy, and always praise and play when she shows interest in the legal toy.

Sometimes a puppy will start to play with the off-limits toy even if you're ignoring her. If you have to intervene and save your shoe from tiny teeth, say *"At!"* loudly, while you keep your face and body language neutral. Again, this stimulates the orienting reflex. Your puppy's brain momentarily turns its attention from the shoe and opens up for new information—as if your puppy is asking, *Now, where did that noise come from?* At that point you can either remove the object, remove the puppy, or wait three to five seconds and then redirect the puppy's attention to an appropriate toy.

One note of caution, however. Some puppies may decide that getting a reaction out of you is a fun game. *Interesting. I chew the shoe, my human pays attention to me. Great!* So keep watch for this—and if you notice that it seems to be happening, stop the game.

When the game is over, puppy-proof the floor again—put the illegal object out of puppy's reach.

For a variation on this game, make the legal toys even more interesting by putting a tiny smear of peanut butter on them. You can also use a taste deterrent on the illegal object.

Taste Deterrents

If you want a little help modifying chewing behavior, one thing you can try is spraying or spreading something that tastes bad on off-limits objects. You can buy taste deterrents at pet supply stores. They're usually packaged in pump spray bottles and are formulated with a bitter taste.

To use taste deterrents, spray or spread a bit on anything you don't want your dog or puppy to chew—furniture, rugs, shoes, or your dog's leash. Of course, if you're concerned about stains, test it first on a place that doesn't show.

Taste deterrents are particularly useful because once they're applied, the object will continue to taste bad for at least a few hours. So they work even when you're not around.

If you have a dog who's very enthusiastic about chewing a particular object—the corner of a rug, for example—you may need to reapply the deterrent from time to time, because the bad taste will fade after a while.

And don't assume taste deterrents are a complete substitute for management and training. For one thing, some dogs don't mind taste deterrents. Dogs can even develop a liking for them.

And because chewing is an inherently rewarding behavior, even a momentary bad taste might not bother a dog enough to stop. Once a dog has developed a solid chewing habit, taste deterrents may be less useful.

Puppies may be known for chewing. But they aren't the only chewers. Although many adult dogs are less compulsive about chewing than puppies are, they still enjoy it. And in some cases, adult dogs can be problematic chewers as well.

Boredom, Stress, and Chewing

Chewing can be an outlet for a dog who's bored. A dog who doesn't have enough stimulation or exercise may turn to chewing to compensate.

Think about it. Say you have a dog, and you work outside your home. On any given day, you might be away for 8, 9, or 10 hours. What does your dog do during that time? If the answer is "wait," then you may have a very frustrated dog on your hands. That pent-up energy has to go somewhere. Destructive chewing may become that dog's outlet.

So how much stimulation and exercise does your dog need? The answer to this question depends on many factors, including your dog's breed, age, and temperament. If she's a purebred or resembles a purebred, you can research that breed for a general understanding of her exercise requirements.

Younger dogs, as a rule, are more active than older dogs.

Dogs' stimulation needs also vary by individual. Observe your dog. Notice how obedient she is on a day when you provide more exercise and stimulation, compared with her behavior on a day when you provide less exercise and stimulation. In many cases, dogs get into less mischief when their people plan acceptable ways for them to burn off their physical and mental energy.

And that includes destructive chewing. If you give your dog enough stimulation—including providing acceptable chewing toys—you can go a long way toward preventing the kind of chewing you don't like.

Stress is another factor that seems to affect dogs' chewing behavior. Some dogs may chew more, for instance, when they are left alone, because being separated from the rest of the "pack"—meaning you—makes them anxious. (See chapter 10 for more on dogs who become very upset when they are left alone.)

Bad Habits

Sometimes destructive chewing is simply a bad habit. Your dog—or puppy—gets a taste of the rungs on your dining room chairs. For whatever reason, he likes the feeling of chewing on wooden chair rungs. Maybe they're just the right thickness. Or maybe oak is the perfect texture. Unfortunately, since you're not in the habit of inspecting chair rungs once a day or so, you don't notice your dog's newfound love. Weeks pass. One day, your puppy vomits wood splinters on the kitchen floor. At first you're curious—where on earth has the puppy found wood to chew? Then it dawns on you that the color of those splinters reminds you of . . . something. And all at once, with a growing sense of horror, you remember where you've seen that type of wood before . . . your heirloom dining room set.

But it's too late. Your beautiful dining room chairs have been scored by sharp little puppy teeth. Worse yet, your dog has a habit. When he feels like chewing, he heads for your dining room.

Yes, you can break a dog's bad habits, just like you can break your own. But it's far easier to prevent a bad habit from being formed in the first place.

Self-Rewarding Behaviors

Whether your dog chews to alleviate anxiety or boredom, or simply because she's developed a chewing habit, it's important for you, the human, to know what you're up against: a self-rewarding behavior.

To understand what a self-rewarding behavior is, it's helpful to use a human analogy. Say you have a job that is okay, but not particularly fun for you. Better yet, imagine you have a job that you truly dislike. But you still get up in the morning and get yourself to work. Why? Chances are, it's because of your paycheck. You need the money, you enjoy spending it, spending it keeps the roof over your head. The job itself isn't rewarding. But you do get a reward for doing it: your paycheck.

Now compare that to something you enjoy doing for its own sake. It may be going to a movie, eating a nice meal, playing a round of golf, kissing someone you love, or jumping onto your snowboard for a trip down the slopes. These are self-rewarding activities. Nobody needs to pay you to do them. Nobody needs to add any extra reward. You do them because, all by themselves, they give you pleasure or satisfy a need.

Dogs are no different. For dogs, certain behaviors are self-rewarding. Eating is one of them. Chewing can be another. Even if you never praised your dog for chewing, chances are she would still chew.

So does it matter that chewing is self-rewarding? Yes, and here's why: Anytime you try to stop a dog from chewing, you're up against some pretty tough competition. Think again about the things in your life that are self-rewarding. Have you ever left for a vacation—even though you knew you had a lot of work to do back at the office? The thought of that work, piling up, wasn't particularly pleasant. But it still couldn't stop you from enjoying your trip, could it?

This example can give you an idea of what your dog experiences when she's settled in for a nice chew. Say your dog is a bit bored. You're not around, and there's nothing else around to keep her occupied. Chewing the edge of a rug alleviates her boredom. That's a powerful motivation.

This is why taste deterrents, while useful, sometimes don't work. The reward of chewing can be stronger than the unpleasantness of the bad taste (which wears off after a bit of chewing anyway).

This is also why punishing your dog for chewing can be ineffective. To go back to the vacation analogy, your boss or colleagues might be able to persuade you to postpone a vacation because of your work-load—for a while. But if you want that vacation badly enough, even veiled threats about your future job security may not have an effect. And incidentally, your co-workers' behavior probably won't do much for your relationship with them, either. You'll start thinking them unreasonable if they use guilt or threats to make you feel uncomfortable about taking a well-earned break once in a while.

Punishing a dog for chewing can have much the same effect. It may work temporarily. It may encourage your dog to chew only when you're not around. Or your dog may begin showing aggressiveness to protect her chosen chew toy. For example, she might try growling at you to tell you to leave her alone and let her chew.

A better strategy is for you to outwit your dog. Use your brains to stay one step ahead of her chewing and to make sure that when she does chew, it's the kind of chewing that's okay. The basic elements of this approach are:

1. **Recognize that dogs do chew.** Expecting to have a dog who doesn't chew is as unrealistic as expecting to have a preschooler who never wants to run in the house.

2. **Stay a step ahead of your dog's chewing by using management.** If you have a puppy, or a dog whom you know chews inappropriately, it's up to you to arrange things so she can't chew the wrong things. Crates and tethering are two valuable management tools. (See chapter 4 for more on using crates and tethers.) You can also use gates to restrict your puppy or dog from rooms where you keep furniture, rugs, or other objects that are off-limits to chewing.

3. **Direct your dog's chewing in acceptable ways.** You should also give your dog objects that she is allowed to chew. And when she does chew them, sweeten the pot by praising her or even giving her treats.

Directing Chewing Behavior

One of the best ways to prevent destructive chewing is to channel your dog's chewing behavior in acceptable ways.

This means you have to do more than decide what you don't want your dog to chew. You have to also decide what you *do* want your dog to chew.

In some cases, it's easy to tell what's off-limits for chewing. You don't want your dog to chew on things that are expensive and irreplaceable. It's also a good idea to avoid letting your dog chew on things that closely resemble objects that are expensive or irreplaceable. For example, if you give your dog an old shoe to chew, your dog may learn that chewing on shoes is okay. So the next time he wanders into your bedroom, he may pick out a brand-new top-of-the-line limited-edition running shoe. Not good.

You also don't want your dog to chew on things that might make him sick. This includes things that splinter, shred, or come apart in any way. In most cases, if your dog swallows something he shouldn't, the foreign object will either come back up or be passed. But if the object gets stuck—causing an intestinal blockage—the consequences can be deadly. Even objects that don't seem particularly dangerous, like dental floss, plastic wrap, and coins, can make a dog very sick.

Surprisingly, the list of dangerous objects also includes chew toys. That's right: Many "toys" you can buy at your local pet supply store can pose serious risks to your dog. Part of this depends on how vigorous a chewer your dog is. Some dogs can play with a flimsy squeak toy for years without leaving so much as a scratch. Others will decimate the toughest toy in a few hours.

It also depends on the toy. Some toys are made of thin, flexible plastic or rubber. These can be chewed up more easily than toys made of thick, hard rubber. Rope toys can disintegrate, after a while, into pieces of string that can be dangerous to your dog. Toys with bells or squeakers inside are another potential hazard. If they're cracked or torn open, your dog could swallow the pieces inside.

The key is to use common sense. Watch your dog. If you have a strong, persistent chewer, don't leave her alone for long periods with suspect chew toys. If you dog does begin to dismantle a toy, take it away immediately, including any scraps.

With that caveat in mind, however, chew toys are a wonderful tool. Chew toys give your dog a way to channel chewing behavior. Your dog can chew to her heart's content—without destroying your house.

Toys, Toys, Toys

According to the American Pet Products Manufacturers Association, most dog owners buy at least one toy per year for their pets. Here are some examples of available chew toys that your dog may enjoy.

✓ **Stuffable, hard rubber toys.** The gold standard for this type of toy is durability. The best are made to withstand serious chewing for long periods. Because this type of toy is so durable, in most cases you can use one to keep your dog occupied when you aren't around to supervise. Just make sure you've watched your dog with the toy a few times first—powerful dogs who chew intently can tear apart even the most durable rubber toys.

Another nice thing about these toys is that often they're either hollow or have holes in them. This lets you add that special something to keep dogs extra interested: food. You can put treats inside. Or, to keep your dog occupied for even longer periods, you can stuff them with food. For example, consider serving a portion of your dog's daily ration of kibble as toy stuffing. You can moisten kibble until it's mushy, pack it into the toy, and leave it with your dog when you go off to work in the morning. Your dog will be able to settle down for a nice long chew session while you're not there.

Some people freeze their stuffed toys to make it even harder for their dogs to work the goodies free.

✓ **Rope toys.** This type of toy, which looks like a piece of rope knotted at both ends, is a great chew toy. However, many dogs can pull rope toys apart after a while, turning them into piles of string. At this point, it's time to throw the toy away—if your dog swallows the pieces, it could cause tummy upset or even intestinal blockage.

✓ **Edible chew toys.** This category of toy includes a wide variety of products, including bones, hunks of cured leather (rawhide, pigs' ears and hooves), and molded, composite products made of everything from cornstarch to nontoxic plastics. Your success with this type of toy may vary. Watch rawhide and related toys in particular. Some dogs can't be left unsupervised with rawhide toys: They chew pieces off and swallow them, which may cause tummy upset. It's not unheard of for rawhide to cause intestinal blockages. Once again, the key is to know your dog. Watch how intently she chews, whether she's able to chew the toy apart—and if she can chew it apart, how quickly she does so. If she likes to shred rawhide, you know you can't leave her alone with this type of toy.

Some people purchase marrow bones—essentially sections of cow femurs—to give to their dogs. You'll find these in pet stores or, in raw form, in many supermarkets. Dogs find marrow bones to be delightful, but again, watch your dog. Pieces of bone can chip off and be swallowed. Marrow bones are also very hard, and dogs may be able to crack their teeth on them.

✓ **Plush toys.** Dogs, like kids, love plush toys, but unlike kids, many dogs like plush toys because they like to chew them apart. And because plush toys can be destroyed relatively quickly, they probably aren't the best choice for unsupervised play. On the other hand, what is cuter than a dog playing with a stuffed animal?

Reinforcing Positive Chewing

Once you've picked out some chew toys for your dog, put together a plan to direct your dog's chewing in positive ways.

Here are some things you can do to train your dog to chew the right things.

1. **Make safe chew toys available.** Again, the key is the word safe. If you have a powerful chewer, even the most durable toys may not be okay for unsupervised chewing. But in most cases, even if you leave the house for a few hours, you can leave a chew toy

with your dog. This gives him an accepted outlet for chewing—
which will help prevent destructive chewing.

2. **Make acceptable objects more attractive than unacceptable
   ones.** Stuffing hollow chew toys is one way to encourage your
   dog to chew them, instead of off-limits objects. Even a smear of
   peanut butter or cheese spread can help direct your dog's chewing behavior to the acceptable toy.

3. **Reward chewing behavior you want to strengthen.** If you
   "catch" your dog chewing something that you want him to
   chew, praise him and give him a little treat.

4. **Rotate the chew toys.** Acquire a selection of toys—but don't
   keep all of them out all the time. Put some away for a few days
   at a time. That way, you can bring out a "new" toy every once in
   a while, to help keep your dog's interest high.

Last But Not Least: It's Just Stuff

One final word about chewing. Accidents happen. Especially if your
new dog comes to you as a puppy, chances are, at some point, she's
going to chew something she shouldn't.

The important thing is to try to keep your perspective. First of all,
remember that dogs aren't capable of understanding the value of our
stuff. Your dog doesn't know how much you paid for your patent leather
pumps. And even if she did, she wouldn't know why that makes them
more valuable than your tattered old slippers.

Second, remember that you can't communicate with your dog the
way you can with another person. Seeing your doormat reduced to
shreds is upsetting. But how are you going to explain that to your dog?
By yelling? What would be the point? Sure, she'll know you're upset. But
she won't necessarily know why. Even if you catch her in the act, the
most she'll figure out is that you go ballistic when you catch her chewing
on certain things. It won't teach her that chewing the doormat is bad. It
will only teach her that you may suddenly act scary and aggressive. For

all you know, your dog may not even connect your outburst with chewing. She may decide you act scary and aggressive when the sun's out. Or
when she's in your bedroom. Or when you're wearing a towel wrapped
around your head, if you happened to have just come from the shower
when you caught your dog gnawing your shoe.

Scolding for chewing can also backfire in another way. Believe it or
not, sometimes even negative attention can be fun for dogs. Say you're
sitting quietly reading a book. Your dog is nearby, but he's not having a
bit of fun. He's sitting around doing nothing—he doesn't even have
thumbs to twiddle—but suddenly he notices something. Every time he
chews a bit on the edge of the coffee table, you look up from your book.
You say his name. You may even jump to your feet and chase him off.
*Hooray, now this is some excitement! Soooo much better than just lying around
doing nothing . . .*

See how much better it is to give your dog a nice chew toy instead?
Use your wits and you avoid having your smart little dog learn the
wrong type of trick.

It also helps to remember that the responsibility for preventing
chewing is yours. You're the one who gives your dog access to your stuff.
You're the one who needs to give your dog positive ways to work off
stress or boredom.

At the same time, don't be too hard on yourself, either. Mistakes
happen. But you can learn from your mistakes. You can change the way
you manage your dog. You can work harder to redirect chewing in positive ways.

And finally, remind yourself that stuff is just stuff. Your dog is your
companion. Your buddy. Focusing too much on your ruined shoe may
also end up spoiling your relationship with your dog. And that's a far
greater loss than a silly shoe.

Chapter 6

PLEASE FENCE ME IN!
GUIDELINES FOR MAKING YOUR
DOG'S YARD TIME SAFE

A door is what a dog is perpetually on the wrong side of.
—Ogden Nash

Dogs love to be outdoors.

The problem is, outdoors isn't necessarily a safe place for a dog to be.

Dogs run into trouble when they run around loose—traffic, for instance. The results, unfortunately, are often deadly. One study in the 1980s followed 449 livestock-guarding dogs. These are dogs who, to do their jobs, can't be restrained by leashes or fenced-in yards. Over a six-year period, 38 of those dogs were killed by being hit by vehicles.[*] Those aren't terribly good odds—and these are dogs who live in relatively rural areas. Dogs in suburban or urban homes probably face an even greater risk when they run loose.

---

[*] Lorenz JR, Coppinger RP, Sutherland MR. Causes and economic effects of mortality in livestock guarding dogs. *J Range Mngmnt* 39:40 (Jul 1986), 294.

Dogs who run around loose can also end up lost. Stop by your local animal shelter and you'll see them: wonderful, friendly dogs who ended up where they are because they got loose and separated from their people.

Happily, some of these dogs will be reunited with their original families. Also happily, others will be placed in great new homes. But losing a pet is always heartbreaking, and finding a lost pet is iffy, at best. It's far better to prevent your dog from being lost in the first place.

Before the Recall, Start with Management

If you have a dog who comes when called—a behavior known as a "recall" in dog training—you have some control over your dog when he's not physically restrained. As we'll discuss further in the next chapter, however, it's not necessarily a good idea to rely on your dog to come when called. For one thing, training a recall requires thought, practice, and time. If you're starting with a puppy, even under the best of circumstances it may be two years or more before you have a reliable recall. And many dogs will never come when called with complete reliability. Part of this is due to our own failings as trainers. Part of it may be the dog's temperament. Calmer dogs master a recall more easily than dogs who are easily excited. Some dogs tend to check in with their people fairly often. Dogs who do this may respond faster to recall training than the type of dog who would, if allowed, spend hours away from home without wondering what his people are up to.

And even under the best of circumstances, it may be a bit of a stretch to call any recall "reliable." You could have a dog who came to you immediately the last 100 times you called. But that's still no guarantee he'll respond to your call the 101st time. Even experienced, professional trainers are careful not to put too much trust in recalls. Dogs with solid recalls have been known to mess up. Dogs can get spooked by unusual noises or sounds, or confused about where you are. Something new and exciting—like a dog's first glimpse of a wild deer—could make months of recall training vanish in a heartbeat.

In an Emergency

Because training a dog to come can be a challenge, you should be prepared in case your dog gets loose and doesn't respond to your call.

There are several things you can do in such an emergency. But be aware: These are stopgap measures. Even under the best of circumstances, chances are they'll work only once—not twice, and certainly not repeatedly. So don't think they are a substitute for management and recall training.

1. Run the other way. Most dogs, if they see you running away from them, will turn around and follow you. Be dramatic and convincing about where you're heading. Chances are, your dog will decide it's more fun to see what you're chasing than to head off on his own adventure.

2. Open a car door. If your dog loves car rides, this may entice him to return to you.

3. Act weird. Pretend to find something interesting on the ground. Talk to a blade of grass. Pick something up and hold a conversation with it. Your neighbors will think you're crazy, but it might get your dog's attention, and that's what counts.

For most of us, a recall is a useful tool. Someday, it may even save your dog's life. But it's not a substitute for good management.

In previous chapters of this book, we've looked at management for housetraining and for preventing dogs from developing bad habits, like destructive chewing. Management is also the ideal way to keep your dog safe when you are outdoors.

Yes, coming when called can help you keep your dog safe. But if you use management wisely, you'll never put yourself—or your dog—in a situation where his response to your call is a life-or-death matter.

Outdoor management tools you have at your disposal include fences, tie-outs, and leashes.

Fences

A fenced-in yard is a great way to create an exercise spot for your dog that will also keep her safe. A fenced-in yard gives your dog the opportunity to run and play unrestrained. Physically fencing a yard can also keep other dogs out, further helping to keep your dog safe.

A downside is that fencing a yard can be expensive. In many neighborhoods, fences can't be installed without obtaining building permits and other municipal permissions.

In addition, while fences are a great management tool, don't assume you can rely on them to hold an unsupervised dog. No fence is 100 percent escape-proof. It's not unusual for dogs to learn how to climb chain-link fences, for example. Larger, athletic dogs can jump all but the highest barriers. And dogs can, and do, dig their way out of fenced-in yards. Burying the base of a fence will at least slow down a digging dog. But for a dog with time on her paws, even those extra few inches won't keep her in the yard forever.

How much you can trust a fence depends on your dog. Dogs who are more adventurous and physically strong are more likely to figure out how to breach a fence. It also depends on what's on the other side of your fence. If you have an intact male dog, and a female dog in heat shows up in the neighborhood, you had better not rely on your fence. (This, by the way, is a very good reason to have your dog neutered.) On the other hand, if you have a couch potato who doesn't show much interest in passersby or other activities outside the yard, a fence might be an acceptable way to keep your dog safe.

Why Neutering Is a Good Idea

If you had a magic wand that would instantly address at least one potential health or behavior problem, would you wave it?

Well, you have that magic wand: It's called neutering your dog.

Let's consider your dog's health first. Neutering is a well-documented way to reduce a dog's risk for certain health problems, including tumors that affect the reproductive organs.

But neutering can also help you with training. Intact dogs are driven to go out, find other intact dogs, and mate with them. Neutered dogs, on the other hand, don't have this same drive. So right away, your job as trainer is easier.

Many veterinarians and canine behaviorists also believe that neutering male dogs, in particular, can help prevent aggressive behaviors from developing.

If that's not enough, there's a strong ethical argument for neutering your dog as well. Every year, millions of dogs are euthanized in U.S. animal shelters because they do not have homes. Neutering your dog is one of the few ways you can be certain that you're not contributing to this tragedy.

So wave that magic wand. Get your dog neutered.

Even if you trust your dog, however, your fence probably has another weakness: the gate. Gates are operated by people, and most people make mistakes from time to time. If your gate has to be used by visitors—guests, or utility service people, for example—or by kids, there's an even greater chance it will be left open at some point. You can compensate for this, to some extent, if the gate has a spring mounted on it to pull it shut automatically. But to be on the safe side, use management. Check the gate before you let your dog outside. Put a sign on the gate door reminding others to keep it shut. And supervise your dog when she's outside.

ELECTRIC FENCES

Not all fences are physical barriers. Another type of fence uses an electrical wire buried around the perimeter of a yard. The dog is fitted with a collar that delivers an electric shock if she gets too close to the wire. The collar first gives a warning tone or beep, to give the dog a chance to avoid the shock. Ideally, the dog will learn to keep a safe distance from the wire, which will keep her in the yard.

There are a couple of advantages to this type of fence. They can be less expensive than physical fencing. They can also be placed with more flexibility. For example, they can be used to keep dogs out of gardens.

However, there are also a number of problems with this type of fence. First, there's the concept of using electric shock as a training tool. Even if you decide it's okay ethically, this type of approach carries with it the same potential fallout as other training techniques based on aversion. Receiving an electrical shock is stressful. Even anticipating a shock is stressful. For dogs who are "soft"—particularly sensitive to pain or corrections—or who have problems with fearfulness or aggression, using shocks to train may have serious consequences. It could exacerbate a dog's tendency to be fearful, for example.

There are other ways that this type of fence can backfire. Sometimes they can train the wrong thing. Dogs have been known to associate the shock with the whole yard. Meaning, a dog who was once happy to go outside is suddenly afraid to step through the door. He doesn't realize he gets a shock from getting too close to the edge of the yard—he thinks just going outside is what causes the jolt. Needless to say, this is *not* helpful for housetraining.

There's also the possibility that this type of fence will fail completely as a training tool. For some dogs, the discomfort of the shock doesn't outweigh the rewards of going outside the fence. If you have a dog who lives to chase squirrels, for example, that electrical shock may be a small price to pay for a chance to tree the little furry guy across the street.

Plus, once the dog breaches this type of fence, he may be stuck outside. This gets back to rewards-vs.-discomfort again. Unless there's now a squirrel inside the yard, why would your dog choose to get another shock? Instead, he'll go play or explore somewhere else (or, best case, look for you, if he's had enough excitement for the day).

And last but not least, this type of fence doesn't keep *other* dogs out. So it won't protect your dog from other dogs.

This brings us to a final note about fences. Electric-type fences aren't the only sort that can fail to protect your dog. Even the highest, strongest physical fence isn't a substitute for supervision.

In some parts of the country, pet dogs can become the prey of wild animals, like mountain lions, coyotes, owls, or eagles. A determined wild predator isn't likely to be deterred by a fence.

Fences won't necessarily stop kids from teasing your dog. Sadly, they can't stop a troubled adult from trying to injure your dog.

And finally, dogs left alone in fenced-in yards can find other ways to get in trouble. They can step on something sharp and get injured, or swallow something they shouldn't. So don't rely on the fence to protect your dog. Don't leave your dog outside, unattended, for long periods of time. Supervision is a must.

Tie-Outs

Another option for controlling the outdoor dog is to tether her. This is considerably less expensive than fencing. It's a great way to keep your dog near you when you're outside. For example, if you're outdoors doing yard work or gardening, your dog might enjoy being tethered near you as you work.

Tethered dogs, however, don't have as much freedom of movement as dogs in a fenced-in yard, so tethering is not as useful for exercising a dog.

Cable runs (a leash line mounted, with a pulley, to a cable) give a dog more running space than a staked tether, so they give some exercise to smaller dogs.

Just as fences are not foolproof, tie-outs can also fail. Stakes can be worked out of the ground, particularly if the earth is wet or soft. Over time, even plastic-coated, wire-cable tethers can wear out and break.

Tying a dog can also put her at risk. A tied dog can't escape from potential danger (for example, from other dogs) as easily as a dog free to run. The tie-out itself can entangle a dog.

Tying a dog in a public place is even more problematic, because it leaves her vulnerable to all kinds of mischief, from teasing kids to getting tangled.

So just as with fencing, never substitute a tie-out for supervision. Check your dog frequently if she's tied up outside. Make sure she has an adequate supply of water, and that she can reach it easily. If it's hot out, make sure she's not getting overheated and can get into some shade. If it's cold, make sure she's warm enough.

Don't leave your dog tied up when you leave home. A tied-up dog can get into trouble in a few short minutes. If you're not around to supervise, your dog should be somewhere you know she's safe, such as indoors in a crate.

Leashes

Fences and tie-outs can help keep your outside dog safe in your yard. In other outdoor situations, the way to control your dog is with a leash. See chapter 9 for detailed help on training your dog to walk nicely on a leash.

The Lure of an Open Door

To prevent a runaway dog, there's one other hot spot you need to address: outside doors.

Dogs tend to get very excited about doors—especially the kind that lead outside. And why not? First of all, doors are where you appear when you come home. They are where strangers arrive. It's where the pizzas are delivered. For a dog who loves to greet people, doors are like a big huge treat dispenser.

Doors to the outside are also exciting because of what's beyond them. Most dogs find indoors pretty boring compared with what's outside. When the outside door opens, that really livens things up.

Most dogs can't learn to open doors themselves, of course. But they know humans can. So when a dog sees you approach a door, he knows what happens next. Some dogs also figure out that when you open the door, it's possible to bolt past you and outside. For a dog who likes getting outside for a little off-leash romp, an open door can be an irresistible temptation.

Now, if outside the door is only a fenced-in yard, that's one thing. But if the open door leads to the street or some other dangerous place, a dog who bolts outside is a dog who's not safe.

There are two ways to address this problem. One is management: Prevent your dog from slipping out the door. You might, for example, make sure your dog is always leashed or crated before you open the door for any reason. Confining the dog in another room behind a baby gate, if practical, is another option, particularly in situations where multiple guests are arriving and leaving.

Management is particularly important for puppies and young, active dogs, because it helps prevent a problematic behavior from getting established.

But here's something else you can do: Teach your dog to sit and wait for your okay before going through an open door.

Training Door Manners

To do this, you use going outdoors as your training reward.

First, approach an outside door with your dog. If the door leads to a safe, fenced-in yard, you don't need to leash the dog. Otherwise, have her on a leash.

Then stand by the door as if you're getting ready to open it, and wait until your dog sits. At first, this might take a while, particularly if your dog is psyched about the idea of going outside. But don't let yourself get discouraged. Be patient. Sooner or later, your dog will get tired of prancing and nudging you, and she'll sit down. She may look at you like she thinks you're weird, but she'll be sitting.

That is your signal to act. As soon as she has settled into a sit, reach for the door.

If she jumps back up again—and she might, because she thinks this means you're about to open the door—pull your hand back. Now you're going to start over again, waiting for her to sit.

When you get a sit, reach for the door again.

Repeat this until you can put your hand on the door handle without your dog leaping to her feet.

Then progress to the next step: Open the door a crack. But continue to use the same technique—if your dog lifts her back end up, shut the door, drop your hand, and wait again for a sit.

With time—and probably not a lot of time—your dog will start to understand. *Oh. I see. When I sit, I make my human open the door.* How did this happen? It depends on how you look at it. From your perspective, you used a reward—the open door—to train your dog to sit politely before heading outside. From your dog's perspective, you've been trained to open the door when you see your dog sitting.

At this point, you can add a release word to the exercise. This is the word you can use to tell your dog, *Now you can do whatever you want.* The words *okay* or *free* are often used for this purpose. Once you say it, leave the door wide open for your dog. After a few practice sessions incorporating your release word, your dog will catch on that *okay* means she is free to go out.

Regardless of who's outwitting whom, if you do this consistently, from puppyhood, you will end up with a dog who is less likely to bolt through open doors. It's a great way to keep your dog safe and under control.

Chapter 7

HEY—GET BACK HERE! OUTWITTING THE DOG WHO WON'T COME

How many times all through his life have I not seen him, at my
whistle, start violently and turn his tail to me, then, with nose thrown
searchingly from side to side, begin to canter toward the horizon!
                                    —John Galsworthy, "Memories"

Of all the things you need to teach your dog, one of the most important
is to come when called. The ideal, sometimes referred to as a "solid recall," is a dog who, no matter what, will turn on a dime the second you
give your recall cue, run up to you, and let you touch her and take her
by the collar if you want.

The opposite is a dog who, given a choice between you and the
wide, wide world, with its fascinating smells, sights, and creatures, will
choose the world. This is the dog who doesn't even appear to hear you
when you call. Or if she does, she might pause, turn around, look at
you, then return to whatever she was doing when you interrupted. Or
pause, turn around, look at you—and start running as fast as she can in
the opposite direction.

So why is this important? At the beginning of chapter 6, we covered
some of the dangers faced by loose dogs. But of course, there's also the

selfish, superficial reason: It's humiliating to shout yourself hoarse at a dog who is merrily dashing away. Problems with housetraining or chewing may be annoying, but at least they're somewhat private. When you have a dog who won't come, your neighbors will definitely find out about it, sooner or later. Probably about the time they see you running down the street in your bathrobe waving a leash and shrieking obscenities.

A good recall also makes spending time with your dog more pleasant. For example, if you take walks in fenced dog parks or other enclosures where off-leash dogs are permitted, you'll be able to retrieve your dog more easily when the walk is over. It helps you avoid annoyances, such as times when your dog has discovered something smelly and you'd rather she not roll in it. Or maybe she's heading toward another person and you would rather she keep her distance. In situations like this, a recall can stop your dog and bring her back to you.

Even in your own backyard, a recall is useful. If you're ready to leave the house for an appointment, and your dog is out chasing butterflies in the yard, you don't want to wait until there are no more butterflies. You want to be able to call your dog back indoors and be on your way.

While having a solid recall is important, it isn't the easiest behavior to train. Part of that has to do with the setting where recalls are most needed.

When it comes to training dogs, there are times when you have no competition. Say you're training your dog to sit. The training session is taking place indoors, and there's nothing else going on. You have no competition. The rewards you're offering your dog—whether treat, attention, or praise—are by far the most interesting things in her world right now.

Now imagine that you have taken your dog to a park. There may be other dogs around, which means endless opportunities for your dog to meet, play, and conduct other dog–dog business. And there are other attractions as well—other people, birds and squirrels, dropped food, and passing bicycles.

In this situation, your treats and praise, wonderful as they are, may not be quite enough to keep your dog's attention. It's a bit like asking you to choose between a stick of licorice and a dinner with two of your closest friends at your favorite restaurant.

So when you're outside with your dog, you have your work cut out for you. You need to compete with a whole menu of alluring stimuli.

As if that weren't enough, most dogs tend to become very focused when something catches their attention. When a dog sees something interesting—another dog, or a cat, or a stranger—she may well focus on that, to the exclusion of everything else around her.

It's also important to remember that a dog's senses of smell and hearing are much more acute than a human's. Consider what this means to your dog's awareness. When you step outside, you may notice whether the air smells fresh or not. You may smell a nearby apple tree in bloom, or the exhaust from a passing truck.

Your dog's nose, on the other hand, is awash with countless other smells. Her ears are flooded with sounds people can't hear. In other words, not only is the world outside interesting, to a dog it's also more full than the world we experience.

So when your dog doesn't respond when you call her, it may be she's so engrossed in sensory impressions that your voice can't get through. Just like when you're watching your favorite television drama, or reading that fast-paced thriller, you may not hear it the first time your significant other calls your name.

Despite these challenges, however, it *is* possible to train your dog to come to you.

The Foundation of a Recall

There are two keys to training a dog to come when called:

1. Your dog must know that the rewards for returning to you are better than the rewards for doing anything else.

2. You and your dog must practice the come behavior until his response is a deeply ingrained habit.

It's tempting to think that coming when called is a simple behavior. It's not. Some of the things your dog needs to master to execute a come include: learning to pay attention to you; learning to accept you grabbing his collar and putting his leash on; and learning that coming to you earns a reward.

Let's take a closer look at these foundation steps and how to work on them with your dog.

ATTENTION

One of the most important things you can teach your dog is that paying attention to you is rewarding. This is something you can work on at any time with your dog—inside or outside.

A great way to do this is to use food.

Here's how to do it. First, pick some sort of food reward. What type of treat you use is up to you, but remember that you don't want to exceed your dog's daily calorie requirements. So whatever food you set aside to use for training, subtract that amount from the food you give your dog in his meals that day.

Also, use little bits of food, not large treats like dog biscuits. To really train your dog, you'll want to reward him a lot. Maybe 20 or 30 times a day. If you're handing out 20 dog biscuits a day, they aren't going to seem quite as special by 5:00 P.M. He'll be full, for one thing.

So use small treats. How small? Ever watch a dog sniff under the kitchen table looking for crumbs? Ever notice how, when he finds a grain of rice, or tiny crumb of cheese, or a single molecule of gravy, he gobbles it down as if that were the nicest thing he'd ever tasted? Well, that's the power of food to a dog. It's not the size that matters. It's the fact that it's food. In other words, you can use treats the size of bread crumbs, as long as your dog knows it's food.

Keep your food on your person, but out of sight. In a pocket, maybe. Then, when you're around your dog, reward him when he pays attention to you. This may happen in one of two ways. He might just come up to you from time to time, or look at you. When he does, tell him "yes!" and give him a treat.

You can also get his attention. Call his name, or clap your hands. If he doesn't seem to notice, that's fine; don't worry about it. But if he does look up, offer another treat.

Vary the circumstances of this exercise. Work on it sometimes when there are no distractions competing for his attention. Other times, try calling his name when he's involved in something else—like investigating the kitchen garbage can. Work on it outside as well as in. But don't treat this like a test. Whatever you do, don't punish your dog if he doesn't respond when you want him to. The object is to teach your dog that paying attention to you is always rewarding.

Is Training with Food a Good Idea?

For a dog, eating is one of life's greatest rewards. For this reason, food is a very useful training tool. It's portable. It can motivate your dog even when she's being tempted by other experiences. And you can vary it. For example, maybe you use boring food, like kibble, sometimes, but other times use a special treat, like a bit of roast chicken. Sometimes you might reward your dog with a tiny little piece of food—but on special occasions, the reward might be your dog's entire dinner.

Some people worry that using food to train a dog is too much like paying a bribe. But what is a bribe, really? A bribe is when you pay someone, up front, to either do something or promise not to do something. When you use food to train a dog, though, you never pay up front. You dispense the food *after* your dog has completed a behavior. Yes, your dog will be working for the food. But you've set the criteria.

If you use food rewards, you'll also be in good company. Many top dog trainers use food to train their dogs. Watch the handlers at Westminster or another first-rate dog show, and you'll see that many use food to keep their dogs alert and focused while they're being judged.

You can also train your dog with other types of rewards, like praise. But dogs have a special relationship with food. Using treats to train can really help your dog learn, and learn quickly.

Food is also versatile, because it can be used as a lure as well as a reward:

✓ **Food as a lure.** A treat can be used to get a dog's attention and position her. For example, you can start teaching a dog to sit by holding a treat, in your closed fist, over your dog's nose, then moving your hand back—kind of like you're petting her—until she drops her hindquarters into a sit. (See chapter 9 for a step-by-step guide in teaching a sit using a food lure.)

✓ **Food as a reward.** As rewards, food treats are used to reinforce desired behaviors. They increase the chances that your dog will perform a behavior again. When you use food in this way, your dog may not even know, in advance, that you have a treat on hand. You bring it out and give it to her after she's completed the behavior you're trying to train. In this way, you increase the chances that she'll do that behavior again.

One final note about using food for training: Make sure the treats you're using are safe and healthy. Think about your dog's overall calorie and nutritional requirements. If necessary, use some of your dog's regular mealtime food for training to avoid overfeeding or throwing your dog's diet out of balance.

GRABBING YOUR DOG'S COLLAR

What does it mean, to a dog, when someone grabs her collar?

To answer this question, you need to look at it from your dog's perspective. What happens right after the collar grab? Does she get dragged away from something she really wants to play in, like the neighbor's tipped-over garbage can? Does her playtime at the park come to an end? Does she get scolded or handled roughly?

If a dog thinks a collar grab may mean something unpleasant, she may decide that it's better to avoid it altogether. Smart dog! But unfortunately, that will not help her humans teach her how to come when called. They may end up with a dog who won't come at all. Or who comes kind of close, but shies away if someone reaches for her collar.

So what do you do to train your dog to accept collar grabs? The key is to teach her that grabbing her collar means good things, not bad things. Several times a day, approach your dog, grab her collar, say "yes!" or "good!" and give her a treat. Do this in many different situations: when she's playing, when she's eating, when she's just walking around the house investigating things. Do it outdoors as well as indoors. Practice during times when she can see you coming, and at times when you know you'll surprise her. And also vary your movements. For example, grab her collar quickly sometimes; at other times grab it slowly. Grab her from the back, the side, and the front.

As you work on this, watch your dog. If she shies away from your hand—maybe because she's naturally on the timid side, or maybe because she's had some bad collar-grabbing experiences—you may need to progress more slowly. The key is not to push her; the exercise shouldn't make her uncomfortable.

Over time, your dog will associate good things with collar grabs.

Once you've practiced this for a while, add another step: After you've grabbed the collar, snap on her leash. Say "yes!" again, give a treat—and then take the leash right off. This helps train your dog not to duck or play Keep Away when she sees you coming with a leash in your hand.

It's also helpful to take other opportunities to grab or hold your dog's collar, simply to get her used to having her collar handled. For example, hold her collar when she's on your lap, or when you are down on the floor petting her.

Introducing the Word *Come*

So far, we've looked at two separate training exercises that will help build a foundation for a good recall. But notice that we aren't using the word *come* at all yet.

There's a reason for that. In dog obedience, *come* is an example of what's called a cue. When you use a word as a cue, you want your dog to respond, when he hears it, with a specific behavior.

If this is going to happen, however, you have to be very careful of how you use that particular word. A cue is not a command. It isn't a magic spell. It can't force your dog to do something just because you'd like him to do it.

So if cues aren't commands, how is it that some dogs respond immediately and fluidly to them? Simply this: A particular behavior is so completely and strongly associated with a particular word that when the dog hears that word, he automatically executes the behavior. It's like when we humans reach for our phones the second they ring. We can do it in our sleep, it's so deeply grooved into our brains.

So what does it take to strongly associate a cue with a particular behavior? There are a couple of things that you, the human, have to watch, especially at first. One is that you don't ever use that special word *unless* you are certain you are about to get the desired behavior.

Come is an excellent example. Say you take your puppy or young dog outdoors to your fenced-in backyard to practice the come. You start out, calling "come" just as your dog runs up to the fence to chase a bird. You try again, calling "come" as your dog investigates a new smell next to the garage. One more time, you call "come," only this time your dog has found an old tennis ball; he runs up to you, then darts off to see if you might be enticed to chase him.

You've now used the word *come* three times. And not once have you associated the cue with the recall behavior. Instead, you've associated *come* with chasing birds, smelling the ground, and playing Chase Me. This weakens the word *come* as a cue. It makes the sound of you saying "come" more like background noise than something your dog should care about.

You should also be scrupulous about not associating *come* with bad things. Again, this is especially important when you're first working on recall behaviors. Don't call your dog when he's in the middle of playing, or you'll teach him that *come* means "the fun is over now!" And most of all, never call your dog to "come" and then punish him for something. Doing that is probably the fastest way to ruin the word *come* for you and your dog.

Starting Fresh with a New Cue

So what do you do if you've used *come* to call your dog, but in the wrong way? What if you have a dog who's gotten used to ignoring *come*? What if you've adopted an adult dog who responds to *come* by running away?

The answer is simple: Choose a new cue to call your dog.

Start from the beginning with your foundation exercises on attention and the collar grab. Then, when you introduce your recall cue, pick a new word. Try *here!* or a whistle. Or use *come* in a different language.

In some cases, it may be helpful to choose a cue that has positive associations for you, too. Why not choose a word you use to tell your dog she's going to eat, or get a treat? Calling "Dinner!" or "Cookies!" has some great advantages. Chances are, you'll always say the word with a happy voice. And chances are, when you do say it, you'll back it up with food or treats.

Instead, associate *come* with terrific things.

Start by practicing *come* when you feed your dog her dinner. Most of the time, as you get your dog's food bowl ready, she'll be right there watching. She's seen you pick up her dish, heard you rattle the kibble bag, open the refrigerator, or run the can opener. So now, as you get ready to put the dish down, quickly step back away from her a few paces. Say "come" as she reaches you and the bowl. Then stand still, say "yes!" and put the bowl down.

Another time to practice using the cue *come* is when your dog is already focused on you and coming toward you. Watch for times when she's running up to you enthusiastically. Maybe she runs up to you when she sees you take her favorite toy down from the shelf. Or maybe when she sees you pick up her leash, she knows you're getting ready to take her on a walk. When this happens, as soon as she starts running up to you, say "come!" When she gets to you, stand still, say "yes!" and then play with her or start your walk.

Play—Another Motivator

Most dogs regard food as a terrific reward. But many dogs also love to play—and playing can be a great way to reward them.

Does your dog get excited when you get out a ball, Frisbee, or tug toy? Do his eyes light up, does he wriggle all over, are his eyes glued to yours? If so, you have a powerful reward at your disposal. Simply use a short play session to reward your dog when he executes a behavior you like.

Say you have a dog who loves to chase Frisbees, and you're working on the come. You go outside with your dog, and when he's on the other side of the yard, pull out your Frisbee. When he sees you have it, and starts running up, say "come!" Then, when he gets to you, say "yes!" and start your Frisbee game.

THE NEXT STEP

The next way to practice the come takes advantage of dogs' curiosity and sociability. You may have observed that your dog will follow you reflexively if you move quickly away from him. If you jump out of your chair in the living room during a commercial break, for example, and head for the kitchen, will your dog often scramble up to follow? Unless he's sick, injured, or sleeping soundly, chances are he will.

So try this. While on a walk (using a retractable leash), or outside in a fenced-in yard, watch for a time when your dog doesn't seem too interested in anything around him. Then suddenly exclaim "oh!" or "wow!" in an excited, happy voice. Back up quickly, or turn and run away a few steps. Chances are, your dog will wonder what is going on. He'll turn to see, and possibly even run up to you. If this happens, and he's approaching you enthusiastically, say "come" and pull a surprise goodie out of your pocket, like his dinner in a plastic bag, or a favorite toy.

Practice, Practice, Practice

The exercises we've described so far are all based on associating *come* with wonderful things.

The other part of training a solid recall is practice. You want your dog to have executed a recall so many times, under so many different circumstances, that responding to your cue is automatic.

When you start training a recall, you must be careful to never use the *come* cue unless you're certain that your dog is going to come to you. But sooner or later, you'll have to test *come* when your dog is paying attention to something else. At this point, you're adding a new level of difficulty and complexity to the behavior.

The key is to watch your dog closely, and be ready to back down a level if she isn't ready to progress. For example, say you have been working on the come in your yard. So far, you've only used the cue when your dog is already running up to you. After a few weeks of this, wait until your dog is on the other side of the yard, but not very interested in anything around her. Call "come!" If she doesn't respond, don't try it again until you have practiced the simpler come exercises for another few weeks.

But if she responds immediately and runs up to you, terrific. You've successfully begun associating *come* with a behavior. Give her a wonderful reward—part of her dinner or a fun play session. You can now add this exercise to your training regimen: calling your dog when she isn't around any distractions.

After a few weeks of this level of difficulty, you're ready for the next step: calling her when there *is* something else around competing for her attention. You still work in your yard—a place she's explored many times, so it doesn't hold all that many surprises. But now wait until something interesting crops up. Maybe a squirrel runs through a tree over her head. Or a dog next door comes outside, too. Now try "come" and see what she does. Just as before, if she doesn't respond to you, you know this is too advanced for her right now. But if she does, let her know how great she's doing with a special treat.

After you've mastered this level, you can try an even more difficult scenario. For example, invite a friend over and see if your dog will leave another friendly person when you call.

If you are diligent and consistent with your recall training, you will have a dog who runs up to you reliably when you call. And that's terrific. You've mastered something that has frustrated many a dog owner. You'll be able to enjoy your dog more—and your dog will be safer as well.

A Few Other Recall Do's and Don'ts

✓ **Posture.** Watch your posture when you call your dog. Dogs who are timid or small may feel uncomfortable if you bend over or stretch out your hands. Standing up straight, with your hands at your sides, encourages your dog to come closer to you when you call.

✓ **Tone of voice.** Listen to your voice. Use a happy tone. And practice "come" in a medium voice, not a yell. If your dog is paying attention to you, he'll hear you. If he's not, even yelling won't help.

✓ **Vary the end of the exercise.** Vary what happens when your dog comes to you. For example, at different times you might touch your dog's collar, snap on the leash, or neither. Once in a while, snap on the leash, then take it right off and let your dog go play again. This way, your dog won't associate the sight of the leash, combined with "come," with the end of playtime.

✓ **Special surprises.** Another great way to keep come exercises exciting for your dog is to plan some special rewards. Hide something really fun in your jacket pocket, or somewhere around your yard, like in a tree or on a fence. The surprise might be a beloved toy, part of your dog's dinner, or a special treat. Then, when your dog performs a successful come, you can deliver an unexpected reward. This helps teach your dog that coming when you call is appealing even when there are other interesting things going on.

✓ **Retractable lead and long-line training.** Using a retractable leash or long line (a lightweight rope attached to the dog's collar) can help you control your dog while practicing and rewarding the come. Just be careful: The longer the leash, the greater the risk of injury should your dog be accidentally jerked.

Chapter 8

Down! Stop It! Don't Do That! Outwitting the Dog Who Has Baaaad Manners

Although large and getting larger, it is his opinion that he is a lap dog and as such entitled to climb on my chair whether I am in it or not.
—Jack Alan, "From Pillar to Post or How to Raise a Dog"

Sometimes dogs seem to act so much like four-legged, furry people that we start thinking of them as if they were family members.

But all too often, they don't act like people at all. Instead of saying *hi* and shaking our hands to greet us, they jump up and jab at us with their paws. Instead of sitting nicely on their own furniture, they use furniture we'd like to keep off-limits. They swipe food off our counters without asking permission. In short, some dogs just don't have good manners.

Of course, that's actually not quite true, if you look at things from a dog's perspective. When two well-socialized, confident dogs greet each other, what do they do? They jump on each other. They mouth each other. They bark and paw each other and wrestle. And they both love it. To a dog, that's wonderful manners. Wonderful doggy manners.

But when a dog uses doggy manners on a person, *then* the difficulties begin. Especially when the person being jumped on, mouthed, barked at, and wrestled with didn't invite it.

So the trick is to teach a dog—who may have wonderful doggy manners—to choose completely different behaviors when he's around people.

It all comes back to helping our dogs fit in our lives.

Setting the Right Expectations

Whether you already have a dog or are reading this book to prepare for one, a good place to start is by asking yourself just what around-the-house manners you'd like your dog to have. It helps to think about your daily routine around your home, and how your dog might affect it. (Or does affect it, if you already have a dog.)

Here are some areas you may want to think about.

GREETING PEOPLE

Jumping up on people to greet them is a pretty natural behavior for most dogs. But it can also create problems. When dogs jump up, they can muddy or tear people's clothing. Even worse, if the dog is large, or if the person being jumped on is small or frail, the dog could knock the person over. So ask yourself how you'd like your dog to greet people.

In many cases, the ideal would be for the dog to sit and wait to be petted.

AROUND YOUR DOG'S STUFF

This is another dog manners hot spot. How do you want your dog to behave when a person comes near her food dish? Or her favorite toy? Or her bed? Sometimes dogs develop a behavior called resource guarding. When they think someone is going to take something valuable away, they'll try to protect it. They'll growl, show their teeth, snap the air, or even bite.

AROUND YOUR FOOD

Do you want a dog who swipes food anytime it's within reach? Chances are, you don't. Be prepared, particularly if you have a tall dog—and are in the habit of leaving food out on counters or your kitchen table. "Counter-surfing" is a hard behavior to change once a dog has learned it. A related issue is how you'd like your dog to behave during your meals. Do you want him pushing his nose into your lap, begging for tidbits? Or lying quietly in the next room?

DURING QUIET TIMES

How would you like your dog to behave when you're relaxing? Watching television? Reading a book? Again, from your dog's perspective, it's not necessarily rude to pester you when you're trying to relax. It's your job to teach her how to behave when there's nothing exciting (to her) going on.

These are a few areas to think about. There are many more. For example, how would you like your dog to behave when he's picked up something in his mouth? Would you like him to drop it or let you take it from him? When the phone rings, will you mind if your dog gets excited and barky? And so on.

By considering these kinds of questions, chances are you'll end up with a picture of how your ideal dog would behave.

Great so far.

Now it's time to get realistic.

Ideal dogs are . . . ideal. And sometimes it's hard to achieve ideals in real life. Not that you can't get pretty close. You can. But there's another factor you need to watch as well: If you expect too much, too soon, you set yourself up to get pretty frustrated.

For starters, how old is your dog? Puppies are high-energy individuals. Just like kids, they have a harder time than adults with "people manners." So if you have a puppy, figure that it might take a couple of years for her to master everything.

Another factor is your dog's temperament. Dogs who are naturally more excitable can take a bit longer to learn good manners. And some dogs are just more likely to exhibit behaviors we don't like.

You may also want to cut yourself a little slack while you're at it. Particularly if you tend to be a perfectionist. Unless you've trained many, many other dogs already, you're bound to make some mistakes. Things might shape up a bit more slowly than you'd like. That's okay. The nice thing about dog manners is that most of these behaviors aren't a matter of life and death. The other nice thing is that you can use management to control your dog until she's mastered her indoor manners.

If you have a puppy, a good goal is to try to invest a little time—5 or 10 minutes—every day in working on indoor manners. If you have an older dog, investing 5 or 10 minutes several days a week may be all you need. Do this, and with time you'll get where you, and your dog, want to be.

Management

When it comes to indoor manners, you have four basic tools at your disposal. One, you've met before: management. Whenever possible, you should try to manage the situation so that your dog doesn't get into trouble—or develop bad habits.

When it comes to indoor manners, the key to managing your dog is to know your dog. Don't kid yourself if you can't quite trust him to behave. Instead, find ways to keep him out of trouble. If he jumps up on people, for example, put him on a leash when the doorbell rings so you can prevent it.

If your dog swipes food off tables or counters, cultivate the habit of cleaning up leftovers immediately. Put dirty dishes down in your sink, instead of leaving them where your dog can reach them. Remember that food is a great reward—if your dog succeeds in swiping a sandwich off the counter even once, he'll be on the lookout for sandwich number two for the rest of his life.

Calm Is Good

Management, of course, isn't a long-range substitute for training. You need to work on your dog's manners, too. But until you teach him the right way to behave, use management to keep him from practicing the wrong way to behave.

Now let's look at some other tools for teaching good doggy manners:

1. Reinforcing calm indoor behavior.

2. Training your dog in some basic good manners.

3. Teaching your dog self-control.

We'll start with calm behavior.

As you observe your dog, you'll notice that sometimes he's calm, and sometimes he's not. Call it his state of arousal. At one extreme, you have a dog who's dozing or even fast asleep. He's relaxed. His eyelids are droopy or closed.

At the other extreme, you have a dog on high alert. You can tell by his body language. His ears may be pricked or lying flat; his hackles may be standing on end. His tail may be held up high, or straight out stiff; it may be wagging or tucked between his legs.

He may be running around—or he may be standing stiffly, making himself tall, as if he were standing on tiptoe. If he's frightened, he may be slinking and ducking his head.

If he's a vocal dog, he'll be barking, growling, whining, or howling. If he's anxious, he may salivate, scratch at things, or chew.

Each of these signals has its own combination of possible meanings. (See the appendix for a list of resources for learning more about reading your dog's body language.) The point here is not to worry about what your dog is feeling, but simply to understand that he's aroused.

Now, between that state of complete arousal and the state of sleep is a continuum. Here you'll find combinations of those signals. Say you have an adult dog, and he's on the floor, napping, and the doorbell rings. He lifts his head. He's still lying down, but his ears are pricked and his tail starts to wag. This is a dog who is fairly relaxed, but alert. That's one point on the continuum.

Now the door opens, and it's your best friend who, unbeknownst to you, has just adopted a puppy and has brought her over to meet your dog. In runs the puppy—and up jumps your dog. Now he's moderately aroused. He's standing and his tail is out stiff, as he lets the puppy jump up and nip at his tail and neck.

Now suppose the puppy succeeds in getting your dog to play, and suddenly you have two dogs running and wrestling in the house. At this point, you're nearing the full-arousal end of the continuum.

You tell your friend that maybe it would be better to take the puppy outside. So the puppy is removed, and your dog now passes along the continuum the other way. For a while he may pace the house a bit, sniffing. Maybe he comes over to you and pushes his nose into your hand to be petted. Finally he settles down, flops onto the ground with a sigh, licks his front foot a couple of times, and starts to doze again.

As you watch your dog, you'll see him pass through this continuum over and over, depending on the time of day, what activities are going on around him, and, of course, his temperament.

What you'll also notice is that, generally speaking, the less aroused he is, the more appropriate his behavior is for an indoor dog. A dog who is relaxing on the floor, sleeping, or playing quietly with a chew toy is a dog who is not getting into trouble. He's not jumping up on someone. He's not running around the house accidentally tripping people.

So how do you encourage your dog to stay at the calm end of the spectrum when he's inside? By reinforcing calmer behavior—and not reinforcing aroused behavior.

Sometimes this requires us to watch how we reward our dogs. After all, aroused behaviors are often cute behaviors—at least at first. It might be hilarious when your eight-week-old puppy scrambles along when you run to answer the phone. But when she's grown into a 70-pound adult dog who jumps up and starts barking anytime the phone rings (including when the phone ringing is a television phone, not a real phone), it's not so funny anymore.

As this example suggests, we also need to watch our own behavior. When it comes to arousal, dogs often take their cues from us. If you jump up excitedly and run to the phone, chances are your dog will jump up and run also. If you wait for a couple of rings, then walk to the phone calmly, your dog may ignore you, or watch you for a second and then go back to whatever she was doing before.

If you tend to be an excitable or nervous person, try modifying your own responses a bit when you're around your dog. You'll be more likely to end up with a dog who acts calmer.

Here are some other guidelines for teaching your dog to be calmer while indoors:

✦ **Try to reward your dog for calm indoor behaviors several times a day.** For example, if you see that your dog is stretched out and relaxed somewhere, approach him quietly. Pet him calmly, praise him in a quiet, gentle voice, and quietly give him a small (not terribly exciting) treat. The goal is to give him attention without getting him excited.

✦ **When your dog approaches you for attention, observe how aroused he is before you respond.** If he's too excited and pushy—if he paws you, jumps up on you, or nudges you—ignore him. Look away and avoid eye contact. After a while, he'll give up and sit down. At this point, calmly pet and praise him. Once you've done this a few times, make the game just a little bit harder. For example, if he used to nudge and paw you, don't pay attention to him *unless* he only nudges you before he sits. If he paws you, he gets no attention at all. Then, once he's learned that pawing never works, make the game a little bit harder again. Now only pay attention to him if he nudges you once or twice before he sits. And so on—until you have a dog who knows that if he wants attention, he has to "ask politely" by sitting near you calmly.

✦ **Leave the high-energy games outdoors.** Use your judgment here. If you have a toy-breed dog, games of Fetch and Tug are probably fine for inside (as long as you're not playing on a slippery surface). But for larger breeds, or if your dog tends to get too wild or barky, choose different kinds of indoor games, such as doing tricks or practicing behaviors like sit and down.

Basic Behaviors That Help with Manners: Sit, Down, Stay

A number of basic obedience behaviors also help with manners. When your dog responds to cues like *sit* or *down*, you have another tool for controlling her in situations where good manners are important. Trainers sometimes call this "asking for an alternative behavior." For example, say you have a dog who jumps up on people. You train her to sit when you say "sit." After many repetitions, your dog becomes very fluent with this behavior, responding consistently to your cue.

Now, someone comes to your door. Your dog rushes up to greet the guest. You (or the guest) say "sit" and the dog drops into a sit—instead of jumping up on the guest.

This won't work unless you have practiced enough with your dog that the sit behavior is solid. But if you have, you have a great tool at your disposal. After all, even the most versatile dogs have trouble jumping up and sitting at the same time.

Sit

There are several key behaviors that can help a lot with indoor manners. Two of these are sit and down. Train your dog to respond to cues with these behaviors, and you have a terrific start on controlling your dog when you need him to display good manners.

To train this behavior, it's helpful to use a technique called luring: Use a treat to get your dog to put his body in a sit position. To see how powerful a technique this can be, get a nice, tempting treat and find a boring place, like the living room or kitchen. The fewer people or animals around, the better. If you have trouble eliminating distractions, you can even try shutting yourself and your dog alone in the bathroom.

Now close the treat into your fist and show your fist to your dog. Does he immediately glue his nose to your fist? If you move it, does he follow it wherever it goes?

Now move your fist, with your dog's nose still glued to it, smoothly back over his head—kind of like you're petting him from his nose to his neck and shoulders. Don't keep your hand too high—you want his head to end up at the height it would be when he's sitting. As he moves his head back to keep his attention on your great-smelling hand, chances are he'll drop into a sit. Say "yes!" and give him the treat.

Notice that you haven't said the word *sit*. Why not? Because your dog, smart as he is, wasn't born knowing what *sit* means. You have to teach him. But before you teach him that, you need to show him that when he assumes the sit position, it earns him a reward. You have to show him that a sit position means something different from standing or lying down or jumping.

Now use the luring game again to get him back into the sitting position. If he's still sitting, get him to stand. Walk around a bit to get him to stand back up again if you need to. Then lure him back into a sit again, say "yes!" and give him the treat.

Now do the same routine a third time. Only this time, try to be a little more subtle in how you get your dog to drop into a sit. For example, instead of moving your hand all the way through the motion, try just putting your fist down to your dog's nose. You may find that he anticipates what will earn the treat and sits right away. If he does, say "yes!" and treat.

Repeat this exercise two more times, for a total of five repetitions. Then take a break. That's the end of your first session. Some other time—later in the day, or tomorrow—practice another three to five repetitions. Three to five sessions a day, six or seven days a week, is a comfortable amount of practice. You'll soon notice that your dog will sit five out of five times during almost every session (four out of every five sessions is a good goal). When you're at that state, it's time to "name" the behavior—that is, to add the cue.

Cues vs. Commands

When I was a kid, I thought professional trainers could command their dogs to do certain behaviors, like sit or come. I thought they did this through a kind of power they had over their dogs. I figured that the dogs knew what *sit* meant and knew they'd be in big trouble if they didn't obey their trainers—kind of like the trouble I got into if I didn't obey my parents.

So when I tried to get dogs to do something I wanted them to do, I would speak words as if they were commands. *"Sit!"* I would say in a loud, commanding voice. Of course, the dog wouldn't necessarily sit—particularly if he hadn't been trained to associate the word *sit* with the behavior of sitting. To the dog, I might as well have been saying, *"Blgsh!"*

So much for that theory.

Today I have a different idea of how to train dogs. I now think of words like *sit* as signals or triggers, rather than commands.

To understand the difference, consider this analogy. Say I'm driving my car and I'm waiting at an intersection for a traffic light to change. When the light switches from red to green, I automatically lift my foot off the brake and press the gas pedal. I'm not thinking about it, I just do it. Why? The light isn't commanding me to drive my car forward into the intersection. Instead, it's signaling me to initiate a new behavior. Over years and years of driving, I've come to associate the flick of green light coming on with pressing the gas pedal. Now the behavior is fluent. I do it even when I'm talking with a passenger or fiddling with the radio dial.

In dog training, verbal cues work much the same way. By carefully and thoroughly associating a cue like the word *sit* with a specific be-havior, we end up with a dog who automatically sits when he hears the cue. To the dog, the cue becomes a signal initiating a new behavior.

K. M.

Adding the Cue

To add the cue, first make sure you have the dog's attention. Say her name if you need to. Then say that word *sit* right before you put the food lure in front of her nose. Keep your luring hand still until the *t* in the word *sit* is out of your mouth. Then use the lure if you need to. When your dog's rear reaches the floor, immediately say "yes!" and give the treat.

Be quick with your "yes!"/treat. Some people even do this in front of a mirror so that they can see exactly when the dog's bottom makes contact with the floor.

Now repeat the exercise with the cue *sit* for a total of five times. Take a break, and later on, practice again for another five-repetition session.

Once your dog reliably responds to "sit!" by sitting, it's time to add some variations. The first is to practice while keeping your luring hand perfectly still. Your dog, at this point, will probably interpret your moving hand as a signal to sit. That's fine; you may even want to incorporate a silent hand signal into your training. But you also want your dog to respond reliably to the verbal cue. So try saying "sit" while keeping your hand still. If you get a sit, respond with a "yes"/treat. If you don't, give the dog a peek at the food you're holding—without moving your hand. Or try moving your hand very slightly. That's usually enough to jump-start your dog to sit.

Over time, you should also work on the sit in gradually more distracting situations. For example, you might now try saying "sit" when there are other people in the room. You can also work on it outdoors, both on and off the leash. But remember not to set your dog up for failure. If she's too distracted to respond to the *sit* cue, go back to working without distractions—or with lower-level distractions—for a while.

You can also start varying the rewards. Try saying "sit" before you give your dog her dinner. When she sits, say "yes!" and put her dinner dish down. Or use a favorite toy as a reward.

You can also set up practice sessions to work on the sit when visitors arrive. Recruit a friend to come to your house. Be prepared with a particularly scrumptious treat. The doorbell rings, you open the door, your

friend steps in, and your dog rushes forward in full welcoming mode.
You say "sit!" If your dog sits, say "yes!" and give her the treat. Then
have your friend kneel down to greet the dog.

If your dog doesn't sit—if she's too distracted to notice the cue—
that's okay. It means you're not ready to use *sit* in this situation yet. Go
back to training the sit in less demanding scenarios for a few sessions.
Take it slow and easy, and before you know it, you'll have a dog who will
sit reliably on cue—giving you a great tool for controlling your dog
when she needs to show her best manners.

Down

Training the down is very similar to training sit. Use the same luring
technique, only this time use your treat-filled fist to lure your dog into
the down position—that is, lying on the floor.

Close a treat into your fist, and move your fist down to the ground
so that your dog follows. Wait, if necessary, until he drops into the down
position, ignoring any other behavior, such as his pawing at your hand.
When he downs, say "yes!" and give him the treat.

As with training the sit, don't worry yet about saying the cue.

Now use the luring game to practice the behavior again. If your dog
is still down, get him to stand by standing up yourself or walking
around. Then lure him back into a down again, say "yes!" and give him
the treat.

The third time, be a little more subtle with your luring motion. Perhaps you just lower your hand toward the floor. If your dog downs, say
"yes!" and treat. Repeat this exercise two more times, for a total of five
repetitions. Then take a break. You can practice another three to five
repetitions later (for a total of three to five sessions per day).

When your dog will down five out of five times during almost every
session, add the *down* cue.

After you've done this, you can work on alternating the sit and the
down. Vary when you treat. For example, have your dog do "puppy
push-ups" by saying "sit, down, sit, down." Then say "yes!" and treat.

Just as with the sit, start practicing the down around increasing levels of distraction. Vary the environment—practice during walks, for example. Another great time to work on down is when you are seated.

Macaroni vs. Sphinx

Dogs tend to lie down in one of two ways. First, there is the "sphinx" down: The dog's belly is on the ground but his legs are under him.

The other type of down is a "macaroni down." A dog in this position is rolled partly over on his side. Dogs assume this position when they are relatively relaxed. It's also a bit harder for dogs to jump back up when they're in a macaroni down. For this reason, some people prefer their dogs to assume a macaroni down on the *down* cue.

If your dog tends to choose the sphinx down, and you'd rather *down* meant a macaroni down, use your lure to get your dog into the macaroni down position. Then, after you have him in the down, keep the lure near his nose and draw it along the floor toward his hip. As his nose follows the lure, his hips will turn, and he'll flop over into a relaxed position.

One final note: If you want consistent macaroni downs, don't reward your dog when he does a sphinx down. Only reward him for a macaroni down.

Stay

When your dog can hold either a sit or a down for 10 seconds, you can start working on the stay. You can use a lure to teach this as well.

Begin by cueing a sit or a down. Then, with treat in hand, do something your dog will interpret as meaning you are about to go away. Usually all it will take is a slight change in body language. For example, try turning your head away and breaking eye contact. Or shift your position foot to foot in place as if you are going to move. Or move away—but only one step away. As you do this, however, stay within range, and keep your dog's focus on the treat you're using as a lure. Praise her and, after three to five seconds, return and give her the treat.

After this, gradually increase the difficulty of the exercise. For example, take two steps away. Stay away for gradually longer periods.

You don't need to use a special cue for the stay behavior. Instead, think of the sit and the down as positions your dog holds until you release her.

In chapter 6 we discussed using a release word, like *okay* or *free*, to tell your dog when it's all right for her to go through a door. You can use the same word now to release your dog from a sit or a down. Simply say "okay" and then give your dog some general praise and pets.

Work on the stay, as you worked on the sit and the down, for short sessions of three to five repetitions per session, three to five sessions per day.

The Four D's

One of the things dog trainers strive for when they train behaviors is what's known as fluency. A dog is fluent when he can perform by himself, on cue, no matter what the circumstances. For example, suppose your dog had learned the sit indoors by the couch. Will he understand what *sit* means outdoors, next to another dog? Not necessarily. This is what canine behaviorists mean when they say dogs don't "generalize" well.

So how do you achieve fluency? By using "the Four D's"—distance, duration, different environment, and delivery of the reward—to vary the difficulty of the exercises.

1. **Distance.** Practice behaviors like the sit and the down when your dog is at a distance from you. Begin when he will sit and stay reliably 80 percent of the time when he is very close to you. Then start moving away from him, a little at a time. (If you do this out-

side, make sure you're in a place that is safe for your dog, like a fenced-in area, or keep your dog on a long leash.)

2. **Duration.** Gradually lengthen how long you leave your dog in a sit or down before giving the release word. Vary the length—make it sometimes longer and sometimes shorter. For example, one time it might be 25 seconds, the next time 10, the next time 40 seconds, and the time after that 15.

3. **Different environment.** If your dog performs well in his usual calm training environment (home, yard, training class), it's time to complicate matters a little by introducing distractions or taking him to different training sites. For example, will your dog sit and stay in your living room if you walk to the closet and put on your overcoat? Will he come if called while the doorbell is ringing? At the park? As with distance and duration, work on this gradually—don't overwhelm your dog with unfair distractions.

4. **Delivery of the reward.** At first, you should give your dog his treat every time he performs the behavior. But after the first two or three weeks, start rewarding him more randomly. As with the duration exercise, make the reward schedule variable. Say you're working on the sit. You might ask for a sit three times in a row before you offer a treat. Then the next time, you might ask for a sit two times in a row, then only once, then two times again.

As you incorporate the Four D's into your training exercises, concentrate on only one at a time. If you are working among Distractions, decrease the Distance you are from your dog and the Duration, or length of the exercise.

You should also set aside varying the Delivery of the reward if you're working on more difficult versions of an exercise. For instance, if your dog has mastered a reliable sit indoors, but now you're practicing outdoors, reward every time again for a while. This makes it easier for him to earn his treats, and helps you keep his attention.

Resource Guarding: Prevention Is Best

One of the most troubling behaviors dogs can develop is resource guarding.

In chapter 3 we described a series of exercises that you can use with puppies to help them learn that it's fun and rewarding to let people take toys from them. We also recommended that you hand-feed your puppy. This helps puppies learn that people's hands give good things more often than they take good things away.

Well, these exercises aren't only for puppies. They're a good idea for adult dogs, too.

There is, however, one important caveat when working with adult dogs: If your dog is already showing resource-guarding behavior, strongly consider getting professional help. Your dog has already decided that she needs to "protect" her toys or food from you. Doing exercises like *my turn* or hand-feeding could potentially backfire. You could unintentionally strengthen the behavior you're trying to resolve.

See chapter 17 for information on how to pick a professional trainer or canine behavior specialist.

When You Need a Little Space

Sometimes solving an indoor manners problem means training your dog to go somewhere else for a while.

Consider your dinnertime, for example. Dogs looooove their people's dinnertime. They love it when someone drops a bit of food—accidentally, or accidentally-on-purpose. Many dogs quickly develop begging behaviors as a result. The minute you get yourself something to eat, your dog is there, by your side, looking up at you with those irresistible eyes.

Some people don't mind their dogs begging. But if you would rather enjoy your meal without your dog watching every morsel as you put it into your mouth, you need a way to tell him to go someplace else.

Another example is when you have a guest who isn't a "dog person." Dogs don't always pick up on human signals. Sometimes it's up to us to notice when a dog's friendliness isn't appreciated—and to take steps to get our dog to move away.

Or maybe you just need a bit of peace and quiet. You've come home from a hard day at work and you've spent a good five minutes saying hello to your dog. Now you want to sit and read the paper for a little while—without having soggy throw toys dropped repeatedly in your lap.

What you need is a behavior we can call the "go-to-place."

Before you train a go-to-place, you need to first work on the sit/stay until your dog is fluent with that behavior. This is because sit/stay is the foundation for go-to-place. The difference is that for the go-to-place, you're asking your dog to sit/stay in a specific spot.

First, choose the spot. Ideally, it should be out of the way of foot traffic, but someplace where your dog can still observe family activities.

It can be helpful to put down a mat or dog bed to make the spot visually clear for your dog.

Next, get five treats. Close one in your fist and lead your dog to the designated spot. Say your new cue, "place," then "sit." Walk away for a short period, then return, give your dog the treat, and use your release word to release him from the sit/stay.

Repeat this exercise four more times, varying the length of the stay.

For the next session, stop about 12 inches away from the mat or dog bed. Extend your hand if you need to, to get your dog to continue into position. Say "place" and "sit." Reward your dog, and repeat the exercise as before, varying the length of time he remains in his place and using your release word after you've given him the treat.

For the next session, stop a bit farther away from the designated place. If your dog continues to the place without you, fantastic. If he needs a bit of help, try gesturing in that direction with your luring hand. Cue "place" and "sit" as soon as he gets to his place.

As your dog becomes familiar with this exercise, you'll be able to stop farther and farther away from his place, and he'll continue on to it without you.

Now you can add another exercise. Put your dog on a leash. Put a treat on the mat or bed while holding him back from it. Lead him away, then let him go. Cue "place" when he reaches his place, then "sit." Reward him again, as before, for staying in his place until you release him.

As you practice this exercise, vary how far away you hold your dog before you let him go pick up the treat.

It's also important to ignore your dog after you've given the release cue. If you pay attention to him after he's left his place, you're rewarding him for leaving. You don't want to do this.

On the other hand, it is smart for you to go to his place while he's holding his stay and petting and praising him. That way, he won't associate go-to-place with being ignored or left out of the fun.

Once your dog will respond to the place cue by going to his spot, you can start adding difficulty using the Four D's. For example, work on Difference in Environment by having a helper ring the doorbell or knocking before you cue "place." Start with the doorbell or knocking noise only. When your dog masters this, make it harder by cuing "place," then opening the door after your dog has gone to his place.

Self-Control

By training your dog behaviors like sit, stay, my turn, and go-to-place, you're giving yourself some control over your dog.

But some trainers also believe that exercises like this help dogs learn self-control.

Think about it. Suppose you have a dog who loves people. When a visitor comes to your house, it's her nature to get excited—and to show it. And it's her nature to show it in doggy ways, like jumping up and pawing.

But you want your dog to control that behavior. So as your dog wriggles up to say hello to the person at the door, you say "sit."

Now your dog has to master her natural inclination—to jump up—and instead do something pretty unnatural—sit.

You're not forcing her. You're not holding her, pushing her hindquarters down into a sitting position.

She's doing it herself. She's controlling herself.

Get to that point with your dog, and you're right to be proud of her—and of yourself.

Chapter 9

STRAIN, COUGH, LUNGE: OUTWITTING THE DOG WHO PULLS ON LEASH WALKS

His whole life is a waiting—waiting for the next walk in the open, a waiting that begins as soon as he is rested from the last one.
—Thomas Mann, *A Man and His Dog*

One of the nicest things about living with a dog is the walks. Picture this idyllic scene: It's a warm, spring morning. The sun is shining, the birds are singing. You have just finished your morning paper when up prances your dog, leash in her mouth. You snap the leash on her collar and head out for a nice leisurely walk around the block . . .

The good news is: Yes, that dream can come true.

But before you get too carried away, you need to inject a little reality into your plans. Because, unfortunately, your dog's idea of a "nice walk" might be completely different from yours. Your dog might be perfectly happy dragging you down the street as she lurches from smell to smell. If she spots another dog, she might try to dash over and make friends—never mind that she has to dash across the street, with you in tow, to get there. Or maybe she'll get excited and run in circles around you, wrapping your ankles in the leash.

Now, if your dog is relatively small, you'll be able to control her through brute strength. It may not be pleasant—even a small dog can exert enough pull on a leash to tire the average arm—but at least it's manageable. If, on the other hand, your dog is big enough, look out. You can end up on the ground. Or with a wrenched shoulder or back. Or "dog-walker's elbow." (Yes, there is such a thing!)

So what are your options? You can't really do without walks, especially if you live in an urban or suburban setting, where off-leash walks aren't an everyday option. Leash walks are an important source of exercise for many dogs. And even if your dog has other ways to get exercise, chances are you'll need to manage her on a leash occasionally, such as on trips to the vet.

Bottom line: Walking nicely on a leash is an essential behavior for pet dogs.

But as with recalls, walking nicely on a leash is a complex behavior. It takes some planning and some smarts to make sure your dog masters it.

What Kind of Leash?

When you prepare to select a leash for your dog, you'll find a variety of choices.

The most common, inexpensive type of leash is made of woven nylon, with a metal clip on one end and a loop for your hand on the other. This basic style of leash is a good start for you and your dog. Make sure you choose one long enough so that your dog can move a few feet away from you without putting tension on the leash.

Another type of leash that is popular among dog owners today is the retractable leash. This type of leash is a long cord that retracts into a handle when you push a button, rather like a retractable tape measure. Retractable leashes let you give your dog room to roam—some brands are available in lengths up to 26 feet—when you are both inclined. But if you need your dog to be closer to you, you can reel him in.

If you use a retractable leash, however, be careful if your dog gets excited or runs (for example, if he starts playing with another dog). If the cable gets wrapped around a person's or dog's legs, it can cause friction burns or even cut the skin.

There are also a number of specialized leashes, including leashes that can be mounted on bicycles and leashes with clip handles. There are even leashes with flashlights on them for night walking. And if you—or your dog—happen to be a fashion hound, you'll find leashes made of leather, and nylon leashes in designer colors.

What's *Walking Nicely* Mean, Anyway?

It's probably helpful, for starters, to define what *walking nicely on a leash* really means. There's no right answer to this question. It will depend on your personal preferences and tolerances. For example, you may want your dog to always walk on your right-hand side, or your left, or you may not care—it may be fine with you if he switches sides as the mood strikes him.

But in most cases, what people want is a slack leash. What this means, in practical terms, is that, no matter what, your dog doesn't pull on the leash. Even when the walk is just starting, and he's excited, and he sees a robin bouncing across the neighbor's yard. Even when he believes there's a spot that he just *has* to sniff up ahead.

Many people find it helpful to train two different types of loose-leash behavior. One is the formal heel. During a heel, your dog will stay very close to your side and give you his complete, polite attention. This is an important behavior when you need to control your dog in specific situations, such as around other people. For example, if you're walking up the sidewalk and you see a kindergarten class approaching, with 20 kids skipping and eating ice cream cones, you need to be able to pass them without a major incident. In situations like this, it can be useful for your dog to walk in a heel position.

If you live in a crowded urban environment, the formal heel position ensures your dog will be a good canine citizen. Your leash won't trip other pedestrians. It will also help you keep your dog away from people who may not react pleasantly or calmly to your dog, such as people who are fearful of dogs.

If you plan to participate in obedience competitions, you'll need to train your dog to perform a formal heel. In most cases, however, a less formal behavior is just fine. This behavior should have a different name than *heel*. We can call it "let's-go." For this behavior, you don't care what your dog does as long as he doesn't pull on the leash and make you both uncomfortable. Your dog can sniff and explore. He can walk ahead of you or behind you. The rules are minimal. In fact, you may have only one rule for the let's-go: Don't pull on the leash.

The trick to training either heel or let's-go is to make it more rewarding for your dog to keep the leash loose than it is to pull.

How do you do that? To start, it's important, again, to assess the challenge. Training a dog to walk nicely on a leash has many of the same components as training a recall (chapter 7). At some point, this will be a behavior that your dog will do outside—and outside is a high-distraction environment. When outside, your dog's senses are continually flooded by interesting sights, sounds, and smells. So when you do any sort of training outside, you are competing for your dog's attention. In other words, outside training shifts the value of your rewards.

Understanding the Reward Hierarchy

Question: When is a reward not a reward?

Answer: When it's being compared with something even better.

Think about it. Say someone offers to pay you five bucks to sit on a mall bench for five minutes. *Cool,* you think. *This is easy money.* So you sit down, and all of a sudden an announcement comes over the mall public address system saying that your name was picked in a drawing for a new car on the other side of the mall—and you have only five minutes to claim your prize. Your choice is to stay where you are—and earn five dollars—or leave, and win a car.

So what are you going to do? Chances are, you'll jump up and make a mad dash for the other side of the mall. Forget the five dollars.

Your dog is no different.

When you are inside, and you're the only one home, and there is nothing else going on, your dog may happily perform any number of tricks for you for the stingiest of rewards. But when there are other things around that your dog thinks are exciting, you're going to have to up the ante a little bit.

Let's take food as an example. Under boring conditions, you can train your dog with boring food: kibble, cereal bits, and the like. If you're trying to train around distractions, however, your choices need to be more attractive. Smelly treats are one option—think fish, garlic, or cheese. If your dog normally eats kibble, bits of "people food" will have a bit of magic. Food is more rewarding to a hungry dog than one who has just eaten dinner, as well.

But you can't stop here. Food is a great reward for dogs, but many other things are, too. If you observe your dog, you will probably discover that most or all of the following things are very important to her: playing with people; playing with other dogs; sniffing; riding in a car; going outside; going on walks; running; digging; retrieving. Depending on your dog, any one of these activities (or quite possibly others not on this list) may be more rewarding than even the most delectable treat.

Your job is to figure out which rewards mean the most to your dog. Does she ignore a piece of roast chicken when she sees another dog across the street? If given a choice, would she play with another dog or greet a human? Does she start spinning in place when she

sees you pull out a favorite toy, or did she miss that because she's
spotted a rabbit in the backyard?

Once you know what rewards mean the most to your dog, you're
better prepared to train her—even when there are other things competing for her attention.

On the bright side, however, leash training lets you use another,
specific reward that your dog may find extremely important: the ability
to go somewhere.

To understand how this works, it's helpful to look at how walking
nicely on a leash affects your dog.

The Walk from a Dog's Perspective

We've looked at what *walking nicely on a leash* means to a human. It's
only fair that we also take a look at leash walks from a dog's perspective—or at least make a reasonable guess.

Let's start with the leash itself. To a human, a leash is a device to
manage a dog—to keep a dog nearby; to prevent a dog from running off
after (or away from) a car, bike, or critter.

But what is a leash to a dog?

Since we can't really switch places with our dogs, we can only spec-
ulate on this answer, of course. But it's probably safe to say that, for a
dog, a leash is a sensory experience—it's what causes pressure on the
dog's collar or harness. And as such, the leash is but one sensation amid
a flood of experiences. Furthermore, this leash sensation doesn't mean
anything inherently. Your dog doesn't "know" that a tightened leash
means he's walking too fast for you.

For all he knows, a tightened leash is a signal that he should pull
harder.

A tightened leash, and the pressure it puts on your dog's collar, may
excite him. Strange as it may sound, a tightened leash may signal that he

should pull. For example, suppose your dog always feels the leash tighten up just when there's something good up ahead he wants to investigate. He may come to associate a tight leash with *excitement ahead!* Who knows what he might learn—while all the time you're convinced that pulling on the leash is a bad thing.

Rewarding a Loose Leash

So one of the smartest rewards you can use to train your dog to walk on a leash is, at first, the least obvious: You need to make sure she knows that when the leash is loose, good things happen.

And as we've hinted, one of those good things is: the freedom to *go*.

If your dog wants to walk somewhere, that becomes the reward for keeping the leash loose. Here's how it works: If your dog puts tension on the leash, you stop. Act as if your dog is tied to a post—and you are the post. Don't say anything. Don't do anything.

It may take a few minutes, but sooner or later your dog will slacken the leash. At this point, you can start to walk again. The lesson you have begun to teach your dog is:

Tight leash: "Dog gets nowhere."

Loose leash: "Dog free to walk."

For this to work, consistency is very important. If you ever let your dog learn the opposite lesson—that *tight leash* means "sometimes, dog gets to walk," because you give in and follow—you undermine the effectiveness of this technique. Your dog might become an even more determined puller—because, as behavioral scientists will tell you, an intermittent reward sometimes does the best job of all at reinforcing a behavior.

In fact, it's likely that some dogs with serious pulling problems developed the behavior because their people let them pull—some of the time, or all of the time. Pulling became rewarding, because pulling got the dog what she wanted—the freedom to get to the next exciting spot up the street.

On the other hand, if you show your dog that the leash must be loose before she can go greet that other dog, you're rewarding the behavior you want. And so it becomes more and more likely that your dog will give you a loose leash.

You can further strengthen the value of the reward by adding food treats and toys. For example, you may notice that when you stop walking, your dog will turn around and look at you. She becomes curious about why you're just standing there. At this point, you are getting attention as well as a loose leash. That's great! Say "yes!" (so she knows she's done something good) and give your dog a treat. Then resume walking.

You may also notice that, at times, your dog doesn't try to pull. This is a training moment. Say "yes!" so your dog knows that this is a behavior that gets rewarded. Then give her a treat.

A variation on this is to do something that gets your dog's attention. For example, call your dog's name. When she looks up, the leash will slacken. Change direction slightly and encourage her to walk with you. Another way to get her attention is to jiggle the leash a bit, to throw her slightly off balance. This may make her step over toward you to regain her balance; she may also look at you, which will slacken the leash as well. Again, catch this behavior with a "yes!" and a reward.

However, if you try this—deliberately getting your dog's attention—don't repeat it too many times. If it becomes a habit, you'll end up training the wrong thing. You'll train your dog to release tension on the leash when you call or jiggle the leash—and only then.

Remember, what you really want is for your dog to keep the leash loose by herself. So no matter what, your main focus should be to watch when she slackens the leash without needing any intervention from you.

THAT EXTRA-SPECIAL SOMETHING

As you work on loose-leash training, it's also important to keep your dog excited. Keep him jazzed. Don't give the same old rewards all the time—you want your dog to know that giving you a loose leash is tons more fun than anything else out there on your walk.

If your dog loves toys, bring out a favorite toy as a reward. Or try bringing your dog's dinner along on your walk one evening. Hide it if you can, so he doesn't know you have it. Then, when he gives you a loose leash, say "yes!" and pull out his dinner.

It's also helpful to hide rewards so that you're not always carrying them. Hide some special treats in the crotch of a tree you'll pass during your walk. Your dog will think you're terrific—and you'll be training your dog to be ready to please you, because he never knows what reward you might be able to produce.

Special Tools for Leash Training

Since leash walking is a popular activity for people who have dogs, it's no surprise that there are a number of tools designed to help you train your dog not to pull.

Some of these tools lend themselves to punishment-based training: Their design lets a trainer make pulling uncomfortable for a dog. Others offer the dog more control and are appropriate for positive training.

CHOKE AND PRONG COLLARS

Choke collars are slip-rope-style collars. They're often made of metal chain, but can also be nylon or leather. For many years, trainers taught people to use "choke chains" to intimidate or control their dogs with brute strength. For example, a person might quickly tighten the collar around a dog's neck if the dog pulled on the leash. This tightening sensation, it was thought, would upset the dog and deter him from pulling. (Note that traditional choke collars can be very dangerous on unsupervised dogs—if the collar gets hung up on something, the dog could be strangled.)

Prong collars (also sometimes called German choke collars) are designed so that when they are tightened, protruding ends of the chain links pinch the skin of the dog's neck. Because they hurt the dog, they have a stronger potential deterrent effect.

Choke and prong collars have worked to train some dogs. But they are not necessary—there are other ways to train dogs to walk nicely on a leash. In addition, these types of collars can cause your dog to associate discomfort with experiences you encounter on your walk. Here is a possible scenario: You are walking with your dog on a choke or prong collar and you see another dog. Your dog becomes excited and begins to bark and lunge toward the strange dog. The choke or prong collar inflicts discomfort or even pain on your dog. *Your dog now begins to associate pain or discomfort with the experience of encountering other dogs while on walks.* So the next time you see another dog, your dog becomes even more excited and stressed. He may begin to perceive other dogs as outright threatening. And so begins a vicious cycle: A dog who starts out simply excited ends up fearful or aggressive toward other dogs while on walks.

For these reasons, we strongly recommend you avoid choke and prong collars as training tools.

LIMITED SLIP COLLARS

A limited slip collar, also known as the half-check collar or martingale, restricts slightly when tension is placed on it. This prevents a dog from pulling free—something that can happen with flat buckle collars, especially if your dog has a small head and ears, like a Doberman or Greyhound. But it doesn't tighten snugly like a traditional choke collar. For this reason, this type of collar is well suited to positive-based leash training.

CONTROL HARNESSES

A control harness has a collar with straps attached that pass under the dog's front legs. The leash is attached to a ring on the back of the dog. This type of device uses discomfort to train, but the discomfort is relatively mild and is under the control of the dog, not the human.

Here's how it works. As you walk with your dog, you never pull or jerk the leash, but simply hold it quietly. If your dog moves too far away, putting tension on the leash, the tightened leash will put gentle pressure on the harness around her chest and torso. This is likely to make her stop pulling. When she does, you say "yes!" and give her a treat or praise her.

HEAD COLLARS

Head collars use a loop over the dog's muzzle so that when the dog is on a leash, you have control over her head.

Not all head collars work the same way, however, so if you decide to explore this type of tool, be sure to research this type of collar carefully to make sure it will accomplish what you expect (see the appendix).

In addition, we recommend that you teach yourself how to introduce your dog to the head collar, as well as how to use it, before you begin training with it. For example, the manufacturers of Gentle Leader brand head collars offer a training video. Take advantage of this to help ensure that you make the head collar a positive experience for your dog.

One final note on leash training tools. While some of them can be helpful, they aren't a substitute for good training. If your dog is rewarded for pulling, she'll pull—even if you're using the fanciest, most sophisticated "no-pull" training tool ever invented. So avoid rewarding her for pulling. Then reward her like crazy when she doesn't pull. Be patient, because you're competing with all the excitement of the outdoor environment. And be consistent, because that gives the fastest, most solid results.

Puppies and Leash Walking

So far, we've given an overview of the basics of training a loose leash. But if your dog is a young puppy, you have a secret weapon: Puppies like to follow people.

If you have a puppy younger than six months, see for yourself. The next time you're playing, get up and walk away, slapping your thigh and calling your pup's name in an excited, happy voice. Chances are, your puppy will come after you, to see what you're up to.

You can use this behavior to lay a foundation for future leash walks. Practice this in the house or a fenced-in yard. When you have your puppy's attention, say "let's go!" and walk. When your puppy follows, say "yes!" and give him a nice treat. Over time, gradually lengthen the period between the *let's go!* and the treat, so that your puppy has to follow you closely for longer and longer times to earn the reward.

When your pup catches on that *let's go!* means "follow me, I've got treats!" attach a leash to his collar and hold it during these sessions. But don't ever, ever use the collar to pull your puppy. If you lose his attention, drop the leash before there's any tension on it. You don't want a tight leash to start feeling normal to your pup.

Training to Heel

The let's-go is a behavior that is pretty relaxed. Your dog can walk anywhere and do anything—as long as the leash is slack.

The heel is a more formal behavior. When you give this cue, you want your dog to stay very close to your side, walking in the same direction you're walking and giving you complete, polite attention. Your dog should never give more than a glance toward distractions.

To visualize the correct position for a heel, picture a seam along the side of your pant leg. Your dog's nose shouldn't fall behind the seam, and her shoulder shouldn't get ahead of it. And she should be as close to you as she can get without touching you. You may also want to imagine a little oval by your side: This is where your dog should be positioned.

Your dog should stay in this position no matter how slow or fast you walk. Even if you stop, and cue your dog to sit or lie down, she should sit or lie in that same space by your side.

For some obedience competitions, the heel position is on the person's left side. For other events, heeling on both sides is required.

Even if you don't plan to enter obedience competitions, you may find it useful or valuable to train your dog to heel by your right side as well as your left. Cases where alternate-side heeling is useful include:

+ If you have a disability or other condition that makes it easier for you to work with your dog on the right.

✦ If you like to be able to switch your dog, depending on traffic or other potential hazards.

✦ If you have two dogs and want to walk with one on each side.

✦ If your dog looks up at you a lot, alternate-side heeling can help keep her neck muscles symmetrical.

✦ If you're left-handed and want your right hand free.

And finally, if your dog happens to be blind in the left eye, you might want to position her so her seeing eye will be on the outside.

The heel is a more precise behavior than the let's-go, but you can train it using the same approach: Make "inside the oval" the most rewarding place to be.

Here are some tips as you teach your dog how to heel:

1. Keep sessions short—only a few seconds at first. You want to set your dog up to succeed.

2. Use random rewards to keep things interesting.

3. Here's a great time to use one of your magic tricks. Hide a toy somewhere on your practice path, like the limb of a tree, the top of your car, or a picture hook down the hall. When your dog has done a great job of getting into heel position, say "yes!" then run together to find the toy and have a game.

4. Use curbs, fences, or walls to help control your dog by limiting how far she can move away from you.

FROM SIT TO HEEL

Here's a program for training your dog to heel. You start by teaching your dog to sit in a heel position. You'll then move to heeling while walking. Finally, you'll reinforce and strengthen the heeling behavior. This program has several stages. For best results, make absolutely sure you and your dog master each stage before moving on to the next.

1. SITTING IN HEEL POSITION

First, you need to train your dog to sit at your left side, facing the same direction you are. Remember the imaginary oval that marks the heel position; you want your dog to be sitting in this oval.

If you've taught your dog to sit in front of you, it may take a few sessions for her to catch on that you're looking for something different, so be patient.

As you'll see, this is a variation on the same luring technique described in chapter 8. Start with five delicious treats. Put one in your left hand, and position your hand down at your left side, luring your dog by her nose until she's sitting in the correct position. Because she's excited about the treat, it may take a few seconds, but sooner or later she'll drop into a sit right where you want her. At that point, say "yes!" and give her the treat.

You can use your surroundings to help get your dog in the right position. For example, you can stand near a wall or fence so that there is only enough room on your left for your dog.

Repeat the luring four more times, then give your dog a break. That's enough for one session.

The next session, you'll probably notice that she performs the sit, in the correct position, more quickly. Eventually she'll do it almost all the time, as soon as you hold the treat in the right position. When she does it right 90 percent of the time, add your cue: Say "heel," pause one second, then say "sit."

Use the *heel*/pause/*sit* cue as you're positioning your hand with the treat. Then, when she gets into position, say "yes!" and give her the treat, just like before.

2. THE FIRST STEPS

Now it's time to start training the next step: moving forward while staying at the heel position. You're going to continue to use luring for this step as well. Let your dog know you have treats. Again, start with five treats. Only this time, instead of giving your dog the treat after she sits, walk forward a step or two. Use the lure like a magnet to take her nose where you want her to go. Then stop and wait for her to sit in the heel position again. At first, you may need to say "sit" to cue her. But very quickly, she'll learn that when you stop, she should sit. Either way, after she sits, say "yes!" and give her a treat.

Just as before, do this a total of five times, then stop for that session.

As with other behaviors, you can train for three to five sessions a day, but do take breaks between sessions.

As this step becomes smooth and successful, add your cue. Say "heel" as your dog walks with you. But don't walk more than a step or two at first. Set your dog up for success by keeping it very simple and easy. You know she's succeeding when you can see that she always sticks close to your side during your heel training sessions.

3. CHANGING DIRECTIONS

For this stage, again start with five treats. Sit your dog in the heel position. Now take a step or two to the left or to the right, luring your dog around with you. If she keeps in good heel position, and either stays sitting or sits quickly when you stop, that's the behavior you want. Say "yes!" and treat. Repeat four times and then break.

Soon you and your dog will look like a smooth team, almost like you're dancing. At this point you can walk in tight, 180- and 360-degree turns, clockwise and counterclockwise—or even spin around in place. Your dog will clearly move with you, as if Velcro were attaching her to your leg. But don't spend too long at a time. Three separate 30-second practice sessions are better for your dog than a single minute-and-a-half session.

4. TREAT FOR WALKING INSTEAD OF SITTING

So far you have been giving the treat when your dog sits. Now begin to give the treat once in a while as the dog is moving along with you nicely.

Add variations to the exercise. Sometimes, reward her for sitting, like before. Other times, say "yes!" and give her a treat while you're walking instead. This is called a variable schedule of reinforcement.

Think of it as a way to keep your dog guessing—making her more excited about earning her treat.

Your goal during this stage of the program is to perform about 15 steps of heeling, during which you reward your dog five times at random.

5. VARY THE TYPE OF REWARD

For this stage, use the same technique you did for teaching the let's-go. (See chapter 6.) Vary your rewards. Sometimes you might end a short session of heeling with an *okay*, then run away and play a game of Tug-of-War or Fetch. And sometimes, give no more than a smile or a pat.

Other times, you should make it obvious that you don't have toys or food with you. Before a practice session, hide some rewards. Then plan your brief heeling segment to take place within a few feet or a few yards of the rewards. Use *okay* as your release and run to a reward.

But even now, stick to very short, positive sessions. And always quit while your dog is still enthusiastic.

Once your dog has a lot of fun practice with the heel, you'll find it's a great tool for specific occasions on your walks. Continue to use *let's go* for most of your walks. This lets your dog enjoy her walk, sniff, take potty breaks, and do almost anything except pull on the leash. Reserve *heel* for when you need a little more control for short periods.

Then, when the need for a heel has passed, use *okay* to release her from the heel position.

Use Your Release

It's very important to get into the habit of using a release cue, like *okay*, to tell your dog she doesn't need to maintain the heel position anymore. Why? Because if you do, it will always be clear to your dog when she should be heeling—and when she can do her let's-go behavior. In fact, the better you get at communicating with your dog in general, the faster and better your training will go.

A dog who walks nicely on a leash is a wonderful sight to see. It's also a wonderful experience for the dog's designated human. It gets us outdoors, gives us some exercise, and helps us stay acquainted with our neighbors. Yes, it can be a tricky behavior for your dog to master—but if you use your brains, you'll get there, and it will be well worth your trouble.

Chapter 10

PLEASE DON'T LEAVE ME! OUTWITTING THE DOG WHO HATES BEING LEFT ALONE

It is loneliness that makes the loudest noise. This is as true of men as of dogs.

—Eric Hoffer, "Thoughts of Eric Hoffer, Including: 'Absolute Faith Corrupts Absolutely,'" *New York Times Magazine*, April 25, 1971

Dogs are social animals. They like being with their buddies. And for most dogs today, that means their human buddies.

So what happens when you and your family leave the house every day for hours on end? While you're at work, at school, socializing, or running errands, your dog is probably left at home. Assuming you have only one dog, that means he is alone. And being alone is something dogs don't particularly like.

Of course, your dog's specific reaction to being left will vary, depending on a number of factors, including his temperament, how strongly he is bonded to you, and how you've conditioned him to being by himself. Some dogs appear relatively nonchalant about being left alone. At the other extreme we find a collection of behaviors often referred to as "separation anxiety." Dogs with separation anxiety freak out about being left alone. And when they freak out, they can become very destructive. They can chew, tear apart, defecate on, and in general destroy furniture, rugs, walls, and anything else they can get their paws or teeth on. Dogs who work themselves into this kind of frenzy may also injure themselves.

Fortunately, these dogs are in the minority. As a dog owner, today, you are more likely to be facing one of the following situations:

✦ You have just acquired a dog or puppy. You aren't sure, yet, how he'll react to being left alone. For you, the job is to design a training program that will help your dog learn to be comfortable while being left alone.

✦ You've had a dog or puppy for a while, and she is perfectly fine about being alone. That's great! But it's still important to take some steps to reinforce this. Doing so will make her happier and better able to withstand other stresses that she may face at some point in her life.

✦ Your dog is giving you some problems when left alone. Dogs in this category don't completely fall apart when left behind, but they do get into mischief. If this describes your dog, then you need a multifaceted program, using a combination of management, enrichment, training, and other tools, to keep your dog safe and happy while you're not home.

Know Your Dog

As these categories suggest, dogs' responses to being left alone can vary dramatically. And your home-alone training will also be different, depending on your dog.

So the first step in helping your dog be comfortable staying home alone is to figure out whether it's going to be a problem at all—and if it is, how big a problem.

In chapter 1 we suggested that, if at all possible, you arrange it so you can spend a lot of time with your dog when you first bring him home. Assuming you're able to do that, use that time to pay attention to how he behaves if you move away. Puppies and some adult dogs follow their people around. If your adult dog does this, it could indicate that he doesn't like being separated from you.

Another key test is what happens when you are out of sight. Does your dog seem to get anxious? If you leave him alone for a few minutes, how does he act upon your return? Is he calm? Has he settled down for a nap? Is he standing up, alert, looking for you? Or does he seem anxious or upset when you come back—for example, is he whining, salivating, scratching at the door or the door of his crate? These are early signs that he may be more sensitive to being left alone.

Later in this chapter, we'll give some ideas for acclimating your dog to being alone—even if he starts out not liking it very much. These exercises work best, however, if you pace them carefully. So as you do them, continue to observe your dog closely. If anything you try causes him to appear upset or anxious, slow down. Pick some exercises that are more tolerable to him. For example, you might shorten the time that you are separated. Or practice being in separate rooms, instead of leaving him alone in the house while you go out.

The key is to make the experiences positive—consistently.

Now, suppose you find yourself in the following situation: Your new dog shows signs of being anxious about being left alone. But you have a full-time job—and you have to be back at work Monday morning. If this is the case, you should consider hiring a dogsitter or placing your dog in a "doggy day care," at least temporarily, while you are out of the house. Work on your home-alone training on evenings and weekends. This will help ensure that your dog's anxiety doesn't get worse as you work on a solution.

Preventing Future Problems

When it comes to separation, the old adage "an ounce of prevention is worth a pound of cure" is wonderful advice. You're much better off teaching your dog, from the start, that it's okay to be left alone sometimes. This is far easier than retraining a dog who has learned to become anxious or destructive when alone.

So how soon should you start? The answer is: from the very first day your dog or puppy comes home to live with you.

Start slowly and simply. Create times when you are home, but at a distance. Spend time in one room while your dog is securely crated or tied in a different room, but within sight of you. Vary this by placing yourself out of sight for short periods. For example, when you go into the bathroom or bedroom for brief periods, close the door behind you.

Make sure, as you do these exercises, that your dog is okay while you're away. Leave a favorite toy before you depart, or something for your dog to chew on. Then pick it up and put it away again when you return. This shows your dog that *fun things appear when my person goes away*. (Later, we'll offer ideas on how to pair separations with good things.)

The key is to make the separation periods a positive experience for your dog. Otherwise, you may be training him to be anxious.

Help your new dog or puppy practice staying alone in the house for short periods as well. Leave him inside while you run out to the garage to get something from your car. Take a short walk around the block, or a short drive to the grocery store.

Again, as you do these exercises, strive to make them a positive learning experience for your dog. And one other important note: If you discover that your dog is fussing about being left alone, don't reappear *while* he's fussing. If he's whining or barking, for example, time your reentry into the house or room so you come back while he's behaving relatively calmly. Otherwise, your reappearance will reward him for the whining or barking.

Other Ideas for Your Home-Alone Training

As you work with your dog on these simple separation exercises, it's useful to also follow a few additional guidelines to make them more effective.

KEEP DEPARTURES NONEMOTIONAL

When you leave, leave quietly. Don't fuss over your dog. Don't pet her and tell her you're sorry to go and how much you'll miss her. Follow the same strategy when you return. Walk in calmly. Don't even greet your dog. For the first 20 minutes after your return, ignore your dog completely. If she needs to be taken outdoors to potty, do so, but maintain a calm, detached attitude.

Yes, this can be a hard rule to follow. After all, your dog is also your friend—and you probably miss her, a lot, when you're apart. But if you're emotional about leaving and returning, she'll likely pick up on it. She might learn to focus on your departure and associate your leaving with unsettled vibes. So exercise some self-discipline. If it helps, set aside some other times to go overboard with your dog. Throw a "glad to be together" party—just make sure your party is at least 20 minutes before, or after, you are away.

Remember, if you pretend your comings and goings are not a big deal in your dog's life, you help her learn that, too.

PLAN WALKS AND EXERCISE SO THEY *DON'T* COINCIDE WITH YOUR DEPARTURES

This tip is closely related to the last one. Taking your dog for a long walk or otherwise exercising her before you leave can be helpful. It can help her burn some of her energy so that she's more likely to relax quietly while you're gone. But make sure these exercise sessions end at least 20 minutes before you leave. Otherwise, the contrast between your being there and your departure may be too dramatic; your leaving will not only mean you're gone, but that the fun exercise time is over.

REWARD YOUR DOG FOR CALM GREETINGS

Observe how your dog behaves when you reappear after an absence. Is he excited? Does he jump, bark, whine, scratch at you or the door of his crate? If so, then your job is to withhold any rewards. You don't want to reinforce this behavior. Wait a while instead. When your dog calms

down, that is the time to greet him. This is a classic tool for outwitting
your dog: Eventually he'll learn to get your attention by acting calm.
Then when you're not home, he's less likely to behave frantically.

REDIRECT YOUR DOG'S FOCUS DURING SEPARATIONS

Help your dog adjust to these beginning home-alone times by giving
him a special toy, or feeding him a meal, just before you leave. By doing
this, you help associate the experience with good things. You also help
switch his attention from your impending departure to something more
positive.

Another thing to try: Encourage your dog to focus on other people.
If you have a friend you can trust to handle your dog, ask the friend to
do your dog's favorite things with him every once in a while—take him
for a walk, play with him, or give him his dinner.

MAKE QUIET TIMES A REGULAR PART OF YOUR DOG'S DAY

When you are home during the day, break up your dog's schedule with
periods for dozing and relaxation. Don't have him out and running
around all day long. You want him to learn that life isn't always fun,
games, and excitement. Sometimes things are boring. So from time to
time, put him in his crate or confine him to his play area. Provide him
with a chew toy for a period of quiet, solitary activity.

When Separation Is a Serious Problem . . .

The majority of dogs, with some thoughtful help on the part of their
people, can learn to adjust to periods of alone time without too much
trouble.

But some dogs react to being left alone by becoming upset or destructive.

This doesn't always mean your dog is suffering from bona fide separation anxiety, however. Here are some guidelines that can help you figure out what's really going on with your dog.

THE UNDEREMPLOYED DOG

Some dogs create problems when they're left alone because they are bored. They have lots of time and energy, and not enough to do. When left alone, this type of dog builds up her energy. Finally, she just can't stand it anymore—she needs a kind of release valve. And her release valve may be destructive chewing, scratching, barking, or digging. This isn't separation anxiety. This is a dog who needs more stimulation and exercise.

THE OVERENTHUSIASTIC DOG

This is a high-energy dog with lots of enthusiasm for life. He's often easily stimulated. The problem is that when this dog is alone, he may discover that doing things you don't like—chewing on your bathroom floor linoleum, for example—is terrific fun. This dog may also be okay some days, but if something happens that excites him—like a package delivery guy ringing your doorbell—it could trigger unwanted behaviors.

The overenthusiastic dog may be destructive when left home alone—but again, the problem isn't true separation anxiety. Your best approach with this dog is to make sure he's getting plenty of exercise, and has lots of stimulating toys to keep him busy when you're not around.

THE DEPENDENT DOG

This is dog who suffers from true separation anxiety. She is an anxious dog who is bonded to one individual in particular—and becomes extremely upset, consistently, if separated from that person. If you set up a video camera to record this dog, you might see pacing, drooling, whining, scratching, chewing, or howling in the direction the special person was last seen or heard. The anxiety is usually at its worst right after the departure.

If she barks, it will be high-pitched and frantic.

If someone else tries to comfort the dependent dog, it may have a slight effect, but she'll remain focused primarily on her special person.

THE WORRIED, FEARFUL DOG

Some dogs display a high level of insecurity and fearfulness in general. In this case, however, the dog's anxiety isn't associated with a particular person. Therefore, this isn't true separation anxiety. Nonetheless, some of the steps you can take for the dog with separation anxiety would also help with an insecure dog.

A Mischief Maker

Dogs who are left alone sometimes find clever ways to have a good time.

Many years ago, we lived in New Mexico in a pueblo-style house. There was a block wall around the entire yard, and this is where we left Honcho, our adolescent German Shepherd, while we were at work.

Well, one day when we came home, Honcho greeted us with a big, wet smile on his face. To our chagrin, we discovered that someone had turned on our hose. The backyard was flooded. There were places where the water was an inch or more deep.

We turned off the water and talked to the neighbors. They hadn't seen any prowlers. So we phoned in a "malicious mischief" complaint to the police and hoped for the best.

But the next day, when we got home, we found the hose back on again.

It wasn't until the third day that the mystery was solved. We'd invited some friends over for a barbecue, and they brought their dog, Zeus, Honcho's brother. After a little while we noticed the two dogs standing near the hose spigot—and, as we watched, Honcho turned on the water with his mouth, and invited his brother to play in the water with him!

In the weeks that followed, we tried to teach Honcho to turn the water off, but we never managed to do it. So instead we got him a large swimming pool to play in—and when we had to leave for work, we took the handle off the spigot first.

T. R.

A Question of Degree

In some ways, defining *separation anxiety* is a matter of degree. How intense are the unwanted behaviors? How long do they last? How destructive does the dog become?

It's also helpful to consider the dog's behavior in general.

For example, dogs who are overly dependent or anxious will be less likely to notice you, your cues, or rewards. Say you try giving a food-stuffed chew toy to your dog right before you leave the house to go to work in the morning. A relatively relaxed dog will be thrilled. He'll immediately start working at the toy. He may not even notice that you've walked out the door.

A highly anxious dog, on the other hand, is likely to completely ignore the toy. He may not even take it in his mouth. It will drop, unnoticed, on the floor or the floor of his crate. Instead, his entire focus is on the extreme discomfort he's feeling in anticipation of your leaving. After you go, the toy, and the food inside it, will be neglected for as long as he feels distressed. (If it's empty when you come back, by the way, that's evidence your dog does calm down for part of the time you're not there.)

Here are some other behaviors that indicate a dog is feeling upset, frightened, or anxious:

+ Trembling.

+ Sweaty paw pads.

+ Change in toilet habits.

+ Tense muscles or mouth.

+ Dilated pupils.

+ Drooling.

+ Freezing into a statue-like pose.

+ Running away.

+ Hiding.

✦   Sudden change in mood or activity level.

✦   Extreme, repetitive behaviors such as barking, pacing, licking, or
    whining.

If it's your leaving that causes your dog to exhibit these behaviors,
she may direct them toward the place where you were last seen. She
may scratch or chew at the door you exited, for example, or periodically
stop in front of it and stare at it.

How do you know if your dog is exhibiting these behaviors if you're
not there to observe them? You have a couple of options. You can install
a video camera, digital recorder, or Web cam in your home. These de-
vices let you record, or remotely observe, your dog's behavior while
you're not there. Another option is to sneak back and look in a window.

You may also find clues in your dog's body language as you prepare
to leave. These might include scratching his body, yawning, excessive
sniffing, flicking or thrusting the tongue forward, or "shaking off" (the
gesture dogs use when their fur is wet).

Note that dogs who are upset by your leaving may not show their
anxiety the entire time you're gone. Sometimes dogs kick up a fuss for
the first few minutes you leave, then settle down. Other times dogs
begin showing these types of behaviors in anticipation of your return.
For example, if you walk back into your home at 5:45 P.M. every day,
your dog might anticipate this, and may start acting up at 5:35.

Needless to say, if this is how your dog reacts to your leaving, the
training techniques we've described so far in this chapter may not make
much difference, particularly at first. You need stronger stuff.

Management

Once again, we come back to our old friend management. The dog who
becomes intensely anxious about being left alone may become destructive. He may even injure himself. So you must confine the dog somewhere where you know he'll be safe and where he can't chew through

your door, or tear apart your couch cushions, or crash through a window, or eat your kitchen linoleum.

For most dogs, this means being crated while you leave.

However, it's important to use extreme care when crating a dog who becomes anxious about home-alone times. *If you get in the habit of only putting your dog in the crate when you leave, your dog may learn to associate the crate with being left alone.* The crate may become a terrible thing, in his eyes, because going into it means "my person is about to go away."

How do you keep this from happening? The key is to pair putting him in his crate with lots of different things, not just *I'm going away for a long time now:*

+ Give him his dinner, a chew toy, or a special treat when you put him in the crate. This helps him learn that going into the crate means positive things.

+ Even a busy person can find times to multitask. If the phone rings, take it and your dog to the crate. Put your dog into the crate with a treat. Keep the door open, but block it by lying down and relaxing on the floor in front of the opening. It's a good break for you, and the dog can enjoy a scratching or one-handed massage while you have your phone conversation.

+ From time to time, put him in his crate when you're not leaving the house. Sometimes you may even be in the same room. Other times you may be leaving the room, so you're out of sight, although you'll still be home. Give your dog a favorite toy when you do this to make sure it's a positive experience.

+ Vary how long he's in the crate. For example, put him in the crate when you're going on 10-minute errands, sometimes—not only when you're heading to work for the day.

+ When you are preparing to leave the house for several hours, don't wait until the last minute to crate your dog. Instead, get him in the crate and settled 20 minutes before you leave.

Another important management tool is to make sure your dog is getting enough exercise and stimulation. All dogs need physical activity to burn off energy. A dog who has adequate exercise is less likely to divert his energy into unwanted behaviors. Remember, however, to take care with the timing of that physical activity. Don't get your dog all worked up and excited just before you leave. A 20-minute break between vigorous physical activity and your leave-taking is a good rule of thumb. So plan your dog's physical fun to coincide with periods when you won't be leaving right away.

Desensitization

Another tool you can use to help a dog who fusses when you leave is desensitization. In this technique you expose your dog to something that makes her upset or anxious in a carefully controlled manner. You begin by exposing her to a version of the thing (or experience) that is very mild—so mild, in fact, that it doesn't upset her at all. Then, gradually, you raise the intensity of the experience. As you do this, however, you make sure never to make the intensity so great that it upsets your dog. You keep the experience positive. With time, this helps your dog learn to tolerate something that was once upsetting.

For home-alone training, desensitization can help your dog learn to tolerate the moments in which you leave and immediately after you've left. By helping your dog get through this crisis period, you ensure you don't leave her in a frantic state.

This exercise works best if you do it during a time when you don't have to really leave your dog. For example, if you're on vacation from work, that's a great opportunity to do *I'm leaving now* desensitization.

Start by noting what signals your dog interprets as meaning you're about to leave the house. Perhaps she starts to show anxiety when you pick up your car keys or take a coat from the coat closet.

Your goal now is to show her that picking up the keys or taking a coat from the closet doesn't necessarily mean you're leaving the house.

Let's use the car keys as an example. Several times during the day, pick up your car keys. Make sure your dog notices you doing this. Jingle them a bit if you have to. Then put them right down again.

After a while you'll notice that she is desensitized to your picking up the car keys. She's realized it doesn't mean you're leaving. She'll begin ignoring it.

So now start picking up your car keys and walking toward the door you normally use when you leave to go somewhere. Again, make sure she notices you. Put your hand on the door handle—but don't open the door. Instead, turn around, put the car keys back where they are kept, and go back to whatever else you were doing.

With time, you'll see your dog become nonchalant about this activity, too.

Now add opening the door to the sequence. Don't go outside. Just open the door, then close it again.

Then add stepping outside.

Then add stepping outside and staying outside for one minute.

Then add stepping outside, going to the car, and slamming the car door. (This assumes your dog can hear a car door slam. If she can, chances are she associates that noise with your leaving.)

When your dog no longer associates this sequence with your leaving, add starting the car engine. Then pulling the car out of the driveway. Then pulling out of the driveway and not returning for a few minutes.

If you proceed through each of these levels gradually, making sure your dog is comfortable with each step along the way, you'll go a long way toward helping her learn that these signals don't mean she's going to be left by herself for long periods.

The key is to proceed slowly. How slowly? It completely depends on your dog's reactions. Some dogs may stop associating a particular step with you leaving after just a few repetitions. With other dogs, it may take dozens of repetitions over a long period of time. The key is to keep your focus on your goal, remain patient, and repeat each step as many times as it takes.

Will this be fun to do? Probably not. The fact is, if desensitization is working well, it's about as exciting as watching paint dry. Nothing seems to be happening. But as with painting, if you try to test it too soon—put your fingers on the paint—you end up spoiling what you've accomplished so far. You'll have to go back and patch your work, and it will end up taking longer than it would have if you'd waited. So the key is to be very, very patient.

As you do this, you should also watch what time of day you do the exercises. For example, suppose you leave for work every morning at 7:30 A.M. Your dog is a clever one. She may realize that when you pick up your car keys at 7:28 A.M., that means something entirely different than if you pick them up at 2:00 in the afternoon. So make sure you hold your desensitization sessions at the time of day you normally leave the house.

Now, suppose you start this on the first day of a two-week vacation, and your dog has made wonderful progress. Reinforce it when you start work again. Every once in a while, pick up your car keys like you're about to go somewhere—but then put them back down.

Or get into your car, start it up, then shut it off, come back inside, and have another cup of coffee.

Combine this with the other techniques we've described—including ignoring your dog to keep your partings low-key, and giving your dog fascinating chew toys to play with while you're gone—and you may find that your dog's home-alone problems become history.

Beware the Unintentional Reward

Sometimes we unintentionally reward dogs for unwanted behaviors. This mistake is particularly easy to make with a dog who becomes upset at being left alone. Think about it: What is the best possible reward for a dog who doesn't like being parted from you? Why, having you close by, touching her and talking to her, of course.

So for a dog with separation problems, it's important to ignore unwanted behaviors. Don't "comfort" your dog because she seems upset or anxious that you've been gone, or are about to leave. This is a time for tough love, not sympathy. The same goes for negative attention. Say you come home and find your dog shaking the last feathers out of your new living room throw pillows. Tempting though it may be to make a fuss, you need to hold your tongue. Ignore your dog. The last thing you want her to learn is that tearing up throw pillows might make you magically appear—upset, yes, but still very much home.

We talked earlier in the chapter about keeping both partings and greetings calm. This is a good practice for any dog, because it helps the dog learn that your departures and arrivals are no big deal.

It's even more important for the dog who shows signs of separation anxiety. For this dog, it's particularly important that you ignore him for 20 minutes before you leave, and for 20 minutes after you return.

It's also useful to control how you reward attention-getting behavior at other times during the day. Some dogs become very skilled at training their humans to pay attention to them. Practice ignoring your dog unless he's engaged in quiet, desirable behaviors. Praise and pet him lavishly when he's lying quietly with a chew toy. Pour on the attention when he's napping.

But if he paws at a closed door to get to you, don't open it—all that will do is train him that pawing doors earns him the ultimate reward. Ignore him if he barks at you to get your attention.

If he's in his crate, only let him out if he is relaxed and quiet. If you let him out right after he barks, scratches, or whines, he'll be sure to try that behavior again.

Other Ideas to Help with Separation Problems

It's tempting to think that separation anxiety is a disease, like the flu. If it were, then every case would have the exact same cause. But like many behavior-related syndromes, separation anxiety can have different causes from dog to dog.

And sometimes looking for the cause can help you develop a solution. Here are two areas to consider.

HEALTH

Sometimes behaviors we label separation anxiety have a physical cause. You should be particularly suspicious if a dog who was fine, for years, about being left alone has suddenly developed symptoms. In this case, a variety of physical disorders, ranging from allergies to hormonal imbalances, could be to blame. So have your dog checked over by a vet. Describe the symptoms and how they developed. Be prepared to give additional information about your dog, including his diet.

Some breeds of dog have a higher incidence of certain diseases or imbalances, so you might also want to do some research on your own to supplement your vet's work.

Some vets are now prescribing psychotropic drugs for pets with problems such as separation anxiety. These drugs are identical to those used by humans for depression, anxiety, and similar troubles. Some may have significant side effects, so do your research, and consider using these drugs only as a last resort.

TRAUMA

Sometimes a dramatic change or event in a dog's life might trigger separation problems. The death of a beloved human or animal companion is one example. Moving is another. Think back to when your dog's symptoms began. Were they always as bad as they are today, or did they worsen significantly at some point? Then review your lives to see if anything happened that corresponded to the onset of the behaviors. You may not be able to reverse the event, but at least you'll have some insight into the situation.

As you work to figure out why your dog has separation problems, consider consulting a canine behaviorist or instructor—it can be a huge help to talk to someone with interest and experience in the intricacies of canine behavior. You may find that a professional can discover clues you may have missed.

And Finally, A Word About Leaving Dogs Alone

Before the industrial age, more humans lived and worked on farms. They didn't go off to factories or offices for hours every day. Even as recently as the 1970s, most U.S. families had at least one stay-at-home adult.

Today we live in a very different world—and so do our dogs. More and more, dogs live with families where all the adults leave every day to work. Because many people commute to their jobs, their workdays can easily stretch to nine or more hours at a time.

This means that many family dogs are left alone for nine or more hours, five days a week.

When you think about it, it's not surprising that some dogs react to this by developing unwanted behaviors. Dogs, as we noted at the start of this chapter, are social creatures. They wouldn't normally choose to be isolated for long periods. By asking them to stay alone for hours each day, we're forcing them to adapt to less-than-ideal situations.

And this, in turn, raises the question of what our responsibility is to our beloved canine companions. Even if our dogs seem to accept being left alone, is it really fair for us to do it?

So what are the options for a contemporary western household? One, of course, is to choose a companion animal who's better suited to being alone for long periods. And in some cases, curing a severe case of separation anxiety means rehoming the dog with a person or family who doesn't have to be away as much.

Fortunately, there are other options available in many communities. Hiring a dog walker to come to your home and exercise your dog once a day is one possibility. Another is to use a "doggy day care" service.

Perhaps a responsible, dog-savvy neighbor would be willing to visit your dog and play with him once a day for a few dollars a week.

Finally, take the time to give your dog things to do when you're not home. Leave chew toys, food-stuffed toys, and puzzle toys (that dispense bits of kibble or other food as your dog kicks or nudges them around) when you leave. Turn on the television or radio. Hide tiny treats or kibble around the house before you go, so that your dog can spend the day hunting for them.

By enriching your dog's environment, you not only alleviate the boredom that can lead to separation problems, you also help ensure you have a happier dog.

Chapter 11

BARKBARKBARKBARK:
Outwitting the Dog Who Barks Too Much

Bow wow wow
Whose dog art thou?
Little Tommy Tinker's dog.
Bow wow wow.
  —Nursery rhyme

Dogs bark.

Some of them bark a lot.

And the ones who don't bark a lot still may bark at times you'd rather they didn't.

That's the bad news. The good news is that you can outwit a barking dog. It can take time. It can take some sleuthing on your part, to figure out why your dog barks and to build a training program to stop the barking—or to at least make it tolerable.

Let's start by looking at some of the reasons dogs bark.

Hey, Hey, Hey!

It's estimated (although not without a lot of debate) that the average, educated American knows as many as 60,000 words. Dogs' vocabularies are pretty limited by comparison. This fact became the basis for a gag in a classic Gary Larson cartoon showing a scientist who figured out how to interpret dog barks. The dogs in the cartoon are all shouting one thing: "Hey, hey, hey!"

Humor works because it oversimplifies, of course. Dogs do say more than "Hey, hey, hey." Nor are their "words" confined to barking alone. Dogs growl, whine, bark, and howl. Occasionally they grunt or sigh. Some dogs come up with special sounds, even mimicking human words.

But even the most vocally inventive dogs depend on their human companions to interpret much of the time. Dogs bark to express a range of emotions, probably including excitement, fear, frustration, aggression, anxiety, and anticipation, to name a few. So how do we figure out which is which?

It isn't always easy. Sometimes we can pick up clues from the sound of the bark itself. Is it high- or low-pitched? Is it a long, drawn-out barking episode or a couple of barks, and that's it? Is the barking interspersed with whining?

It's also important to watch the dog's body language. Look for signs of arousal, like raised hackles, outstretched tail, or stiff, on-the-toes stance. Some dogs, when concerned about something, pace stiffly. Dogs who are happily excited, on the other hand, may dance and twirl.

And last, but definitely not least, pay attention to the environmental circumstances. Barking is often triggered by something that happens around the dog. It may be straightforward, like the phone ringing, or it may be more subtle. An animal passing under a window at night may be invisible to us humans, but a very noticeable intruder to a dog.

You may not always be able to identify the trigger that sets your dog off. But chances are, your dog never barks for no reason. And knowing what makes your dog bark can help you figure out how to modify that behavior—assuming you want to modify it. After all, having a dog bark at suspicious goings-on outside your house, at night, is usually a good thing.

Why Bark? Why Now?

Every dog is different. Nonetheless, most dogs bark for one of several common reasons.

In some cases, the barking isn't problematic. If your dog barks at squirrels in the backyard, and you don't particularly mind, then the barking isn't a problem for you. You may want to work a bit on keeping the barking sessions short. But in many households, the occasional bark is fine. It's part of having a dog in the house.

In other cases, barking becomes intrusive. If a dog barks too often, or for too long at a time, it can become stressful to the dog's human family. It can anger neighbors: Barking is one of the most common nuisance complaints in towns and cities. Communities, in turn, try to control the problem with noise ordinances. These laws vary from community to community, and sometimes carry stiff penalties. As a result, if your dog is a problem barker, you could end up being fined, or even have your dog impounded.

So what is *problem barking*? The answer depends, in part, on your tolerance for barking—and the tolerance of the other humans around you. But generally, a dog is a problem barker if he barks for long periods (for example, more than a few barks at a time), or barks too frequently (more than a few times a day), or both.

Dogs who bother neighbors or break noise ordinances are problem barkers.

And finally, as we'll see, sometimes barking indicates other problems, such as boredom or anxiety. A dog who barks to release pent-up energy, or because he's frantic about being left alone, needs help, regardless of whether there are any people around to hear it.

The first step in helping a problem barker is to understand why the dog barks. So let's take a look at some categories that can help us figure this out. But as you do, keep in mind that your dog may fall into more

than one of these categories, depending on his temperament and the circumstances of the barking.

ATTENTION

Some dogs bark to get someone to pay attention to them. These are
usually very social dogs. They aren't usually bonded to a particular person or group, but are happy getting any sort of attention from just about
anyone. They may have a history of using other behaviors to get attention as well, like digging or chewing.

Dogs who bark for attention usually have a somewhat high-pitched
bark. They might bark, pause and look or listen to see if anyone responds, then start barking again. During the pause, the dog might wag
her tail, circle, bow, or show other behaviors intended to initiate play or
get attention.

It's possible to train a dog to bark for attention—even if you didn't
mean to. Dogs who find attention rewarding may learn to bark more
when they figure out you'll kick up a fuss about it.

A Lucky "Roo"

My Corgi has a tendency to bark for attention. Because I noticed this
early on, and carefully ignore her when she uses her *look at me!* bark,
this has never developed into a full-blown behavior problem.

But I was also a bit lucky—I was able to teach her an alternate vo-
calization for getting attention. She was a puppy, and I was in working
on some basic obedience behaviors, like sit. Suddenly, she let out a
"roo." If you've ever had a Corgi, you may have heard this noise: a
kind of a short, modified howl. Fortunately, I had a little warning—she
holds her nose up and puts her ears back when she's about to roo—
so I was ready to quickly give her a treat. It worked. She immediately
added rooing to her repertoire, and since the sound is very cute

(unlike her attention bark, which tends to be high-pitched and earsplitting), she's had lots of positive reinforcement for this behavior in the years since. As a result, to this day she is more likely to roo for attention (or dinner) than to bark.

K. M.

OFFENSIVE BARKING

Some dogs use barking to protect themselves or their property, possessions, or territory. These dogs will bark at anything or anybody they think is encroaching on them. Dogs who bark for this reason combine the barking with confident but aroused body language: alert expression, pricked ears, tail held high. The dog will tend to advance toward the perceived threat, not back away. The bark itself tends to be lower-pitched than an attention bark. It will often start as a growl that escalates into a bark. The barking itself tends to be intense, but of short duration, maximizing the startling effect.

Dogs who bark for this reason mean what they say. If the perceived threat gets too close, the dog may carry through with his threat.

You can think of the offensive barker as using his bark like a spear: It's a weapon he brandishes to warn threats away.

If you believe your dog is an offensive barker, consider consulting a canine behaviorist or instructor. This type of barking behavior can signal a dog's willingness to act aggressively—so it's better to have experienced help in understanding and modifying the behavior.

DEFENSIVE BARKING

Defensive barkers, on the other hand, use barking as a shield. They bark to protect themselves.

This type of dog tends to be worried or anxious. The defensive barker will have ears laid back, tail tucked, legs bent, along with signs of arousal, like raised hackles. He'll tend to retreat as he barks, and the bark will tend to be sharp and high-pitched.

Although this dog will try to get away from the perceived threat, he will bite if he feels he has no other choice. He's scared, and he'll do what it takes to tell the scary thing to back off—especially if his own options for retreat have been cut off. For this reason, you may also want to bring in professional help for working with a defensive barker.

RECREATION

Some dogs bark to amuse themselves. A dog who has lots of energy, and not enough to do, may vent some of that energy by barking. This type of bark tends to be monotonous, broken by repetitive intervals. Barkbarkbarkbarkbark. Pause. Barkbarkbarkbarkbark. Pause. Over and over and over. The bark is usually of medium pitch, and is flat and boring, although some dogs will embellish it with an occasional howl. Because the bark goes on and on, with no change in intensity and pitch, it's obvious that this dog isn't barking at anything in particular. He's just barking.

Dogs like this are bored and frustrated. They may also come up with other unpleasant behaviors to release their pent-up energy, like chewing, scratching, digging, or licking.

ENTHUSIASM

High-spirited dogs sometimes find that barking is a great outlet for their energy and enthusiasm. These are easily stimulated. Movement is often a trigger to begin barking. The bark is high-pitched and continuous. The dog will often move around a lot as she's barking. Her expression will be alert but happy; she'll wag her tail, and often pant.

For this type of dog, barking can be self-rewarding. Think of her barking as a feedback loop. She's excited, her barking is an exciting thing to do, and therefore, her barking excites her even more.

SEPARATION ANXIETY

Finally, there are dogs who bark because they're anxious about being separated from someone. Unlike attention-seeking dogs, the anxious barker isn't looking for attention from just anybody: Only that special someone to whom she is closely bonded will do. This type of bark is often high-pitched and frantic. It may be accompanied by pacing, drooling, whining, scratching, chewing, and howling. These behaviors may be directed in the direction the special person was last seen or heard, and will be most intense right after the departure. See chapter 10 for more information on how to help dogs with this type of problem.

As we can see from these categories, dogs bark for many different reasons. And here's the kicker: *If you don't know why your dog barks, you won't be able to design a program to stop it.* You'll need a different approach for a dog who barks for attention than for one who barks defensively. If you have a bored barker, you'll be trying something different yet. And so on.

So your first step, when you have a problem barker, is to do some detective work. Pay attention to when and how your dog barks. Take notes. Here are some questions that can help you get started:

+ Is there a pattern to the barking? For example, does your dog bark only on Monday mornings? Only when outside, at night, alone? Only when it rains?

+ When did the barking start? Has it been going on since puppyhood? Or did its onset coincide with a lifestyle change—a child leaving for college, a move, a family vacation, new neighbors moving in?

+ Where does the barking take place? Inside? Outside? Both? Does she bark in the car, or on walks?

+ Who is present? Does it make a difference if your dog is alone or with others? If being with others does help, does it matter who is present? Can it be anyone, or does it have to be a special someone?

✦ Where is the dog's focus? Is it on a certain person, animal, or thing, or on nothing at all? If the dog is focusing on something in particular, does it vary, or is the focus always on the same thing?

✦ What solutions have you tried, and how long have you tried them? If the barking has been a problem for a while, it might seem like you've tried everything, but it's still important to answer this question. Write down a list of everything you've done to handle the barking—including trying to ignore it.

You should also pay attention to your dog's body language. In chapter 10 we've listed some behaviors dogs may exhibit if they are feeling anxious. Review this list and make a note if your dog's barking is accompanied by any of those behaviors or body language.

The Big Picture

As you start to understand why your dog barks, chances are you'll also begin appreciating something else: Excessive barking is often part of a broader problem. Therefore, to treat it, you need to look at more than the barking alone. You need to look at the overall health and well-being of your dog.

1. START BY MAKING SURE THERE ARE NO UNDERLYING HEALTH ISSUES

In most cases, problematic behavior, like excessive barking, is exactly that: problematic behavior. But occasionally, the root of the problem is physical. So start by taking your dog to a veterinarian for a complete checkup. Discuss your behavior concerns. Extreme repetitive behaviors, such as barking with no apparent purpose, circling, pacing, or licking, are of special concern.

Food can have an impact on behavior, so tell your vet about your dog's diet. For example, some dogs might develop allergies to certain foods. There is anecdotal information that the protein levels in some dogs' diets might contribute to behavioral issues.

If your dog exhibits symptoms of severe anxiety or extreme repetitive behavior, your vet may suggest prescription medications. You may also want to explore the options available through complementary medicine, such as aromatherapy, acupuncture, touch therapy, nutritional therapy, or homeopathic remedies.

Some veterinarians offer a surgery in which dogs are "debarked," a procedure in which vocal cord tissue is removed or reduced. Results differ depending on the specific procedure and other variables, and not all pet professionals agree it's advisable. Do your homework and get a second opinion. Keep in mind that debarking can't be reversed, and it doesn't address the underlying behavioral issues that caused the barking in the first place.

2. ENRICH YOUR DOG'S ENVIRONMENT

Dogs are social creatures. And today, thanks to our modern lifestyles, many dogs are left alone for long periods while their human companions are occupied outside the home. Sometimes, problematic barking behaviors crop up as a result.

So if your dog tends to bark excessively when left alone, look for ways to keep her more occupied. (Chapter 10 deals extensively with helping your dog become more comfortable about being left alone.)

3. MAKE SURE YOUR DOG HAS PLENTY OF EXERCISE

Dogs need physical activity on a daily basis. Walk your dog in the morning before you leave for work, or spend 15 minutes playing catch or some other active game. Then do the same in the evening. By giving your dog a healthful outlet for burning physical energy, you help prevent her from developing problem behaviors.

4. TRAIN YOUR DOG TO DEVELOP QUIET HABITS

Often barking problems occur because we aren't proactive enough in teaching our dogs to offer quiet behaviors.

How often do you praise or treat your dog when he's relaxing quietly? If your answer is never or hardly ever, then it's time to add this to your training program:

✦ Keep a supply of treats in your pocket. At random times during the day or evening, when you observe your dog engaged in relaxed, quiet behavior, say "yes!" and toss him a treat.

✦ If your dog barks when you're not home or around, make sure you never walk back into the house or yard while he's barking. This technique uses a high-value reward—your return—for not barking. Here's how it works. Say you have gone out to the grocery store, leaving your dog in the house. On your return, you notice that your dog is barking. Don't go inside. Wait outside, for as long as it takes, until your dog falls silent. Only then, open the door. If the act of opening the door causes your dog to bark again, shut it quickly and wait for silence again. Over time, make your dog wait, silently, for longer periods before you go into the house. If you do this consistently, your dog will learn very quickly that being quiet makes you appear. And that's using your wits.

✦ Ignore your dog when he's barking. If your dog learns that barking earns him attention—even disapproving attention, like yelling—then you're losing the barking battle. This can be a hard thing to do. But if you combine this with rewarding quiet behaviors, your dog will learn that to get your attention, he has to be quiet.

The Extinction Burst

When dogs have learned that a certain behavior earns a reward, it can take time to teach them otherwise. And you might find that you hit some bumps in the road as you go along.

Barking is a great example. As you work on retraining your dog, you may encounter what behaviorists call an "extinction burst." Even though the old, unwanted behavior seems to be fading, it may crop up again—sometimes dramatically. Say you've implemented a program where you ignore your dog when he's barking. You seem to be making some great progress. Then, all at once, he starts going a little crazy. He starts barking again to try to get your attention. Only this time, it may seem like the barking is worse than ever.

Stick with it! An extinction burst does *not* mean your training isn't working. *As long as you remain consistent,* over time the barking behavior will decrease.

5. Establish an alternate behavior

Sometimes it's useful to train your dog to do something in place of barking. For example, if your dog barks when you appear at the door at the end of the day, plan ahead and come home with a ball or toy. Before your dog can bark, toss the toy to redirect his intensity toward it.

You can do the same thing anytime your dog barks, habitually, under specific circumstances. If your dog barks when the phone rings, train him that the phone ring means "sit and you'll get a treat." Do the same if he barks when he sees other dogs during leash walks.

Training an alternate behavior takes time and consistency. You need to plan in advance and be ready to reward your dog when he offers the new behavior. But once you've done it, you'll have solved that particular barking problem.

6. Management

Sometimes the fastest way to address barking is to control the environment around your dog.

As you do your barking detective work, think about how you can manage your dog to prevent barking in the first place. Enriching your dog's environment, as discussed above, is one important management technique.

Others include eliminating the triggers that set off the barking behavior. Perhaps your dog barks at squirrels that come to a bird feeder on your deck. Try moving the feeder to a different location, out of the dog's line of sight.

If your dog tends to bark outside on weekends, when your neighbor's kids are playing in the adjoining yard, perhaps you need to keep your dog indoors at those times.

Sometimes, you'll find that people themselves behave inappropriately, stimulating your dog to bark. Some children (or even, sadly, adults) find it exciting when they learn that they can get dogs to bark by teasing them. If you discover that this is happening with your dog, you have several options. Involving the other person in training your dog not to bark may be useful. Explain that you are teaching your dog to bark less, and you need help in the form of ignoring the barking and only paying attention to the dog when he is quiet. (See chapter 14 for more tips on outwitting kids and dogs at the same time.)

Sometimes a second fence, inside the fence that separates two yards, can ensure a little extra distance between your dog and neighbors who may not understand the importance of leaving your dog alone.

Helping the Anxious or Frightened Barker

If you believe your dog barks because she's anxious or underconfident, you need to add other approaches to your training program.

A dog who becomes anxious when left alone needs help in becoming comfortable in that situation. Chapter 10 addresses the needs of dogs who have separation issues.

If you decide your dog is a defensive barker, your job is to teach her that "scary" things aren't scary after all.

A great way to accomplish this is to associate the scary thing with a food reward. For example, suppose your dog barks defensively when a stranger walks by your house. Prepare in advance by having with you a supply of treats (break them into tiny pieces to make them last longer) or your dog's dinner. Then, when a stranger comes into sight, immediately offer your dog as many treats as she wants. You can do this by offering one treat after another, in quick succession. Or hold up a bowl of food or treats and let your dog eat as much as she wants.

Don't worry if your dog continues to bark or whine as you feed her treats. It may seem like you are rewarding her for her behavior, but with a frightened dog, you're actually sending a different message: You're pairing the sight of the scary thing with food. Over time, this will change the dog's idea of what it means when a stranger walks by. Instead of meaning "something scary is about to happen," it will mean "something wonderful is about to happen."

One caveat before you begin this program. Make sure your dog is barking defensively, not offensively. If you're not sure, review the descriptions at the start of this chapter—or consult a canine behaviorist or experienced instructor for help interpreting your dog's behavior.

When you have a frightened barker, it's also useful to work on overall confidence. To do this, you need to pay close attention to what frightens your dog. Your goal is to strike a balance between overwhelming and overprotecting her.

One way to achieve this balance is to observe your dog to learn how close something has to be before your dog becomes upset. There is an imaginary line around your dog that behaviorists call "the critical distance." If a perceived threat remains outside this line, your dog will be alert and watchful, yet calm. The instant the threat crosses this line, however, your dog will start showing defensive behaviors, including, possibly, barking.

When training an underconfident dog, this line is your constant companion. Once a perceived threat is inside your dog's critical distance, training becomes much more difficult, perhaps even impossible. The reason: Your dog's sensory system becomes completely focused on the threat. In all likelihood, she will completely ignore the treats or other rewards you offer her.

On the other hand, you need to expose your dog to perceived threats to teach her that she doesn't need to be afraid of them. The solution is to let her see the scary things while they're on the other side of that line. Let her watch the scary thing while it's far enough away that it doesn't bother her so much. And while she's watching, give her lots of yummy treats. This way, she'll start to associate the experience with positive things: food.

And what you'll notice, over time, is that the critical distance will begin to shrink. Something that was once terrifying when it was two blocks away will be okay at one block. Then 20 feet. Then 10 feet. And finally, with work and patience, at sniffing distance.

Sometimes, underconfident dogs react to specific bogeymen. You might observe, for example, that your dog barks at people wearing hats. Try having everyone in your family wear hats around the house. This will acclimate your dog to hats, and help alleviate the fear-barking behavior.

Building the confidence of an anxious dog can take time and patience, but it can also help reduce this type of problem barking.

Desensitization for Barkers

Some dogs bark at particular stimuli. Often it's a particular noise. As you gather information about your barking dog, you may discover that sirens, thunder, doorbells, or ringing telephones invariably set off a bout of barking.

One way to address this type of problem barking is through systematic desensitization. The basic technique is as follows: You set up training sessions in which you expose the dog to the bark-inducing noise at very, very low levels. How low? That's easy: low enough that your dog doesn't react by barking.

For example, if your dog barks at thunder, record a thunderstorm. Or buy a tape or CD recording of the bothersome noise. (Some dog supply companies sell recordings specifically for this purpose.) Then play it back at very low volume so your dog can hear it. Watch your dog carefully for signs of impending barking. If it looks like he's about to bark, turn the volume down.

Now play the sound frequently at that volume. Do it at various times of day or night until your dog becomes so used to it, he doesn't react at all.

Now turn the volume up slightly. Again, watch your dog to make sure the added volume won't trigger barking.

Play the sound at this volume until, again, he doesn't react to it.

Then turn it up some more.

This technique works best when you pair it with removing the trigger. For example, if you're working on thunder, start your program at a time of year when you won't be experiencing real thunderstorms. If fireworks are your problem, start work in the fall, not a few days before the Fourth of July. If it's sirens, and you can't be sure when an ambulance or fire truck will pass your house, try arranging a stay at the home of a family member who lives in a quieter location, and do the desensitization there. Otherwise, a sudden exposure to the trigger, at full volume, may undo your work and you'll need to start all over again.

Triggers aren't always noises. Sometimes *you* might be the barking trigger. For example, suppose you notice that your dog starts barking when you pick up his leash for a walk. You can also desensitize your dog to this. The trick is to show your dog that picking up the leash doesn't always mean "we're going for a walk." Do that, and the leash will become far less exciting.

Start by only looking at the leash, but not touching it. At first your dog will get excited when he sees you look. But over time he'll realize that your looking at the leash doesn't mean a walk is coming, and he'll stop paying much attention to it.

Now is the time for the next step: reaching for the leash, but not picking it up. Again, at first, your dog will probably react to your reaching by getting excited. But again, over time, he'll learn that it's no big deal.

Progress to picking the leash up, then putting it right back down.

Then pick it up, hook it to your dog's collar, unhook it, and put it back down.

Practice each of these steps several dozen times a day. Of course, every once in a while, you'll take your dog for a walk. But all the same, he'll learn that your taking the leash is usually a pretty boring thing. And as a result, the barking behavior will fade.

Last But Not Least: Relax

Barking can be annoying and disruptive. It can startle us when we least expect it. It can upset people around us, who then upset us in turn.

So it's all the more important for us to maintain a little perspective. Dogs bark, and some dogs are naturally more barky than others. It may not be realistic for you to expect your dog to be perfectly quiet, under all circumstances. To a certain extent, you may need to accept your dog's barking.

This doesn't mean you need to put up with excessive, constant barking. But sometimes compromise can be a great thing. Perhaps you can permit your dog to bark outdoors in the yard, during times when you know your neighbors aren't home. Another option is to allow your dog only three or four barks when she's excited. Then say *"At!"* or clap your hands to redirect her attention (the orienting reflex, introduced in chapter 4) and give her something else to do, like playing with a favorite toy. Do this a few times. Then, the next time she starts to bark, wait to see if she pauses. If she makes the decision to stop and look at you, say "yes!" and give her a nice treat or some other reward.

If you try this, however, make sure you pay attention to whether your dog is barking in order to earn a reward. Does she start to bark again as soon as she's swallowed her treat, for instance? Ignore her.

But if later that evening, she barks because she's heard a noise outside, but then stops barking and looks at you after a couple of yips, reward her like crazy. She's catching on.

Approaches like these let you meet your dog halfway, and reduce your own stress by setting your training goals a little lower.

Relaxing may also help reduce your dog's barking in another way. Dogs pick up on their human friends' emotional states. When you're excited, anxious, or upset, it may cause your dog to become more aroused, which can trigger barking (as well as other unwanted behaviors). Cultivate a more laid-back, relaxed response to life. When the phone rings, don't leap up and dash over to pick it up. Let it ring a couple of times, then saunter over nonchalantly to answer. Do the same when someone comes to the door.

Your dog picks up cues from you. If your heart starts thumping when you see a stranger walking up the street, perhaps you can find a technique, such as deep breathing, to help modify your response. And you may find that this will have a positive influence on your dog.

The same goes for how you react to your dog's barking. If you become angry or upset when she barks, you're adding to her arousal. This can make it even harder for her to control her barking.

Many experts believe that when people learn to relax, they live happier, healthier lives. You may also find that when you relax more, your dog is happier and healthier, too.

Chapter 12

BEST-FRIEND-IN-TRAINING: OUTWITTING THE DOG WHO ISN'T NICE TO OTHER PEOPLE

Mother used to send a box of candy every Christmas to the people that Airedale bit. The list finally contained forty or more names.
—James Thurber, "The Dog That Bit People"

They say that dog is "man's best friend."

Unfortunately, that turns out to be an oversimplification. Dogs, like people, are individuals. Some warm up, quickly, to any and all humans. But other dogs don't.

And this can be a problem. Most of us have lifestyles that bring us into frequent contact with other people. Neighbors and strangers pass our homes. Visitors stop by. Friends and strangers, like door-to-door salespeople and mail carriers, come to the door. Family members may show up, too—and sometimes stay a while.

And if that's not enough, many of us also want—or need—to take our dogs with us when we go places. This means that our dogs will come into contact with other people as well.

As long as our dogs are part of our lives, other people will also be part of our dogs' lives. So ideally, we'd like our dogs to be relaxed and confident around other people, including strangers.

Fortunately, you have some control over how your dog reacts to people.

So You Think You Want a Guard Dog

Many dog owners believe that one advantage of having a dog is protection. There is merit to this idea. If you're out walking with a big dog at your side, it's probably less likely that another person, looking for trouble, will bother you. Many home security experts believe that a barking dog helps deter break-ins, perhaps because when a dog barks, it's harder for a burglar to keep the break-in a secret.

But there's a huge difference between this and having a dog who's likely to bite another person.

Dogs can be trained to attack people, of course. But this is a sophisticated behavior that should be undertaken only with qualified professional help—and only if you are ready to take on an enormous commitment of time and effort. This is a point that cannot be overemphasized: If you try to teach your dog to be a guard dog, and you don't know what you're doing, you may end up with a dog who is unpredictable or unstable. And all it takes is one mistake—one person being bitten—and your dog could end up being seized and euthanized, while you deal with the fines, the lawsuits, and the guilt.

Instead, what the average pet owner should do is this:

✓ **Work on training.** If you're seen with a dog who is paying attention to you, and does what you tell him to do, it sends a strong message to other people. They'll realize that your dog is bonded to you and takes cues from you. If someone is looking for a victim to mug or attack, this makes you a much less attractive target.

✓ **Don't suppress alert barking entirely.** Dogs' sensitive senses of hearing and smell are wonderful assets around the house. Dogs can tell that something strange is happening outside even if we are oblivious. Most of us don't want dogs who bark excessively. But don't go to the opposite extreme and teach your dog to never bark, ever. Permitting or even rewarding two or three short alert barks is a great way to ensure your dog lets you know if something unusual is going on. Rewarding excited barking at truly unusual events—for example, someone rattling a window or knocking on the door at 3:00 A.M.—is also probably a wise idea.

Understanding Your Dog's Reactions

It's helpful to start with some examples of how dogs may react to people, including strangers and people they've met before.

EVERY HUMAN IS A NEW BEST FRIEND

For this dog, everyone he meets is like a birthday present. Whether the person in question is kid, adult, male, female, and regardless of physical attributes, this dog's reaction is the same: He runs up, wriggling with joy, ready to be petted, play, or generally have a good time.

STRANGERS ARE OKAY—BUT ONLY OKAY

This dog is demonstrative with familiar people, but doesn't get excited about meeting strangers. When he does greet strange people, he'll tolerate being petted and fussed over, but will remain aloof.

SOME PEOPLE ARE OKAY; OTHER'S AREN'T

Dogs in this category vary in their reactions to people. They may be fine with women, but not men—or vice versa. Some dogs are bothered by people of particular racial heritages, or wearing certain types of clothing.

Beards sometimes trigger unwanted reactions in dogs. Dogs sometimes react differently to children than to adults.

A dog's reaction to people may also depend on other circumstances, such as location. For example, a dog might be fine when visitors come to his home, but act fearful or even aggressive toward the staff at the veterinary clinic.

MOST PEOPLE ARE SCARY—I WANT TO GET AWAY

At this end of the spectrum, we find dogs who feel threatened by other people. This tendency may express itself in a number of different ways. As with evaluating other types of behavior issues, you'll find clues in body language. Does your dog show signs of anxiety when around strangers or certain individuals? See chapter 10 for a description of behaviors that may indicate anxiety. Do any of these behaviors seem to crop up when your dog is around people? In addition, does she try to avoid people? When you have visitors, does she run to greet them or disappear, hiding in another room?

If your dog shows signs of anxiety around people, and handles it by trying to evade contact, she's probably in this category.

Dogs who are fearful may also become aggressive, however. See the next category for more about this.

PEOPLE ARE SCARY—I'D BETTER SCARE THEM AWAY

Dogs in this category also show signs of anxiety. They may also attempt to escape contact with people. But in addition, they show aggressive behaviors. This is often labeled "fear aggression." These dogs are not confident at all—in fact, they are anxious or even frightened. Their aggression is defensive: They raise their lips, snarl, snap, or even bite because they think it's a useful way to make the human go away.

PEOPLE ARE INTRUDERS—MY JOB IS TO WARN THEM OFF

Finally, we have dogs who aren't frightened of people, but have no intention of becoming friends, either—and in fact, view people as unwanted intrusions who need to back off. These dogs are confident. They may use behaviors, such as barking or growling, to make it clear that the intruder isn't wanted. They have a pretty good idea that reacting aggressively toward people will make them go away.

This type of dog may not show these behaviors when he's away from home. But if he's in the yard or house and a visitor comes, it can mean trouble.

One of the key differences between dogs who fall in the last two categories is whether a dog tends to be offensively aggressive or defensively aggressive. In chapter 11 we talked a bit about offensive and defensive barking. Offensive barkers use their barking like a spear: It's a weapon to warn away something that makes them feel threatened. Defensive barkers use their barking like a shield: It's more for protection than warning. The same distinction holds true for dogs' reactions to people. Some dogs react to people offensively: They choose behaviors intended to warn people off. Others react defensively: They choose behaviors intended to protect themselves.

How do you tell the difference between a dog who is offensively aggressive toward people and one who's defensively aggressive? The key is to observe your dog closely. What is her body language and facial expression? If she looks aroused but confident—alert expression, pricked ears, tail held high, standing "on her toes," then you probably have a dog who is offensively aggressive. A dog who rushes an approaching human, barking or growling, is probably offensively aggressive.

If, on the other hand, your dog shows submissive body language—ears laid back, tail tucked, legs bent—then you probably have a fear-aggressive dog. Usually, a fear-aggressive dog will first try to get away from the threatening human. But if she can't—if she's cornered or forced to be too close to the frightening thing—she'll growl, snarl, bare her teeth, snap, or even bite.

It's also important to understand that sometimes, dogs give out mixed signals. For example, a dog may seem offensively aggressive toward people who are a fair distance away. But if a stranger gets too close, the dog's body language may shift from confident to fearful.

Dogs who show signs of either offensive or defensive aggressive-ness, of course, present their designated humans with a special problem. Already in this book, we've noted that certain behaviors warrant profes-sional help. If your dog appears to show any sort of aggression toward people—strangers, friends, or family members—please consult an expe-rienced trainer or canine behaviorist.

Socialization: The First Step

As we covered in chapter 3, socialization is a critical component of a dog's upbringing. Socialization, in the world of dog training and behav-ior modification, refers to exposing a puppy or dog to a rich variety of experiences before she reaches 16 weeks of age.

Doing this helps to normalize those experiences. And the more ac-customed to an experience a dog is, the more she's likely to react to that experience in a relaxed and calm manner.

Socializing puppies to people is a critical part of helping our dogs fit comfortably into our lives. Today's dogs, after all, generally end up liv-ing around people—all kinds of people. So as we raise puppies, it be-hooves us to make sure they'll grow up comfortable around people—all kinds of people. Puppies who are exposed to many different kinds of people are likely to be more comfortable around people when they be-come adult dogs.

But don't assume that once a well-socialized puppy reaches adult-hood, your work is over. Make sure you continue to give her the experi-ences she needs to ensure she continues to be comfortable approaching, and being approached by, people.

But Even If You Start Late . . .

So what if you have a dog who wasn't properly socialized as a puppy? Perhaps you've adopted a rescue dog, or some other dog who wasn't raised under ideal conditions. Perhaps you adopted a puppy before you learned that socialization was important. Perhaps you allowed your puppy to be frightened by a person—such as a veterinarian—and now need to undo that old lesson.

Well, guess what? You *can* teach an old dog new tricks. Technically, after your dog has passed the age of 16 weeks, it's too late to work on socialization—because technically, *socialization* refers only to the developmental period that occurs during puppyhood.

But what you can do is something very similar: desensitization. You literally help your dog become less sensitive to experiences that might otherwise arouse or even frighten him. By exposing your dog in a gradual, controlled way to people, in time you will see at least some improvement in his ability to handle people-related situations.

How's Your Dog Doing Today?

Whether you're beginning with a puppy or retraining an older dog, it's useful to put a desensitization plan together. This will act as a map, showing all the possible situations you may want to incorporate. After you understand where you're going, you can begin the work of desensitizing your dog.

The first step, then, is to understand how your dog reacts, today, to the people she meets. Once you know that, you can develop a desensitization plan and work on modifying your dog's behavior around people if necessary.

Suppose, for example, you've observed your dog acting stressed, overly excited, frightened, or aggressive toward a person (or around a group of people). If this is the case, you know you have a particular issue or set of issues you need to work on.

It's also important to think about what people your dog will encounter during her life, and under what circumstances. Where do you live? What people will your dog likely encounter as you go about your lives?

But remember to plan for the unexpected as well. You and your puppy may live in an isolated mountaintop cabin today, but what if you move to a crowded city neighborhood 5 or 10 years from now? Is it possible you'll someday travel with your dog? Will you always walk your dog in your home neighborhood, or might you sometimes want to walk her someplace completely different?

As these questions suggest, you're better off exposing your dog to a broad range of people experiences. This will help ensure that, even if your life takes an unexpected turn down the road, your dog will be able to adapt.

So, to summarize, you should plan to expose your puppy or dog to:

+ Lots of people—and

+ different kinds of people—in

+ different kinds of situations.

For example, think about the diversity of people your dog might meet during his life:

+ Women and men.

+ People of different heights and weights.

+ People of different races.

+ People in a wide variety of dress—skirts, coats, slacks, shorts—in every conceivable shape and color.

+ People wearing hats, sunglasses, or other things that change their appearance or the appearance of their faces.

+ Bearded men and people with different hairstyles.

+ Uniformed people, including firefighters, police officers, and veterinarians.

+ People in wheelchairs, or using crutches or walkers.

+ Children, including infants, toddlers, and school-aged children.

+ People carrying things, like umbrellas, suitcases, or grocery bags.

+ Runners, people who limp, and bicyclers.

Ideally, you want your dog to feel at ease when she sees, or is approached by, any person—no matter his appearance, his dress, or how he moves.

You should also plan to expose your puppy or dog to different numbers of people. You may not always have the luxury of being around only one or two people at a time. So you need to prepare your dog to be comfortable around groups or even crowds of people.

And finally, consider the context of your dog's people experiences. A simple example is proximity: how close the people are. To your dog, seeing a stranger at 50 feet may be a completely different experience from having a stranger close enough to touch. Your desensitization program should take that into consideration.

Or consider your dog's veterinarian. A veterinarian is a person— but a person in a very particular environment. First you have a strange place, full of strange smells, other people, and other animals. A visit to a vet's office often means your dog will be enclosed in a relatively small space, and will be approached and handled by more than one stranger, not just the vet. Some of the things these strangers do may feel uncomfortable to your dog, or even painful. And finally, the vet will likely be wearing a uniform of some kind, rather than street clothes. All these elements combine to make a specific, unique experience for your dog. Be ready for this by planning to desensitize your dog to that specific experience.

Another example is a crowded city street, with people pressing around you and your dog. Compare that to a quiet suburban sidewalk, where you encounter fewer people and have more space to maneuver around them.

Each of these people-related scenarios represents a unique set of circumstances. As much as possible, your job will be to expose your dog to these circumstances, in a positive way, so that she learns to accept them as okay.

Does this mean you'll have to spend hours of time exposing your dog to myriad situations? Fortunately for most of us, the answer is no. Many, if not most, dogs are pretty relaxed around people. So if your dog falls into this category, your work at people desensitization will be pretty easy. Not that you should ignore desensitization entirely. It's still a good idea to expose her to a variety of people-related experiences periodically.

This helps ensure that, as she ages, she'll continue to believe that meeting people is a great thing.

Other dogs are comfortable in some situations, but not in all. If this is your dog, your job will be to concentrate on the problem areas. At the same time, don't leave the other pieces out entirely. For example, if your dog is okay meeting strangers one at a time, but becomes stressed in crowds, plan to concentrate on crowds—but every once in a while give her a positive experience with strangers one at a time.

In other words, your desensitization plan will be unique to your dog. After all, your goal is to have a dog who will fit into your life. So your plan should emphasize the areas that are most important to your lifestyle and activities.

Easy Does It

We've looked, so far, at the kinds of experiences that may form the basis of your desensitization plan. This is your map. It shows all the possible features of your upcoming adventure. And by tailoring your plan to your dog, you've highlighted the parts of the map that you'll most need to visit—or visit more than once.

But when you get down to the business of actually desensitizing your puppy or dog, you'll need to take your eyes off the map and put them on your dog. Why? Because chances are, you'll need to modify your desensitization program as you go along.

The first step is to make sure you're familiar with the anxiety-related behaviors described in chapter 10. Remember, your dog can't talk. She can't turn to you and say, "You know, I'm feeling pretty uncomfortable around all these people. Can we get out of here, please?"

Instead, you're going to have to interpret her body language, movements, and facial expressions. This is a skill that can take some time to master, particularly if you haven't been around dogs much before. But the better you get at it, the more effectively you can tailor your desensitization efforts to your dog.

The next step is to learn to anticipate your dog's reaction to particular situations.

Why is this important? Because if your dog becomes too anxious, she may not learn as quickly—or even at all. Say your dog is skittish around bearded men. It's far better to train her, initially, to accept a bearded man in the distance. She may be alert or even a bit upset, but if you work to associate *bearded man, a long way away* with positive things, like treats, chances are she'll more quickly learn to tolerate *bearded man, a little closer.*

If, on the other hand, you lead her right up to a bearded man, and let him stand over her and try to pet her, she may become terribly stressed. She may not even notice the treats that you or the bearded man are offering her. This can defeat the purpose of your training.

In chapter 11 we described an imaginary line around your dog— what behaviorists call the critical distance. We discussed how, if a perceived threat remains outside this line, your dog will be alert and watchful, yet calm. The instant the threat crosses this line, however, she'll start showing defensive behaviors, including, possibly, barking.

When desensitizing your dog, you need to be aware of where this line is, because if something that causes your dog stress is inside her critical distance, training becomes much more difficult, perhaps even impossible. Her sensory system becomes completely focused on the threat. In all likelihood, she will completely ignore the treats or other rewards you offer her.

Instead, what you want to do is to see the troubling thing from inside the safety of that imaginary line. If your dog is nervous about people carrying open umbrellas, for example, you want to begin working with her around an umbrella person outside this line.

Then, over time, what you'll notice is that your dog's critical distance changes. Umbrella people who were once disturbing at 50 feet away will be okay at 20 feet, then 5 feet, and finally even when they are within arm's reach.

The trick is to observe your dog so that you control the progression of your desensitization. You have to modify your desensitization plan on the fly, as your dog's responses to people evolve and change.

Associating People with Good Things

So you've got your map, and you've got your eyes on your dog.

Now comes the fun part: actually teaching your dog that people are great.

And guess what? A great way to do that is to use food. The idea is the same as in other reward-based training we've covered in this book. Food is good. Dogs love food. So if they come to associate something with food, they'll love that, too.

In other words: You need to show your dog that people are like his dinner dish.

His dinner dish. Goodness knows, there may be nothing particularly special about that dish. It may be a plain old boring bowl. But what happens when your dog sees you carrying that plain old beat-up, banged-up bowl? Chances are he goes nuts. He knows what it means—it means dinner is coming. So to him, that bowl is like the world's greatest candy dish. It's like a slot machine that always spills a jackpot. He probably can't pass it during the day without checking it, just in case it may have magically filled when he was in the other room. He probably gives it a good lick every once in a while, even when it's empty, he loves that dish so much. And of course, the sight of it when you've just picked it up is enough to make him believe he's in heaven.

So imagine what it would be like to outwit your dog into thinking that people are just as wonderful as his dinner bowl. What if your dog realized that when a person appears, it means he's about to get a tasty treat?

Getting to that point turns out to be fairly easy to do. You collect your dog, and some treats, and take them both to a place where you're going to see people. Then, when you do see people, you give your dog treats. Simple. After a bit, your dog will start to associate seeing people with getting a treat. He may even glance at you when a person comes into sight, anticipating the upcoming tidbit.

Do you need to go through this exercise if your dog loves people already? The answer is, if your dog is a young puppy, it's a good idea. And even after your puppy is officially past his socialization period, the first year or two of his life lays a foundation for later. Teaching him to associate people with good things is part of that foundation.

If, on the other hand, you're working with an adult dog who loves people, this work may not be necessary. Your dog may find greeting people and being petted to be a wonderful reward. Adding treats would be superfluous. So continue to expose him to lots of people. Watch him to make sure he enjoys it. But bypass the treats part unless you detect that his response is changing. (Save your treats for other training activities.)

But suppose you have an adult dog who isn't comfortable around people. Say he's anxious about people in uniforms. Gradually expose him to people in uniforms, feeding him treats as you do so. Over time you'll see his anxiety subside. He may even, one day, be okay with being handled by someone in uniform.

Desensitizing Trips to the Vet

Another application for this is the vet's office. If your dog is nervous at the vet, work to gradually modify that reaction. In this case, you're dealing with both the person and the circumstances of being around that person, so incorporate both into your program.

At what point does the stressed behavior begin? Some dogs learn that a trip in a car means a trip to the vet. For these dogs, just being led to the car is enough to start making them upset. So start by practicing going to the car. Feed your dog treats when you get in. Then get back out. Your dog will start to learn that getting into a car doesn't necessarily mean a trip to the vet. Outwitted!

When you get that far, take it a step further. Maybe that means driving around the block, giving treats to your dog as you drive.

Then drive to the vet's office. Get out of the car and feed your dog treats next to the parking lot. Then drive back home.

When he's comfortable with that, you're ready to actually enter the office. Since you'll be giving your dog treats, you will probably want to get the staff's okay in advance—and be careful about other dogs who are present. You don't want another dog to decide he'd like a treat too, and start a scuffle. So choose a place to feed your dog his treats where other dogs can't join in. Perhaps the vet staff would permit you to work in an empty exam room, for example. Choose a time of day when the office will be less crowded as well.

As you enter the building, observe your dog. How does he react? If he's too anxious to take treats, you may need to refine your strategy. Try picking treats that are a bit more delicious. Or bring his dinner, and feed it to him right at the vet's office.

Then, once you've finished dispensing treats—leave. Your dog will realize that a trip to the vet sometimes means "food time!" instead of "poked, prodded, and vaccinated." So his response to going to the vet's will start to change.

Finally, add contact with the vet and the veterinary staff. Again, you'll need to enlist their help. Have the office staff hand out treats. Arrange for your vet to come into an exam room to give your dog a reward.

And don't forget to make rewards part of your actual vet visits, also. This will help compensate for the prodding, poking, and vaccination part of the experience.

A Little Help from Your Friends

A great way to enhance your people-desensitization program is to get other people to help you.

When you go to a park, and someone approaches, ask him if he'd be willing to toss your dog a treat. When your dog sees that strangers sometimes hand out food, she'll be a long way toward understanding that strangers are okay.

You can do the same thing with people who come to your house. Your mail carrier or package delivery person might be willing to help if you ask. Just explain that you want your dog to know he's a friend—he'll probably appreciate that you are taking steps to ensure that your dog likes him.

If you have a dog who runs away when visitors enter your house, keep a jar or tin of treats by the door. Ask your guests to toss treats to your dog when they come in. But make sure that, other than tossing treats, they ignore the dog. This way, they won't inadvertently frighten her.

Avoid Creating a Dog Who Bites

Early in this book (chapter 2) we talked a little bit about dog bites.

One reason some dogs bite is that they feel threatened. Biting is a reaction to feeling afraid or threatened. So what makes dogs feel threatened? In many cases, we humans do. In fact, one reason that reward-based training is a smart choice for dog owners is that we avoid making our dogs feel threatened. Put yourself in a dog's place for a second. How would you feel if someone were "training" you by hurting or frightening you? You probably wouldn't feel terribly comfortable. You might even end up downright cranky. You certainly wouldn't trust your trainer. And you'd quickly start associating your trainer with pain and discomfort.

Dogs are no different. When we train dogs using punishment and threats, we make them feel threatened.

Of course, many dogs will put up with this type of training without resorting to biting. Again, there's an analogy to humans. We sometimes put up with a great deal of aggravation—unpleasant work or home situations, for example—without yelling, hitting, or finding some other way to show how upset we are.

But some dogs aren't so tolerant. It depends on the dog. If your dog is naturally anxious, for example, even the gentlest correction, like a tap with a rolled-up newspaper, might provoke a bite—or at least a warning, such as a snarl or a show of bared teeth. Why? Because this particular dog is already nervous by nature. He's already in a state of anxiety. So he may react strongly to a perceived threat.

At the other end of the spectrum, a strong, self-possessed dog might be supremely aware that she can defend herself. She might choose to snap or bite just to maintain some control over you. Can you really blame her? She knows she's got teeth, and when she sees you coming at her with that rolled-up paper, she knows what you plan to do. Can you blame her for deciding enough is enough?

In both of these scenarios, humans have, in a sense, provoked a bite. Not intentionally, of course. But when we use a "training technique" that isn't matched to a dog's temperament and tolerance for stress, we can end up with an unexpected—and problematic—response.

Using reward-based training can help us avoid putting our dogs in situations where they choose to snap or bite.

If Your Dog Has Already Bitten

If you're dealing with a dog who has already bitten—even if it wasn't enough to break the skin—you need professional help.

Professional behavior consultants are trained to observe and interpret dog behavior. They're an invaluable resource anytime you feel overwhelmed by your dog's behavior.

But in particular, you should consider contacting a behavior consultant if:

✦ Your dog growls, snaps, or gives you a stony stare when you touch him, stand over him, try to get him off a resting place, or get near his food or toys.

✦ Your dog lunges at or chases, nips, or bites other people or animals.

✦ Your dog seems unduly afraid of anything in the environment.

In addition, if your dog has bitten, you should immediately go into a micromanagement routine. This means you control every tiny detail of your dog's daily routine. Don't leave anything to chance: supervise, confine, and control your dog 24 hours a day.

Why? Because by doing this, you prevent giving him an opportunity to practice the behavior.

Meanwhile, take care in selecting a pet professional to advise you. Not every dog trainer or even behavior expert is knowledgeable about the various motivations for and modifications of biting behavior. See chapter 17 for more information on choosing a behavioral consultant.

In addition to reward-based training, it's important to make sure your dog feels as relaxed and comfortable as possible around people—all kinds of people, in all kinds of situations. Chances are, you'll find this will have its special reward for you, too—because a dog who is comfortable with people is a dog who has fun with people. And when our dogs have fun, we have fun, too.

Chapter 13

WHY CAN'T YOU BE FRIENDS?
OUTWITTING THE DOG WHO
ISN'T NICE TO OTHER DOGS

My neighbor has two dogs. One of them says to the other, "Woof!"
The other replies, "Moo!" The dog is perplexed. "Moo? Why did you
say, Moo?" The other dog says, "I'm trying to learn a foreign
language."

—Morey Amsterdam

If you spend some time in an off-leash dog park, sooner or later you'll see a dog who seems to rub another dog the wrong way. And next thing you know, the two of them will be snarling, baring their teeth, and acting like they want to murder each other.

Now suppose it's your dog who is doing the snarling and snapping. Chances are, if this has happened, you got pretty upset yourself. Most of us humans are taught to control or hide our aggression—if we allow ourselves to feel it at all. So it can be disturbing when our dogs display behaviors that are so counter to our own human code. It can be hard to understand. *What does it mean? Is my dog vicious? Is she trying to hurt the other dog? Whose fault is it that she's acting this way?*

The Dark Side—Or Is It?

Becoming upset at this type of behavior is probably natural on the part of us humans. But we make a mistake if we interpret our dog's behavior exclusively through our own human filter. We can't judge it on the same terms we judge human behavior. We have to take a step back and understand it on its own terms.

That doesn't mean that it's okay for our dogs to cause trouble with other dogs. Just as our companion dogs will come into contact with lots of people during their lives, chances are they'll also come into contact with other dogs—on walks, while traveling, in the waiting room of the vet's office, and so on. If these encounters go smoothly, everybody's happier and less stressed.

But even though dog–dog aggressive displays are undesirable, we need to keep our perspective.

To start, let's give some thought to why dogs might engage in this type of behavior. Let's take a look at some of the reasons that dogs might display aggressive behaviors toward each other.

FEAR

Fear is a defensive type of aggression. It occurs when a dog perceives his physical safety is threatened or when his critical distance is invaded. (We introduced the concept of critical distance in chapter 11.) There is an imaginary line around your dog. If a perceived threat remains outside this line, your dog will be alert and watchful, yet calm. If a perceived threat crosses this line, however, your dog will start showing anxious, defensive, or aggressive behaviors.

Fear seems to be a common, if not the most common, trigger of threats and aggression. Dogs displaying this type of aggression are often called fear biters. The behavior is associated with a combination of defensive and submissive body postures. For example, the dog may bare his teeth and air-snap, but at the same time his ears will be flattened and his tail tucked between his legs.

Fearfully aggressive animals will not generally chase their opponent or continue an attack once the opponent has retreated outside the critical distance.

DOMINANCE

This is a popular label for categorizing threats and aggression. And, like many fashionable labels, it is often misused. So make sure you're really describing how your dog behaves, and not just assuming that, because she's growled or lunged at another dog, it's a dominance behavior.

So what does this type of aggression look like? First of all, the dog's body language will be more offensive than defensive. Unlike fear-based aggression, her posture will be "up": her tail raised, her ears pricked.

Another important clue, in understanding dominance-type aggression, is what triggered it. Often the trigger is that another dog fails to display proper appeasement behaviors (read on for more about appeasement behaviors). It can also be triggered when another dog tries to take possession of a valued resource: a bone, a couch, a toy.

It's important to understand that dominance is not a personality trait. It's not an emotion. It's not some trait your dog might have that needs to be cured or controlled.

Dominance-related aggression is a reaction to a social situation. Period.

POSSESSIVE

Possessive aggression occurs when a dog has a valued resource such as a bed, toy, or food—and she doesn't want to share.

Some authorities combine this category with dominance aggression. It's also been described as territorial aggression, or guarding behavior, or resource guarding.

Possessive aggression can be directed toward humans as well as other dogs. It may have offensive or defensive components, or a combination of both.

PROTECTIVE

When a dog is defending one or more members of his social group, the behavior might be termed protective aggression. Some authorities include maternal aggression in this category. As with possessive aggression, protective aggression behaviors may include both offensive and defensive components: The dog appears ambivalent, or conflicted, as if not sure what to do.

TERRITORIAL

Territorial aggression is shown when a dog is defending his home area or social group. It also may include offensive or defensive components.

Some experts believe territorial aggression is a special type of protective aggression that includes the defense of a home or breeding area.

To understand this behavior, it's important to consider what a dog might claim as his territory. For example, his sense of territory may extend well beyond what you consider appropriate. You think your territory stops at the edge of your yard. Your dog may think differently, however. He may think it includes the road, the sidewalk on the other side of the road, and the neighbor's property.

It may include the park he visits every day. If he's in your car, the car and immediate area around it could be considered territory.

In fact, anyplace where you settle with your dog might quickly be considered *my territory* as far as your dog's concerned.

Is territory aggression the same thing as possessive aggression or protective aggression? You could make good arguments either way. And in fact, this question shows how many gray areas we run into when we try to categorize aggressive behaviors.

PAIN-RELATED

If a dog is in physical pain or discomfort, she might respond by displaying defensive aggression. For this reason, it's important to be careful around any dog you believe might be in pain.

If your dog is older and suddenly starts showing defensive aggression, it's always good to first rule out pain-related aggression as the cause. This is particularly important if the aggressive behavior is out of character for your dog. If this is the case, schedule a visit to the vet.

Pain-related aggression is sometimes classified as fearful aggression. Some authorities put punishment-elicited aggression in this category.

The positive side to pain-related aggression is that sometimes a trip to the vet is all you need to address it.

REDIRECTED

If a dog is prevented or blocked from attacking her primary target, that offensively or defensively motivated aggression can be directed toward any individual who is handy. This might be another dog or a person—including you.

SOCIAL FACILITATION

Sometimes called pack-facilitated aggression, this category applies when one or more dogs in a group display aggressive behavior and other dogs then join in. It's similar to other behaviors that seem to be inspired by nearby dogs, such as when one dog starts to bark or howl and pretty soon all the other dogs around start barking or howling, too.

PREDATORY BEHAVIOR

Predatory behavior is sometimes listed as a form of aggression. Not everyone agrees with this, however. Predatory behavior is related to a dog's instinctive method of obtaining food. It is not displayed as a reaction to social conflicts. Instead, it is directed toward individuals or objects moving away from the dog. Joggers, bicyclists, and skateboarders can stimulate predatory-like behavior. Dogs will also display predatory behavior toward small mammals such as cats, mice, and birds.

Some attacks on children are probably related to predatory behavior. The dog perceives the quick, jerky movements and high-pitched vocalizations of children as similar to the behavior of prey animals.

Stalking, chasing, and nipping at the legs or ankles are characteristics of predatory behavior. A Border Collie working a herd of sheep is engaging in the initial stages of predatory behavior.

Predatory behavior has nothing to do with malice. A fisherman doesn't hate the fish; he just wants to catch it. Similarly, with dogs, catching prey has nothing to do with a dog's emotion. It is entirely businesslike.

Occasionally predatory-related behaviors can come into play between two or more dogs. Some behaviorists call this predatory drift. The dogs are getting along fine, when suddenly something causes a heightened arousal level. This, in turn, triggers a response in which one dog regards the other as prey.

In Dog Terms (Or as Close as We Can Get)

The above list attempts to give us some ideas of why dogs might act aggressively.

But in some ways, the list has only a limited value.

It's an old problem for behaviorists: Human language, for better or for worse, reflects a human way of looking at things. As a result, when we talk about why dogs do things, we need to realize that ultimately, we can't be positive that we're right. We can't get into a dog's head. And even if we could, we might not be able to articulate, in human terms, what's going on in there.

To make it even more complicated, even if we categorize behaviors, such as aggressive behaviors, there's no guarantee that a dog's behaviors will fall neatly within those categories. If you think about it, this is true for humans as well. We can feel angry and afraid at the same time, for instance. Perhaps the same is true for dogs.

For this reason, it's better to concentrate on describing the behavior, instead of labeling it. For example, suppose you're walking your dog on a leash. Up ahead on the sidewalk you see another person, walking another dog. As you approach each other, your dog suddenly begins to lunge and bark at the other dog.

If your first impulse is to label this behavior (*my dog is being dominant* or *protective*, for example), then you are distracting your attention from actually observing your dog's behavior. What was her body language? Did it change as you came closer to the other dog? What were those changes?

Gathering this information is far more important than coming up with a label.

Observing Your Dog

Sometimes dogs react to other dogs with reactive, excitable behaviors. This is probably related to the individual dog's temperament. Some dogs have an unreasonably strong reaction to events compared with how other dogs react. For example, suppose you have enrolled your dog in a training class. If he's a highly reactive dog, he may start spinning, jumping, and barking at the sight of other dogs as you're waiting for class to start. This is completely different from another dog in the room, who stands around, just looking.

Reactive dogs might also exhibit exaggerated behaviors if they see something unfamiliar. Perhaps you come home from the store and leave a package on the kitchen floor. Your dog walks in, glimpses the package, and shies away from it. That's a reactive response. A less reactive dog would be nonchalant by comparison. He may be interested, but his main response would be to walk up to the package and sniff it.

As this example suggests, defining *reactive behavior* involves comparisons. A dog is considered reactive if he displays any behavior (fearful, aggressive, friendly) that goes beyond the behavior of a normal dog in frequency, intensity, or duration.

Another characteristic of reactive dogs is that they tend to have poor impulse control. It's as if their energy builds up, and when they can't hold it anymore, they pop. They bounce into action—whether it's appropriate or not.

This impulse control issue can, in turn, cause problems around other dogs. A reactive dog, for example, might suddenly lose control and snap or bare his teeth at another dog—even though the display wasn't warranted by the second dog's behavior. This, in turn, can trigger dog number two to display aggressive behaviors. The result: a chain reaction—that plays out with lightning speed.

Training: Help for the Reactive Dog

Obedience training is important for any dog. But if your dog is reactive, it's even more important.

That's because training and rewarding appropriate substitute behaviors can help a dog learn impulse control.

Suppose you teach a dog to sit, for example. You can use this to help your dog learn to ignore other triggers around her and react to your cue instead.

Here's how it works. Suppose you're out on a leash walk, and a squirrel darts up a tree across the street. Would your dog sit if you said "sit"? If she's a reactive dog, chances are she wouldn't. She'd bark and lunge at the squirrel, and generally carry on like a maniac.

But suppose you work on the sit with your dog. You start indoors, in a relatively boring environment. Then you increase the challenge: You practice the sit in your backyard. Then, when she's mastered that, you practice in your backyard when the neighbor kids are out playing. And then you give it a try when something really exciting is going on—like when another dog is around. Or a squirrel.

What will happen, with time, practice and patience, is that your dog will learn to respond to your cue, even when there's a squirrel tail twitching in full view. And this is the best part: Not only will this help you control her lunging at squirrels, but it will also help her learn to control herself a bit more. She'll learn that she can check her impulses. And that's a great thing for a reactive dog.

Offensive vs. Defensive

As we consider the range of behaviors that dogs might display toward other dogs (or people, for that matter), we should also remember that there is a difference between offensive and defensive reactions.

In chapter 11 we talked about offensive vs. defensive barking; in chapter 12 we described how these behaviors can also relate to how dogs react to humans. So it should come as no surprise that these categories of behavior also apply to situations involving other dogs.

OF TWO MINDS?

At the same time, as we consider what a dog's behavior and body language tell us, we also need to keep in mind that sometimes dogs can be undecided.

Like people, dogs can sometimes be unsure how to act. Such a dog might display mixed signals. He might be staring at another dog—typical offensive behavior—but backing up at the same time—a defensive behavior. Then he may suddenly lunge forward.

When greeting another dog, the ambivalent dog might mix friendly and fearful signals.

As you observe your dog, therefore, it's important to really watch what's going on. If you see one type of body language—like staring—don't stop right there and conclude your dog is on the offensive. Pay attention to all your dog's signals. And remember that your dog may switch behaviors midstream. A dog who shows offensive behaviors toward other dogs who are a long way off may suddenly show defensive behaviors should the other dogs get too close.

Why Pay Attention?

Clearly, dog behavior is complex. It can take time to learn how to read it. But as we pick up dog-reading skills, we prepare ourselves to prevent dog–dog problems. This is because the better we understand our dogs, the better we become at removing our dogs from situations before they turn ugly.

Think of it like a slide at the playground. When you first walk up to it, or maybe climb up onto the first step of the ladder, there is still time to change your mind and do something else. When you get to the top of the ladder, it's a bit more difficult to back down, but you still have time.

When you start down the slide, however, you're past the point of no return. Gravity has taken over. It's now out of your control.

As your dog's designated human, it's your responsibility to intervene before your dog starts down the slide. You do this by reading her signals. If you have brought your dog to a park, started on a leash walk around other dogs, or walked into an obedience class, how does you dog react? Do you see signs of arousal? Does it appear to be happy arousal or has she crossed the line into anxiety?

Has she become reactive? Is she displaying offensive or defensive behaviors? Or is her body language more neutral?

Note that these signals start out subtly, then build in intensity. Your job is to learn to read them early, when they are subtle. It's easy, for example, to tell your dog has a problem when he's just yanked the leash out of your hand, charged another dog, and knocked her over, leaving her yelping in fear. But by that time, the damage is done. Your dog has learned nothing positive. He's learned nothing about how you'd like him to behave around other dogs.

If, on the other hand, you notice his arousal early—long before he's lunging with all his strength against the leash—you have some control over the situation. At the very least, you can remove your dog. Walk the other way. Leave the room. Whatever it takes.

Communication Between Dog and Dog

Another important lesson for reading dog behavior is that dogs use body language and other signals to communicate with one another.

Worried dogs, for example, try to tell other dogs they are not a threat and will do no harm. This might take the form of signals that they intend to escape. A dog might turn her head, turn her body to the side, or sit suddenly.

Ethologist Nikolaas Tinbergen, in his book *The Study of Instinct* (see the appendix for more information), describes many of these behaviors as "cutoff signals." Dogs seem to use them to postpone or break off conflict with other dogs. You might also think of them as a way to offer a compromise between fighting and fleeing.

Other experts characterize these signals in different ways. Turid Rugaas, a Norwegian dog trainer, has labeled a group of behaviors as "calming signals." She explains calming signals as cues that produce pacifying effects. They help calm the dog who gives the signal, while they also have a pacifying effect on other dogs who observe the signal. Sometimes two or more dogs exchange calming signals in a subtle "dance" that helps each understand that aggression won't be necessary.

Here are some examples and descriptions of common calming signals:

+ **Yawning.** Dogs may begin to yawn as things get tense.

+ **Tongue flicking.** This can be hard to see without practice, because it can happen quickly. Watch for a quick little flick of the dog's tongue over her lips. (Interestingly, both yawning and tongue flicking often appear in photographs of dogs, because posing for a photo session can be stressful for them.)

+ **Scratching.** When a dog scratches herself—even though she doesn't have itchy skin—it may be a calming signal. For example, if a dog sees another dog within her critical distance, and suddenly sits down for an intense scratch with her hind leg, it is likely a calming signal.

+ **Turning away.** This is a very common calming signal. A dog might turn her eyes, head, or entire body away from the problem.

+ **Blinking; averting eyes.** You should also watch your dog's eyes during potentially stressful situations. You may catch exaggerated eye blinks. You may see your dog roll her eyes side to side, or look away with her eyes (even if her head is still facing the problem). These are also common calming signals.

✦ **Sniffing.** Excessive sniffing can be a calming signal. This is a lot like scratching or yawning: It's something that dogs do anyway, but within the context of a stressful situation it's probably a calming signal. After all, why would your dog suddenly have an urge to sniff the ground just as another dog approaches? Surely the other dog is more interesting right now? Well, in fact, the other dog is what has your dog's attention: The sniffing is a calming signal.

Talking to Your Dog

Dogs use calming signals to communicate with each other. But they also often use calming signals to communicate with us.

If you stand over a dog and notice that he glances away from you, that could be a calming signal. Or suppose you call your dog to come to you. He doesn't really want to do it. So he might suddenly pause and sniff the ground. He's not being defiant—the sniffing indicates that he's feeling some stress, but at the same time he doesn't want you to become aroused toward him.

Furthermore, Turid Rugaas theorizes that humans can communicate with and even calm dogs by mimicking their calming signals. For example, you can more quickly gain the confidence of a worried dog by avoiding direct eye contact and turning away. If your dog has trouble settling himself when you've made yourself comfortable on the couch, try some pretend yawns. You may be surprised to see your dog start to yawn back—and almost immediately begin to relax himself.

A final note about calming signals. They don't necessarily carry status significance. A dog who turns his head away or sniffs the ground isn't necessarily ceding higher social status to another dog. Think of calming signals more as the language dogs use to help ensure that their relationships progress smoothly, without miscommunications—just as humans do things like nod at complete strangers we pass in the street.

At the same time, if you observe your dog throwing clusters of calming signals, it can indicate he's feeling stressed. So use this to figure out whether you may need to intervene. For example, suppose you go to the dog park and find more dogs there than usual. You observe your dog, who is generally comfortable playing with one or two other dogs at a time, averting his eyes, yawning, and scratching himself over and over. It might be a good idea to leave and come back later when there are fewer dogs.

(See the appendix for how to learn more about calming signals.)

They Don't Necessarily Want to Fight

As the information on calming signals suggests, it isn't necessarily natural for dogs to become aggressive with one another. Dogs are social animals, and animals who live in groups depend on each other for survival. It's in the group's best interest for everyone to coexist peacefully. In addition, members of groups need ways to avoid or resolve disputes without injury. The reason is simple: An injured member affects the well-being of the entire group.

Calming signals are one set of behaviors dogs use to avert or resolve potential disputes. But we can also place them in a series of broader categories:

+ Avoidance.

+ Appeasement.

+ Submission.

+ Threat of aggression.

+ Aggression.

Let's take a closer look at these categories of behavior.

AVOIDANCE

One choice dogs have is to simply leave—to avoid a threatening situation altogether. A dog who would like to avoid potential conflict with another dog might try to back away. She might try to get behind you.

If a dog is unable to get away—for example, because she's leashed—she may feel forced to choose a different category of behaviors.

APPEASEMENT

Another choice dogs can make to resolve social conflict is to display behaviors intended to turn off or inhibit perceived threats from others. These are gestures intended to calm such perceived threats.

SUBMISSION

Different from appeasement, behaviors labeled as submissive are shown toward people or dogs who have an established relationship with the dog. A dog who rolls over on her back, or lowers herself to the ground, ducking her head and flattening her ears, is showing submissive behaviors.

Some submissive gestures are similar to those meant to communicate anxiety, fear, or stress. But a dog displaying submissive behaviors is not necessarily afraid. How do you tell the difference? It can take practice. Dogs who freeze, tremble, or defecate, however, are more likely fearful.

THREAT OF AGGRESSION

If a dog feels threatened by another dog (or a human, or anything else, for that matter), she may react by sending a warning.

Threatening dogs can be quite dramatic. They can lunge, snarl-bark, and even air-snap—biting at the object of the threat, but without making contact. It can look so awful that sometimes we humans believe what we're seeing is an actual attempt to injure, not just a warning. And in fact, threats and actual aggression are on a continuum, starting with a subtle warning (perhaps a slightly curled lip) and continuing to an all-out attack.

Still, it's important to keep our wits about us as we observe our dogs. Air-snaps, for example, aren't accidents. If a dog wants to connect, she will. An air-snap is an inhibited bite. Is it a serious signal? You bet! But the important thing is to learn from it. It's a warning. Which means you need to do a better job, next time, at intervening before your dog has to threaten again.

So What Can We Do?

Dog–dog aggression can create nagging problems for humans.

We've looked, now, at the forms dog aggression can take. We've considered a bit about why dogs might resort to aggression. And we've looked at behaviors dogs can use to avert aggression among themselves.

All this information can help us to remove our dogs from situations that might trigger aggressive behaviors. Is there anything else we can do?

Part of the answer is to focus on prevention. One key time to work on prevention is when dogs are puppies—under 16 weeks of age. If your dog is a puppy, enroll him in a "puppy kindergarten." This type of class focuses primarily on socialization rather than obedience training.

It may also be useful to arrange private playdates for your puppy. If you do this, however, make sure the playtimes are short—10 or 15 minutes at a time. And beware of playdates with multiple puppies. Rowdy, free-for-all play among large groups of puppies can be overwhelming, or even frightening, to a young pup. It's better to give your puppy a few minutes with one other puppy than expose him to an experience that makes him feel anxious or threatened. (This is true of puppy kindergarten classes as well as private playdates.)

Some experts believe that adult dogs who get practice interacting with other dogs can become more fluent with dog–dog communication. Rugaas, for example, has observed that adult dogs learn to use calming signals more effectively by interacting with other dogs who use them.

However, if your puppy or dog shows signs of dog–dog problems— for example, signs of anxiety or aggression around other dogs—your best bet is to look for professional help.

The reason: Dogs can learn unwanted behaviors as easily as they can learn desired behaviors. And because you're dealing with other dogs—not people, as when working with dogs who are anxious around humans—you may find yourself quickly out of your depth.

And the risks are significant. Say you have a fearful dog who is timid around other dogs. You decide you want to socialize him by taking him to a local dog park. What happens if you, innocently enough, push him too far, too fast? To put it bluntly, you may end up transforming your "plain vanilla" fearful dog into a dog with full-blown fear-aggressive behaviors. He may learn, for example, that the best way to solve his problem is to chase other dogs away with overt threat displays. So now you have an even bigger problem on your hands.

Professionals learn to follow dog signals, in a group setting, even when the exchanges are happening at breathtaking speed. This takes practice. Don't make the mistake of practicing on your dog. Find an experienced behaviorist or dog trainer. Some even specialize in dogs with fearful or aggressive behavior problems. (Turn to chapter 17 for more on how to pick a trainer.)

You'll be glad you did. Because in the case of dog–dog problems, getting help from a more experienced human is often the smartest thing to do.

Chapter 14

Now for a Real Challenge: Outwitting Kids and Dogs at the Same Time

Orvie had more than a longing for a pup, he had a determination to possess one, gave his father and mother little rest from the topic and did all he could to impose his will upon theirs. Their great question had thus become whether it would be worse to have a pup or to have Orvie go on everlastingly asking for one.

—Booth Tarkington, "Blue Milk"

So you have a dog—and a kid. Or more than one kid. Or neighbors with kids.

You, my friend, are seriously outnumbered. As complicated as it is to manage a dog's behavior, that's nothing compared to what happens when you toss in a kid or two. Human children have their own unique behaviors—and unfortunately, they will occasionally clash with your goals for training and managing your dog.

But all is not lost. If you keep your wits about you, it's possible to raise a dog successfully, even if there are kids around.

A Boy and His Dog

Before you get started, it's a good idea to take a look at your assumptions about kids and dogs. There's a romantic notion, perhaps owing to the 1950s television show *Lassie*, that dogs and kids are natural partners. It's true that dogs can be a great source of amusement for kids—after all, they like to run around and play as much as human children do. It's also true that some kids, just like some adults, appear to be naturally gentle and empathetic around dogs.

But it's important to understand that, when you put dogs and kids together, things can go terribly wrong. While it's difficult to pinpoint how many people are bitten by dogs every year (because most bites are probably not reported), it's believed that as many as half of all dog bite victims are children. And when a child is bitten, it's usually in the face. As a result, potential disfigurement is added to the trauma of the bite itself.

It's also believed that the majority of dog bites are inflicted by the family's own pet, or a neighbor's pet. In other words, the person who was bitten knows the dog.

So it's no wonder that the first thing we're going to recommend is that you never leave dogs and children unattended.

Supervision, Supervision, Supervision

Face it, kids can't be trusted to show good judgment all the time. Even the best-behaved kid can do foolish things, like reach for a dog's favorite toy, step on a dog's foot, or fall into the dog by accident. Any of these incidents, innocent though they are, could provoke a dog to snap or bite.

By supervising your dog, you ensure that you can step in before the child makes a mistake. You can calm the play down if it gets too wild. You can intervene if you see the child about to do something that might cause problems.

You can also watch for deliberately provoking behavior on the child's part. Some kids excite themselves by teasing dogs: blowing in the dog's face, poking at the dog, or pretending to take the dog's food or toys. If you're watching, you can stop this behavior before your dog takes matters into her own paws.

Part of supervising your dog includes knowing her well enough that you can spot problems before they escalate. Observe your dog. Note if she shows signs of anxiety. Is she trying to get away from the child? Is she licking her lips, looking away, panting, or trembling? Learn the body language and facial expressions that indicate all is not well with your dog.

Then, if you see your dog giving off any of these signals, step in at once. Remove the dog and put her somewhere she feels secure and protected.

You should also pay close attention to what situations cause your dog to feel anxious or even just aroused. Does she become overexcited when the phone rings? When a thunderstorm comes up? After a ride in the car? When there is another dog around?

Sometimes dogs who can handle one kid just fine have trouble around multiple kids. Having more than one child may mean that the play gets wilder and noisier. Your dog may end up feeling overwhelmed or threatened. Or she may become excited and wild herself.

The problem is that anytime your dog is worked up, her responses may potentially become exaggerated. A dog running frantically around the yard, barking at another dog, is a bit less predictable than a relaxed dog sitting quietly in the living room. So you need to take this into account.

You should also take special care if your dog is sick or injured. Dogs who are in pain may have a lower stress threshold than healthy dogs.

Resource Guarding: Special Hot Spot

We introduced the problem of resource-guarding behavior in chapter 3. It deserves a special mention here, however. Adults can generally remember to respect this behavioral tendency and act accordingly. But kids are a different story. You can tell them to stay away from the dog dish. And most of the time, they'll remember. Then one day, your nephews will start playing catch in the kitchen, and their ball will roll over near the dog dish. Somebody will dart over to retrieve it. And your dog won't necessarily understand that the kid is going for the ball, not his dish.

So what should you do? The best cure is prevention. In chapter 3 we described some exercises to help puppies become comfortable giving up toys, and having people's hands near their food.

But don't rely on the training alone. Supervision is also critical.

And if you have a dog who already shows resource-guarding behaviors, consider getting help from a professional trainer.

Cycle of Violence

Most of the time, when troubles arise between dogs and kids, the problem is lack of supervision, poor socialization skills on the part of the dog, and/or the child's lack of skills or practice on how to behave around dogs.

But sometimes, the problem is more serious. Some children, unfortunately, cross the line from ignorant behavior into genuine cruelty.

Research shows a strong correlation between substantial animal abuse in childhood and later personal violence to humans. As a result, we can no longer dismiss cruelty to animals as an innocent childish prank. In 2001, for example, the American Humane Association reported that in a comparison of men imprisoned for violent crimes versus a group of nonincarcerated nonviolent individuals, 25 percent of the violent criminals reported "substantial cruelty" toward animals in their childhood. None of the nonincarcerated men reported a history of animal cruelty. Further, in a study of 57 families being treated for incidents of child abuse, 88 percent also abused animals. In two-thirds of the cases, an abusive parent killed or injured an animal to control a child. In one-third, a child had abused an animal, using the animal as a scapegoat for anger.

Recent studies also suggest the following:

✓ Children raised with intense coercion may imitate this behavior with animals and people.

✓ Children learn cruel behaviors from adults and may reenact them on animals.

✓ Children abuse animals to release the aggression they feel toward abusive adults or because of psychological trauma.

Sadly, the options for addressing abusive family situations are complex and, at times, limited. However, if you observe a child being cruel to your dog—or any other animal—you should report the incident to the authorities.

If your own child has crossed the line into cruelty—for example, by deliberately injuring or attempting to injure your dog—please seek professional help immediately.

Management

Sometimes your watchful eye is enough to prevent problems from cropping up when children are around. But in other cases, you need to be even more proactive. Management is a particularly useful tool if:

+ You have adopted an older dog and aren't sure if he tolerates children well.

+ Your dog or puppy has a history of becoming anxious or aggressive around children—even if this behavior seems to have subsided or disappeared.

+ Your dog has a history of resource-guarding behaviors—even if that behavior has subsided or disappeared.

+ Your dog is overwhelmed or anxious—for example, he's been tolerating some visiting children for a while, but now shows signs of wanting to get away from them.

You cannot be 100 percent sure your dog will be okay around all children, in all situations, all the time. For this reason, good management, like supervision, is critically important.

USE THE DOG'S CRATE

Use a crate as a haven for your dog. Give him a nice chew toy as well, so he can physically channel his stress. If your dog is particularly upset, consider putting a blanket or towel over the crate to cut down on visual stimulation even more. And make sure to instruct the child or children to leave the crate alone. There should be a no-go zone around the crate. Putting some tape on the floor to show how far children should stay away gives them a gentle visual reminder.

KEEP YOUR DOG LEASHED WHEN ON WALKS

This ensures you have control over your dog should a child appear.

TELL CHILDREN TO STAY AWAY

If you do encounter a child while on walks, in the vet's waiting room, or in other similar situations, explain that your dog "isn't used to children" or "isn't feeling well today" and that the child must keep a distance. It may also be helpful to position your body between the dog and the child.

REMOVE VALUED TOYS, DISHES, AND SO ON

It's a good idea to put away objects that your dog values when children are around, even if your dog has never shown resource-guarding behavior.

DON'T LEAVE YOUR DOG ALONE IN A PARKED CAR

There are a lot of good reasons to follow this rule. You can't be absolutely sure your dog is safe alone in the car. You can't be sure no one is disturbing your dog. You can't be sure the temperature inside the vehicle is appropriate.

But in addition, some dogs become territorial when left in cars. When they see someone near the car, they act out by barking, charge the windows, and become aroused, excited, or worried in general. And if that someone is a child, you can't be certain that the child will be supervised, or will know enough to keep hands and fingers away from open windows. So plan your dog's outings accordingly.

Hey, Kids: No Misbehavin'

When people adopt dogs, they take on a pile of responsibilities. When you add kids to the mix, your responsibilities grow. You not only have to train your dog. You also have to train the kids.

How to teach children is a whole industry itself—a subject well beyond the scope of this book. There are, however, a few rules of thumb that you will probably find helpful. First, don't try to teach too much at one time. Many kids, particularly younger ones, do best with brief lessons, rather than long ones.

It's also important to gear your lessons to each kid's age and developmental stage. For example, a two-year-old isn't going to learn how to pet a dog from long, wordy explanations. But if you hold his hand and pet your dog together, he'll quickly pick up at least some of what you want him to learn—for example, how hard to pet and in what direction.

Adults who have been around kids a lot—who have raised a few themselves or have worked with children professionally—tend to get a feel for how to gear lessons age-appropriately. If you're not familiar with kids, consider getting some pointers from someone who is.

So what are some lessons that you should teach kids who are going to be around your dog?

WHETHER TO APPROACH A DOG

Children need to be taught that before they approach a dog, they have to check with the dog's human companion *and* with the dog. This means they first ask the human companion if it's okay to pet the dog. Then, even if the human says yes, they need to watch the dog. This comes back to the same signals that adults need to mind. Does the dog look relaxed and confident? Or is she showing signs of anxiety? If the latter, the child should steer clear—even if the nearby humans say it's okay to pet.

Of course, not all children will know what an upset dog looks like. It takes practice and experience to learn to read dog! One way to help a child learn is to get down on your hands and knees and act like a dog. Demonstrate body language that says *don't pet me* (turning your head away, backing up, lifting your lip in snarl, ducking your head fearfully) and body language that says *petting me is okay* (head up, face relaxed).

When you see dogs, whether in real life or on television, point out body language and facial expressions, and talk about how to interpret them. Sometimes the lessons can be subtle. For example, in television shows and movies featuring dogs, a dog playing the role of aggressor or attack dog is often showing the body language *confident and excited*. Her ears are pricked, her lips are relaxed, her tail is up and wagging. Discussing this with a child can help him become more skilled at reading dog. Point out to your child what the person on TV is doing and how he (your child) could handle the situation more appropriately.

How to approach a dog

Most dogs are more comfortable being approached by the side than from the back or the front. Walking straight up to a dog, for example, can be interpreted as threatening. Approaching a dog from behind may startle her. So teach children to walk up to a dog's side.

Children should always make sure that the dog sees them as they approach. And if the dog backs up and looks afraid, or comes forward looking angry, the child should not try to pet her.

How to pet a dog

Some dogs are uncomfortable being petted in places where they can't see your hands and arms. Other dogs become uncomfortable if someone reaches over them. Teach the child where to pet dogs:

✦   On the side of the face.

✦   Under the chin.

✦   On the dog's near (closest) shoulder.

✦   On the dog's chest.

Children should always pet the near side of the dog, so that they don't reach over the dog's body or head. They should never pet the top of a dog's head. And children should never be allowed to hug or lean on dogs.

WHEN TO LEAVE A DOG ALONE

Children should be taught to leave dogs alone when they are eating, sleeping, playing with toys, or chewing on something. This helps prevent resource-guarding-related accidents.

RESPECTING DOG'S TERRITORIES

It's also important to help children understand that dogs may not like having people enter their space. For example, if your neighbors have a dog, and your kid's ball goes into their yard, the child shouldn't enter the yard unless your neighbors (or you) are present and say it's okay. Explain that some dogs naturally guard their homes and yards. They may become frightened or feel threatened when someone enters their space.

Children should also be taught to stay away from dogs in parked cars. They must not reach into a car to pet a dog, even if they know the dog.

HOW TO BEHAVE AROUND AGGRESSIVE DOGS, OR DOGS WHO JUMP UP

Children should also be taught how to behave if a dog seems angry or makes them feel scared or uneasy: They should stand perfectly still, like a post. They should not run. They should not move their hands. They should not make any noise or talk, but just stand still. They should let the dog sniff them, until the dog is ready to walk away.

Explain to the child that if they move, talk, or run, the dog will become more interested, and will not leave them alone as quickly.

Dogs who are not trained to greet politely may jump up on children to greet them. Again, the child should be instructed to "be a post."

Yes, Dogs Can Behave Like Predators . . .

We humans become so attached to, and involved with, our dogs that we sometimes forget they're predators. But the fact is that they are. They have the jaws, teeth, eyes, and brains of predators. And they also exhibit behaviors that are common to wild predators.

Biologists Ray and Lorna Coppinger describe the hunting, killing, and eating behavioral sequence of general carnivores as: *orient > eye-stalk > chase > grab-bite > kill-bite > dissect > consume.** They go on to say that we have created specialized breeds of dogs by rearranging this pattern. In some dog breeds, segments of this sequence are virtually eliminated. In others, certain segments are hypertrophied—that is, they have been made stronger or more pronounced.

What's important for the average person to realize is that dogs can, and do, respond to their environment as predators. When a dog chases a Frisbee, that's the *chase > grab-bite* segment of the carnivore sequence. When Border Collies stare at sheep, that's eye-stalking. When a Pug or Pomeranian pounces on a toy and shakes it, it looks so cute. But what we're really seeing is actually the grab-bite (the pounce) and kill-bite (the shaking).

All this has special importance when it comes to human children and dogs. Children's quick movements can trigger portions of this behavior sequence to kick in. If a child runs away from a dog, for example, it can trigger the chase behavior. Depending on the dog, that could in turn lead to a grab-bite or, even worse, *grab-bite > kill bite.*

This is why it's so important for children to learn to hold perfectly still around an angry or scary dog. A motionless, quiet child avoids triggering these potentially disastrous behavior sequences.

You don't need to explain all this to children. For young children, in particular, explaining all this would only overcomplicate your lesson. You want them to learn *what* to do, not *why* they should do it.

But it is helpful for us, the adults, to understand, because it helps us remember—and respect—our dogs' true natures.

* Coppinger R, Coppinger L. *Dogs: A Startling New Understanding of Canine Origin, Behavior & Evolution.* New York: Scribner, 2001, 206.

WHAT GAMES ARE OFF-LIMITS

Teasing dogs can be exciting for kids. When children discover they can get a dog to react by blowing in his face, tickling his paws, or taking away his toys, they will sometimes turn it into a game.

It's important to help kids understand that these "games" aren't fun for dogs. Older children may be able to relate in terms of how they feel when other kids tease them. Young children may need this explained more simply, in terms of the black-and-white rules for playing with your dog.

It's also important to set limits on running and chasing games. Sometimes kids and dogs can run together without losing control. In other cases, a chasing game that starts out as fun can take a bad turn. Know your dog. Does he become overstimulated with this kind of play? For example, does he have a tendency to start nipping at the children's clothing, heels, or hands?

If this is the case, play it smart: Ban this type of game entirely—substitute some of the alternate games described later in this chapter.

Manners

While never a substitute for supervision, training is an indispensable tool for helping your dog do well around children. When your dog responds reliably to cues like *sit* or *down*, you can exert a little more control over situations.

Key behaviors that are useful when your dog mixes with kids are the sit, the down, and *my turn*. Use *sit* or *down*, for example, if your dog is overwhelming a child, such as licking the child's face, which may in turn cause the child to run, scream, or strike the dog.

My turn is useful in situations where a child and a dog want the same toy.

A secondary benefit of obedience training is that it helps dogs develop self-control. Reinforce this by working on obedience behaviors when you are around children.

My Training Helper

I adopted my current dog, a Pembroke Welsh Corgi, when my daughter was two years old. One way I helped ensure the adjustment would go smoothly was to let my daughter help "train" our puppy.

I laid the groundwork by first teaching our puppy the *down* cue and *okay* as a release. Then I began involving my daughter. First, I let her toss treats. I'd say "down" and, when the puppy lay down, my daughter would toss the reward.

Next, I let my daughter use the *down* cue. The only rule was that she had to wait until the puppy lied down before she could toss a treat. I'd put out a pile of tiny bits of treats and let them play for as long as they wanted.

This game proved endlessly enjoyable to my daughter—and our puppy. And best of all, we ended up with a dog who loves to play down with kids. My daughter can now use *down* anytime she wants a little space from the dog. The same goes for visiting children—who also love to play the down game. And as an added benefit, if my daughter is carrying food of her own, our dog doesn't try to take it from her—instead, she lies down in the hope that maybe my daughter will share.

K. M.

Happy Practice

Another important way to make sure your dog can tolerate children is to expose her to children, while carefully controlling the experience to make sure it is positive for your dog.

If your dog is a puppy, that's fabulous: You have the opportunity to make a great start. Plan to expose your puppy to children of all ages, from infants to teenagers. Talk to friends and relatives who have kids, to arrange as many meetings of this kind as you can.

During these encounters, be sure to pair your dog's being-around-kids experience with rewards. And watch your puppy: Make sure it's a pleasant and nonthreatening experience.

For example, suppose you arrange to meet a friend with children at a park. Bring along a bag of treats. As soon as the kids are in sight, give your puppy a treat. This shows her that *seeing kids means I get a reward*.

As the children get closer, observe your puppy. Does she seem happily excited, or does she seem anxious or frightened? If she becomes anxious, exercise control. Don't let the children crowd in and overwhelm her. Instead, stay at the distance at which she is alert, but not terrified, and start feeding her treats. Don't spend a lot of time—maybe five minutes or so, then leave. Then arrange another meeting in a day or two, and see if you can get a bit closer.

The key is for you to remain in control. It's probably useful, in advance, to discuss the ground rules with the kids—and their parents. Let them know that:

✦ You plan to remove your puppy *before* she becomes worried or overwhelmed.

+ They can pet your pup some other time, when she's learned it's okay.

For puppies who are not scared, you can start involving the children in the training. Hand out treats, and let the children toss them to the puppy. (Tossing is better than having the puppy take the treats from the kids' hands. If a kid does feel a puppy's teeth, the child may scream or jerk the treat away, which can frighten the puppy or overexcite her.)

Ask the kids to tell your puppy to "sit" or "down" before they toss the treat. This helps reinforce your obedience training work, and also helps teach your puppy how to say "please" to kids.

You can also enlist the children to work on other lessons, like how to greet people without jumping up. For example, explain that they should turn their backs and ignore the puppy unless she sits.

No matter what, however, as you do these exercises, watch your dog. If you ever observe your dog appearing at all anxious or aggressive around children, please seek professional help.

The Scariest Moment of My Life

When I adopted my first dog as an adult (well, I thought I was an adult, anyway), I knew nothing about the importance of socializing a puppy so she would grow up comfortable around little children.

As a result, I ended up with a 65-pound Doberman mix who became anxious around young children—and, to make matters worse, felt she needed to guard me from them.

One day, during a period when I was sharing a rented house, my housemate invited a friend over. The friend brought along her son, who was about five years old and was as wild, impulsive, and noisy as any little boy can be. I was in my bedroom with my dog when the boy came dashing down the hall to see us. I'll never forget what happened next: My dog quickly positioned herself between me and the door. The child burst in and ran up to my dog—and started petting her on the top of the head. Brett's ears were back flat on her head. Her hackles were raised, her tail was straight out and stiff, and her lips were drawn back in a nasty snarl. Her face was inches from the child's.

My heart stopped. I knew that if that child made a sudden move, it would be over.

In a firm but quiet voice, I told the boy to drop his hands. I called my dog and, thankfully, she came to me.

Later, I talked with the boy's mother to let her know that I needed her help managing her child when she visited.

I also became much more committed to making sure that I didn't put my dog in that kind of situation again.

And I vowed to make sure my dogs were properly socialized to being around children in the future. The alternative is a gamble that isn't worth the stakes.

K. M.

Bringing Home Baby

Adding a new baby to your family changes everyone's life—including your dog's. Your preparations should include steps to help your dog adjust.

KNOW YOUR DOG

It's important to gear your preparations to your dog's temperament. If your dog is a sleepy, laid-back fellow who barely reacts to strange sights or sounds, you may not need to invest much time preparing.

On the other hand, you should plan to put in some extra time if you suspect your dog might have trouble adjusting to a new baby. Is your dog very reactive to strange sounds or sights? Does he have a pronounced startle reflex—for example, if there's a sudden noise, does he jump up, bark, or become frightened or upset? Or does he simply lift his head, look around, and go back to his nap?

Other important signs are tendencies to:

✦   Guard toys, food, and/or family members.

✦   Have high energy levels.

✦   Become overly excited or out of control.

✦   Be touchy about his body.

✦   Be grumpy in general.

In addition, some dogs have more pronounced chase or other prey-drive-related behaviors. These dogs also need special attention.

OBEDIENCE TRAINING

Make sure to work on obedience training as part of your preparation. Brush up on sit, down, and stay, and on greeting people by sitting rather than jumping up. Walking nicely on a leash is also especially important now that you will have a baby stroller to control as well as a dog.

Another useful obedience behavior is the ability to send the dog to a specific target area, such as a special rug, and stay there until released. See chapter 8 for how to train the go-to-place behavior.

BEGIN MAKING LIFESTYLE AND ENVIRONMENT CHANGES *BEFORE* BABY COMES HOME

For instance, if you plan to make baby's room off-limits to your dog, now is the time to start boundary training. Go into the room, but first tell the dog to sit/stay outside the door, or send him to his target area ("go to place"). Make staying outside the room very special and good by giving your dog a pacifying treat such as a chew toy.

You should also get the dog used to the baby's things. Set up your crib and changing area ahead of time. Get a teddy bear or doll and place it in the crib. Choose a life-sized doll that flails her arms and makes baby sounds. A few times a day, take a couple of seconds to go over to the doll. Sprinkle some powder or rub some lotion on the doll to get your dog used to these new activities and smells.

Consider purchasing a tape or CD with recorded baby sounds to get your dog used to them.

If the baby is born in a hospital, you can bring home a blanket ahead of time that has the baby's scent on it. Wrap the doll in it and allow the dog to investigate this novel smell. Be happy and praise the dog. Give him a cookie. This will help him associate the baby with good things.

CONTROL THE FIRST INTRODUCTION

When the new mom comes home, the dog may be so glad to see her that he might forget his manners and jump up. Even if the dog behaves well, Mom might be nervous about the baby, and the dog might pick up on that. So just in case, consider having someone else carry the baby into your home. You may even want to have Mom come into the house first, a few seconds before the baby. This will give Mom a chance to greet your dog and get him settled down. Mom should deliberately keep the greeting calm so the dog doesn't become overly excited.

If your dog is reasonably calm, allow him to sniff the baby all over. If he's excited and out of control, save this step for a time when he is more relaxed.

THE NEXT FEW DAYS

During the first week or so, take special care to ensure that the baby appears, from your dog's perspective, to produce attention and happiness. For example, when you change the baby, toss tidbits or toys to your dog. You can keep a jar of treats or toys on the changing table, or wear an apron with big pockets.

Do the same anytime you're giving attention to the baby, such as during feedings. Make particularly sure you toss treats if your dog is offering sits or downs while you are with the baby.

Also, anytime you're holding the baby, speak softly and lovingly to your dog.

SUPERVISION

Never leave your baby and your dog alone, unattended. Babies squeak and move like a prey animal. While some dogs may simply want to investigate the baby, these sights and sounds could initiate instinctual chase and grab reactions. Don't take that chance.

Toddlers

Beware! Once your baby begins to crawl and walk, the situation changes and supervision becomes *very* important. Never leave toddlers alone with a dog—even if your dog has always been friendly and tolerant toward the child. A poke in the eye, a trip and fall into the dog, or a loud scream into the dog's ear could produce an orienting reflex that might make the dog whip around and knock the child over. Worse, the child's actions might cause the dog to snap. Toddlers can get bitten for natural toddler behaviors—running, screaming, throwing themselves at the dog, or hugging the dog, especially hugging from behind.

Make sure your dog has an area of her own. It should be accessible to the dog and close to family activities, but out of the traffic pattern. This space could be a bed, a wire dog crate or airline kennel, a carpet square—any easily identified space. Take the dog to this area when things become chaotic.

Give your dog a special treat when she's in her safety zone. Over time, she will learn to escape to this area when she wants to be left alone. Respect this—and teach children and their visiting friends to respect it as well. They should always keep away from your dog's safety zone.

Older Children

If you've been diligent, by the time your baby is school-aged, there will be a mutually friendly and respectful relationship between your child and your dog.

But don't make the mistake of allowing children too much freedom to interact with your dog. Supervision is still important to make sure your safety rules are enforced.

The good news is that with older kids, you can design special games that will help channel both your dog's and the kids' energy in positive ways. These games can help reinforce obedience training and self-control while they exercise your dog both mentally and physically.

INDOOR HIDE-AND-SEEK

Hold the dog by the collar or ask the dog to sit/stay or down/stay. Meanwhile, have the child leave. The child should make a big deal of leaving, saying "Good-bye, dog, see ya later." Then the child should get out of sight, hiding behind a chair, under the bed, or in an open closet. Release the dog to find the child. If the dog gets off track, ask the child to say just the dog's name.

Note: This game can backfire if the dog is too rambunctious, so have him sit when he finds the child. If he sits, the child can give a treat to the dog.

This game builds bonds between the child and dog, exercises the dog, and teaches and rewards politeness in greetings.

CARD GAMES

On a pack of blank index cards, write a variety of exercises you and your family members can do with your dog. Make the exercises appropriate for the age of the children and the abilities of your dog. Some examples include:

+ Get a towel and wipe all four of your dog's feet.

+ Get a chair; walk all the way around it with a slack leash.

+ Put your dog in a down; skip three circles around her.

+ Put your dog in a sit/stay while someone rings the doorbell once.

✦ Put your dog in a down/stay in front of the refrigerator, while you remove and then replace some food.

✦ Have your dog stand still, all four paws on the floor, for eight brushes of the brush.

✦ Put your dog in a sit/stay about 3 feet from a player, who then tosses a treat—the dog must catch the treat on the first try.

✦ Put a T-shirt on the dog.

Your child or children can help make the cards by writing the exercises down on them, or illustrating them by making drawings, or cutting or pasting pictures from a magazine.

Then set up the game rules. For example, set the timer for three minutes. Have one person perform as many exercises as possible. This player gets to keep the card when an exercise is successfully completed. When all cards are gone, whoever has the most cards wins.

If a player or a player's parent doesn't like the card, they can put it back facedown and pick up a different one.

Or, instead of working to accumulate the most cards, give each card a value. The player with the highest total score wins.

Here are a couple more ideas for varying the card game:

✦ **Spin-the-Bottle.** Put the exercise cards, facedown, in a big circle with a bottle in the middle. Each player takes a turn spinning the bottle and performing the activity the bottle points to when it stops spinning.

✦ **Tic-Tac-Toe.** With this variation, two teams compete, instead of individual players. First, pick your teams. Then draw a tic-tac-toe grid on a big piece of paper on the floor or table. Place one card on each square in the grid. Get game pieces—plastic cups work well—in two colors to act as markers. To claim a square, the team has to complete that square's exercise. The first team to claim a line of three squares wins.

Kids and Dogs: Not Impossible After All

When you combine kids and dogs, your challenges multiply. But as we've seen, you have lots of tools at your disposal. Use them wisely, and there's no reason you can't outwit your dog—and have plenty of brain power left over to handle the kids as well.

And Sometimes Our Kids Teach Us

Working with kids and dogs together can be a challenge. But sometimes there are unexpected side benefits. Sometimes our kids can even show us adults a thing or two about training.

When our daughter Jennifer was 10 years old, we told her she could have a dog of her own. Her choice was a six-month-old puppy who'd lived in a kennel for a long while before we adopted her. She'd had little or no training.

A few days after we brought the dog home, I happened to look out the kitchen window—and there was Jennifer, giving the puppy a series of hand signals at a distance. Now, this particular signal exercise is taught for Utility Competition—the American Kennel Club's third level of obedience competition. It's an upper-level exercise.

Concerned about Jennifer's self-image, I quickly went to the yard to explain that her dog was just a puppy, she was just a kid, and this was a very advanced exercise. But suddenly, before my wondering eyes, I saw the pup complete three of the exercises correctly!

The moral of the story (besides "Yeah! Kid Power!") is "Set no limitations on your dog." Jennifer didn't. She thought all dogs knew how to do these exercises. After all, all the dogs she'd lived with for her entire life could do them. So, since it never occurred to her that her puppy couldn't do them, too, she trained her pup with the expectation that it would be easy—and it was.

T. R.

Chapter 15

THERE GOES THE NEIGHBORHOOD: WHEN THE PROBLEM IS NEXT DOOR

It is other folks' dogs and children that make most of the bad feelin's between neighbors.
—Ellis Parker Butler, *The Confessions of a Daddy*

Now, here's a funny thing about dogs. Sometimes, you don't even need to have one to enjoy their features and benefits. Sometimes, all you need is to have a dog living next door. Or up the street. Or down the road.

But hey, even if the dog you need to outwit lives at a different address from you, all is not lost. Of course, you will have another factor to deal with—the dog's human—and that can limit your options a bit. But there are still plenty of things you can do.

I Just Love Your Dog, But . . .

Inspiring, adorable, fun—other people's dogs can be any of those things. But they can also be a total pain.

Some common problems with other people's dogs are:

✦   Nuisance barking.

✦   Toileting on your property.

✦   Aggressive behavior toward you or your family members, in-
     cluding your children.

✦   Aggressive behavior toward your dog.

✦   Destruction of property; harming of other pets or livestock.

If you live in an area that doesn't have leash laws, then other problems may also crop up—such as stealing steaks.

Stop, Thief!

Growing up in the country, we were used to visits from neighbor's
dogs—but that didn't mean we were always prepared for the consequences.

It was the early 1970s, and hibachis were popular. Hibachis,
however, are quite low to the ground—or, from the perspective of a
Beagle mix, about nose-high. Which is why, one evening, we lost a
nice big steak: It was swiped—right off the hot grill—by our neighbor's dog.

The moral of the story: If you live in an area where dogs are allowed to run loose, it's a good idea to be ready for them to show up.
In other words, put your hibachi up on the picnic table.

K. M.

In a minute, we'll discuss each of these problem areas. But first, let's
take a closer look at how dealing with other people's dogs is different
from working with your own.

Managing Unwanted Behaviors: Barking, Toileting, and Loose Dogs

When you're dealing with your own dog, management is one of the most effective and reliable tools in your toolbox. One reason for this is that you have so much control over your own space. You can put a baby gate up if you want to keep your dog out of a particular room. You can put your dog in a crate. You can keep forbidden objects out of reach.

When you're dealing with other people's dogs, however, you have a little less control. Take one of the most effective management tools, for example: the leash. With your own dog, you can use the leash to prevent her from running up to people and jumping on them, going onto someone else's property, and a host of other behaviors.

But what if it's another dog? Sure, in some circumstances, it's appropriate to ask a person to leash his dog. In some circumstances, it may even be appropriate to point out that an unleashed dog is unlawful. But that's all you can do: talk. It's not your dog. It's not your leash.

AVOIDING POTENTIAL PROBLEMS

One option is to avoid the problem altogether. For instance, it probably doesn't make sense to take a small child to an off-leash dog park, or to any public place where people let their dogs run loose.

Other times, dealing with other people's dogs means you have to deal with the other people. Management can be the right tool for that, also. After all, if there's a way to prevent a problem entirely, why not try it?

BARKING

Sometimes people simply don't realize that their dogs bark as much as they do—or that it's bothering the neighbors. So if you're having problems with another person's dog barking, try phoning or stopping over at the neighbor's house to mention that the barking has become a nuisance.

Be specific. If you're away from home most of the day during the week, explain that it's evenings and weekends that are most sensitive.

If the neighbor seems receptive, you might also suggest some of the strategies for barking given in this book. You never know: A good chew toy might be all it takes to turn a frustrated barker into a happy—and quiet—neighborhood dog.

If your neighbor doesn't seem to believe the barking is a problem, you might also try recording it. Don't provoke the dog—capture his behavior as it naturally occurs. Try recording it from inside your home, to show how you actually experience the barking. Then use the recording to politely approach your neighbor.

If these steps don't do the trick, some management strategies to consider are:

+ **Rearranging how you use your living space.** For example, if you're troubled by barking at night, can you move to a different bedroom, farther away from the noise?

+ **Soundproofing.** This involves a financial investment on your part—but may be worth it, if you have the resources. And there may be other benefits as well. For example, adding insulation can help soundproof a home—while it also cuts heating and cooling bills. You can also look for special soundproofing windows.

TOILETING

If you have a problem with dogs using your lawn for a toilet, the real problem isn't the dog, of course. It's the human who doesn't pick up afterward.

One option, therefore, is to talk to the human. Perhaps asking, politely, for the human to please pick up after the dog will be enough. In many communities failing to pick up after dogs is against the law; if this is true for your neighborhood, it may help to point this out.

If you're still getting nowhere, it's time to take management into your own hands. Consider:

✦ **A fence.** Yes, a fence costs money. But the nice thing about a fence is that it makes it impossible for other people's dogs, whether leashed or not, to come onto your lawn. If it will bring you peace of mind, it may be worth the cost.

✦ **Some other type of physical barrier.** A hedge might be useful for blocking other people's dogs from using your lawn as a toilet, particularly if your problem is with leashed dogs. Garden ornaments might be enough to keep leashed dogs off your lawn, by making it harder for the dog and owner to maneuver past them.

LOOSE DOGS

If your problem is loose dogs coming onto your property, once again, a phone call or face-to-face request might be all it takes to solve your problem. If this doesn't work, make sure that your property, including other pets, and your family members are safe. For example:

✦ Don't leave pets who also happen to be prey animals—such as rabbits or guinea pigs—unattended or housed somewhere accessible to loose dogs.

✦ Loose dogs have been known to tear through chicken wire and jump fences to get at livestock. So invest in secure enclosures if you keep pets or livestock outside.

✦ Loose dogs have also been known to enter people's homes through their own animal's pet doors. If you're leaving your house for a while, it may be smart to keep any pet doors latched.

✦ Put your garbage in cans that close securely.

Regardless of the specific problem, when you talk to other people about their dogs, it's a good idea to be as diplomatic as possible. Point out how, if the person does things differently, he will benefit—and so will the dog:

"I was thinking that your dog might be barking because she's bored. I have a book with some ideas for helping this. Do you want to borrow it?"

"My vet told me it's best to pick up right away after my dog, to help control the spread of worms. I've been passing the word on to all the neighbors. It's really so much better for our dogs."

"I'm worried that your dog might be hit by a car when he comes out this way by himself. Did you know he goes out into the road?"

You may also find help through neighborhood associations or other support groups.

Training Someone Else's Dog

While management can be useful, it's not the only option you have when it comes to solving problems with other people's dogs. You can also apply the same tools you use to train your own dog.

Here's an example to illustrate how this can work. Suppose your problem is your next-door neighbor's dog. Your yards are separated by a fence. When you go outside, the neighbor's dog barks.

The first step is to observe the dog. Watch her body language and listen to the pitch and intensity of the bark. Use the information in chapter 11 to help figure out why she's barking. Does the barking appear to be offensive, defensive, or recreational? Does she seem enthusiastic or anxious?

These observations will help you formulate a training approach. Suppose you observe that the barking follows the pattern of the defensive barker: sharp, high-pitched barks combined with submissive body language. This tells you she's barking because your appearance makes her anxious or fearful. So right away, you know that scolding or yelling at her could make the problem worse—by making her even more anxious. On the other hand, speaking in a happy, soothing voice may be helpful.

Now imagine a different scenario: a dog who barks at you out of high spirits. He runs around and pants when he barks. His body language is alert and happy: perked ears, wagging tail. Most likely, the barking gets worse if you, or your family members or guests, are doing something active, like playing a ball game.

This dog is most likely an enthusiastic barker. For him, barking may be self-rewarding. The last thing you want to do is reward it further.

So for this dog—ignore any barking. Paying any attention to him will only reward him further—making the behavior stronger. This includes talking to him. It also includes yelling "quiet!" or "no!" or "shut your trap!" Because anytime you respond in any way to the barking, including verbally, you risk making this game more fun for him.

Dogs with Bad Manners

In a perfect world, other people's dogs would be perfectly trained. But most of us have probably experienced the exact opposite. We've been jumped up on, mouthed, or otherwise subjected to the bad manners of someone else's dog.

Worst of all, sometimes other dogs' owners don't seem to notice that their dogs are causing a problem. Maybe they assume that just because their dogs jump on them, nobody else minds it.

Fortunately, there are some things you can do to help curb these sorts of behaviors. In some cases, they may also help the dog's human realize that you aren't enjoying yourself.

- ✦ **Dogs who jump up.** Turn your body away and ignore the dog. Some dogs will learn quickly that they need to sit if you're going to pay attention. If this is the case, reward the dog by turning back and calmly greeting him. Just be ready—you may need to turn your back once more if he tries to jump again. At the very least, your turning away shows the dog's human that you don't like being jumped on.

- ✦ **Mouthy dogs.** Put your hands in your pockets or, if you don't have pockets, clasp them tightly against your waist. Then turn your back on the dog and ignore him. Again, turning away will help show the owner that the dog is bothering you.

✦ **Dogs who pee when greeting.** Don't make eye contact with or talk to the dog. Turn your back on him and give him a chance to settle down before trying to greet him again.

Of course, there are also instances when it's appropriate to simply ask the owner to please control the dog.

Close Encounters with Loose Dogs

When dogs are permitted to roam off the leash, they can create particularly nettlesome problems for their human neighbors:

✦ They can pose a safety hazard to people driving cars or riding bikes. Swerving to miss a loose dog is as unnerving as it is dangerous.

✦ They can disrupt your dog's on-leash walks. It can be difficult to manage an on-leash dog when one or more loose dogs approach.

✦ They can cause property damage and threaten other pets or livestock.

Loose dogs come in several forms:

✦ Neighborhood dogs, known to you, who come by from time to time on their rounds.

✦ Neighborhood dogs, known to you, whom you encounter regularly when you are on walks or bicycle rides.

✦ Strange dogs whom you see on a regular basis.

✦ Strange dogs whom you see infrequently or only once.

✦ Single dogs.

✦ Dogs in packs.

✦ And the most common scenario: dogs who are with humans, but not on a leash, and therefore possibly not under the humans' control.

How you handle a loose dog depends, in part, on the dog, whether the dog is alone, and where the dog is. For example, a lone, stray dog is less likely to be aggressive (assuming he's healthy) than two dogs hanging around, unconfined, in front of their human's house. In the latter scenario, the dogs may feel they should be guarding their property—a factor that won't come into play with a loose dog who is away from home.

IF YOU ENCOUNTER AN AGGRESSIVE, LOOSE DOG WHILE ON FOOT . . .

Your best defense against an aggressive, loose dog is to hold still. Do not make eye contact with the dog. Whatever you do, don't make jerky movements or try to run away. Wait. Most of the time, dogs will lose interest in a boring, motionless person.

. . . OR WHILE ON A BICYCLE

If you're on a bicycle, this is a bit harder, because chances are you are already moving when you realize the loose dog is there. The problem is that your movement can trigger a dog to give chase or even bite. If you are a biker, and you face the possibility of being chased by an unconfined dog, consider carrying a can of citronella or pepper spray to protect yourself. If you're agile enough, you may also try putting the bike between you and the dog: Stand up, shift your weight to the foot that's away from the dog, and swing your near leg over to the far side of the bike also.

If you're on a bike and see the dog from a distance, try dismounting and walking the bike past the dog. By moving past more slowly, you may be less likely to trigger chasing.

Know the Law

You should also know what dog-related ordinances are in effect in your community. Just because you see loose dogs doesn't mean they are permitted. See if there are leash laws that forbid dogs to run loose. Even if there aren't, there may be laws that give you recourse if someone else's dog damages your property or injures a pet or livestock animal. And if a loose dog bites someone, you definitely have legal recourse.

Familiarize yourself with the guidelines suggested by your local animal control authorities. Small communities may not have much funding for their animal control departments. As a result, your local animal control officer may only be on duty during certain hours or on certain days.

Of course, just because there are leash laws on the books doesn't mean you will always call the authorities when you see a loose dog. If you know the dog, sometimes a call to her people is the best first step. They may not know she's loose. Even if they do—and think it's okay for her to run loose—you may be able to persuade them otherwise.

The same goes for situations where someone is with the dog. Many loose-dog complaints fall into this category. You're out walking in a public park. Suddenly, a dog charges up to you. Way off in the distance, you see the dog's human. Assuming the dog is friendly, a conversation with the human may persuade him to leash the dog from now on. For example, suppose you have your kids with you. You may try an approach like this: "I want my children to feel comfortable about dogs. But when they have a big dog like yours run up to them, it scares them. They don't know the dog is friendly. If your dog was leashed, you could control her better and make sure my kids aren't scared."

If you do decide to report a loose dog, plan to give a good description: exactly where you saw the dog; the dog's size, color and markings, breed or breed resemblance; and whether she's wearing a collar. And if you can, identify the dog's owner and the owner's address. This will be a great help to the authorities.

If the loose dog has damaged your property or injured a pet, take photographs of the damage. Better yet, take pictures of the dog in the act.

When Your Dog Is Leashed— and the Other Dog Isn't

Encountering loose dogs when your dog is leashed can be a recipe for trouble. Behaviorists suspect that when dogs are leashed, they respond differently to other dogs, including loose dogs. Sometimes this means that tension between a leashed dog and a loose dog can escalate more quickly than it might otherwise.

The best medicine for this difficulty is prevention. If you know that a particular park is frequented by off-leash dogs, don't plan to walk your dog there.

However, sometimes you can't prevent the problem. If you spot a loose dog while walking your dog, here are some things to try:

+ If you are within sight/shouting range of the dog's human, ask her to leash her dog.

+ Turn around and go the other way. If you can stay far enough away from the loose dog, he may not approach your dog.

+ Go around the other dog—way around. The key is to give the loose dog a lot of space.

These tactics are intended to help you avoid a confrontation with the other dog. But if the other dog gets too close, here are some other ideas you can try in a pinch:

+ Carry an umbrella when you walk your dog. If a strange dog comes too close for comfort, open the umbrella suddenly. Note: For this to work, you need to be sure your own dog is used to umbrellas.

+ If you're smart, you will be carrying treats in your pocket in case you need them to train for your own dog. So if a dog comes too close—if it's an emergency—throw a treat in the strange dog's direction. This may provide enough of a distraction for you to turn away and quickly walk away from the dog. The dog might even decide to gobble the food instead of harassing you and your dog.

If your dog is actually attacked, any intervention on your part can make you a target also. However, a very loud noise—such as picking up a rock and hitting it against a nearby sign—might create a brief lull, long enough for the dogs to reconsider.

✦ ✦ ✦

Dealing with other people's dogs can be more difficult than dealing with our own. We have less control. We don't know strange dogs as well as we know our own. But with patience and thought, in some cases it is possible to solve—or at least lessen—these types of problems.

Chapter 16

TOOLS, TRICKS, AND SOMETHING DIFFERENT: WHEN BASIC OUTWITTING STRATEGIES SEEM TOO EASY

A dog will look at you as if to say, "What do you want me to do for you? I'll do anything for you." Whether a dog can in fact, do anything for you if you don't have sheep (I never have) is another matter.

—Roy Blount Jr., "Dogs Vis-à-vis Cats,"
Now, Where Were We?

So you've mastered all the basics? You've got a pooch who's house-trained, walks nicely on a leash, sits to greet visitors, and wouldn't dream of barking at the window just because there's a colony of groundhogs square dancing on your lawn?

Okay, maybe not. Maybe what you have is a dog who's (mostly) housetrained . . . walks nicely on a leash (when she's exhausted) . . . sits to greet (boring) visitors . . . and only barks at groundhogs when they're sitting on the windowsill, tapping on the glass, and pulling funny faces . . .

In either case, you're ready to have some more fun, right? Hey, why not?

Well that's good news, for both you and your dog. Because with the right tools, you two can work together on much more than just the basics.

Just a Bit of Theory

Most of us know about Ivan Pavlov's experiments with dogs. In the 1920s Pavlov (who was actually studying digestion) noticed that dogs he was studying would salivate when he rang a bell.

Why did they do this? Because previously, Pavlov had rung a bell every time he brought the dogs their food. The dogs learned to associate the bell's ringing with food. So after a time, every time they heard the bell, they would begin to salivate—even if Pavlov didn't have any food with him.

Today behaviorists call this classical conditioning. If a reward (such as food) is associated with a particular stimulus (such as a bell ringing), then the animal (or person) connects the two events, almost as if one caused the other. Of course, we know the bell didn't cause the food to appear. But to a dog, it doesn't matter. The bell is still a wonderful thing.

Some years later, B. F. Skinner discovered something else that turns out to be a great help for dog trainers. He realized that animals (and people, for that matter) learn to operate in the world based on the consequences of particular actions in the past.

For example, suppose you fix a wonderful, home-cooked meal for your significant other. The meal makes a big impression, and you're showered with attention and praise. This is very pleasant to you. And so, chances are, you'll fix another wonderful, home-cooked meal sometime in the future.

What happened? You were rewarded. The reward, along with what you did to earn it, was filed away somewhere in your memory bank. And forever after, when you plan your menus, you'll have that memory—and the lesson that went along with it—ready to go to work for you.

But that's not all. You have also learned a new way to control your world a bit. You don't have to sit back, helpless, and hope your significant other will suddenly burst into the room and shower you with attention and praise. You can try the old *fix-a-meal* trick.

Skinner called this type of learning operant conditioning. The conditioning part is very similar to what happens in classical conditioning: We learn to associate something (fixing a meal) with a reward (attention and praise). But the new twist is that we are in the driver's seat. We can initiate the chain of events that leads to the reward.

So guess what? Dogs learn through both classical and operant conditioning. All the time. And if you've applied some of the techniques we've covered in this book, you've been applying both types of conditioning.

For example, if you've helped your dog become accustomed to a crate by feeding his meals in it, you've used classical conditioning. On some level, your dog associates his crate with food, just like Pavlov's dogs associated a ringing bell with food.

And if you've got a dog who sits when you say "sit," because she knows that doing that means she may get a tidbit of food, you're seeing operant conditioning in action. Your dog has learned to operate a piece of her world to get food.

The Nice Thing About Theory . . .

Like many amateur dog people, when I decided to adopt a new dog, I also decided I wasn't going to repeat the mistakes I'd made with my last dog.

So I went out and bought a bunch of dog training books.

They left me more confused than anything. Every writer had his or her own bag of tricks. Some seemed, intuitively, to make sense. Others didn't. Some were humane. Others seemed downright mean.

Then I picked up a book, *Don't Shoot the Dog* by Karen Pryor, that introduced operant conditioning. At first I thought, *This is more information than I need.* But as I began to understand the theory, a lightbulb suddenly went on: This was the foundation for all those other trainers' techniques—whether the trainers realized it or not. This explained why some of their tricks would work. It explained why some of them wouldn't work, or would only work part of the time.

Furthermore, as I began to work with my new puppy, I realized that I was now better at evaluating myself as a trainer. If something didn't work, I could figure out why. If it did work, I could figure out why.

You don't need theory to train your dog. You can apply techniques from this book, or any other tools-and-tips book, and do just fine.

But what tools and tips can't do is help you troubleshoot problems. And they can't help you refine your training abilities. Theory, on the other hand, can help you do both, because it goes beyond what to do to why it works.

K. M.

Clicker Training

Using operant conditioning is fun, because it's gives you a win–win way to train your dog.

To make it even more effective, you can add a new twist: a secondary reinforcer (also sometimes called a conditioned reinforcer). A secondary reinforcer is a signal that tells your dog a reward is coming. It lets you communicate more precisely to your dog that she's done something right. A secondary reinforcer can be a word you speak, or some other kind of audio or visual signal.

In many obedience-type training exercises we've described in this book, we've suggested that you say "yes!" when your dog gives you the desired behavior. For example, in chapter 8, we gave a technique for training your dog to sit by your side in the heel position. In this exercise, after you lure your dog into a sit, you say "yes!" and then give her a treat. In this context, "yes!" is a secondary reinforcer. It acts like a reward, because your dog knows that when you say it, a treat is coming.

Trainers will sometimes say that a secondary reinforcer "marks" a behavior. This is a useful way to understand how secondary reinforcers work, and how they can help you with training your dog. You can't use complicated human words to explain to your dog what you want. You can't sit down, look your dog in the eye, and say, "Honey, here's what we're going to work on next. You need to learn to move into the heel position. That means you'll move over next to me and stand by my left foot, facing forward. The cue I'm going to use for this is *heel*. So when you hear me say that, I want you to hustle your furry little self into that position for me, okay?"

It would be nice to think your dog could understand all that. But the reality is, she won't.

So instead, you need to catch her when her body is in exactly the position you want it to be in. And you need to mark that event with a signal she understands: a signal that shows her that standing, facing forward, next to your left foot *means something to her.*

In fact, the better you get at marking desired behaviors—behaviors you intend to reward—the faster your dog will learn.

It is for this reason that many trainers, both professional and amateur, use a clicker as secondary reinforcer. Clickers were originally a child's toy, sometimes called a "cricket": a little piece of metal that makes a two-beat *clickclick* sound when you press it and then let it go. Today clickers are widely sold for use in pet training. You can find them at pet supply stores, including the national chains. Many trainers also incorporate clicker training and have clickers available. They can be purchased on the Internet as well.

Clickers have a bit of an advantage over using words like *yes!* as secondary reinforcers. First, the sound is unique. Second, it's a short, staccato signal, making it a bit more precise. Some experts also think that the motor skills needed to press a clicker are a bit more streamlined than the ones we use to speak.

The second two points are important because of another nuance in dog training: timing.

TIMING IS EVERYTHING

The goal, when training a dog, is to mark a behavior. And the better you are at marking behaviors, the better your training sessions will go. This is why good dog trainers emphasize timing.

Here's an example. Suppose you're working on teaching your dog to sit at the heel position. Your job is to mark the sit-at-heel so that you can reward it. But your dog may not stay in that position for more than a couple of seconds, especially at first. She might start to sit, but then almost immediately raise her rear end back up off the ground.

If you time your secondary reinforcer so that it hits the split second your dog's bottom is touching the ground, you'll communicate the right message to your dog. But suppose your mark is a bit late. Suppose you say "yes!" (or click a clicker) as your dog has started to rise back up. Now what you've reinforced is *lifting my rear end at the heel position*.

Is this the end of the world? No. On balance, if your timing is right most of the time, your dog will train just fine. But the better your timing is, the faster your dog will get what you're working on. And make no mistake: The most successful trainers work in a world of microseconds.

Precisely marking behaviors is also why clickers can be better than verbal markers. Even a short word, like *yes*, takes longer to complete than a clicker noise. So go back to the sit-at-heel example. What happens if you say "yes" as your dog is still sitting, but before the *s* sound at the end of the word is over, your dog has started to stand back up? Again, the mark is less precise. Your dog will still learn. But using a clicker instead of a verbal signal will help her learn even faster.

GETTING STARTED

So you're interested in adding the clicker to your training toolbox?

The first step is to show your dog that the *click* noise means a reward is coming. Keep in mind that, in this exercise, you aren't training your dog to *do* anything. Instead, what you're doing is creating a secondary reinforcer that you can use, later, for training.

Clicker trainers sometimes call this charging the clicker. Think of it like charging a battery. A battery has no power unless it has an electrical charge. But once it does have a charge, you can use it for all sorts of fun. So here are the basic steps for charging a clicker:

1. Collect your clicker, dog, and five delectable tidbits.

2. Pick a spot, preferably indoors, that is pretty boring—not too many distractions about.

3. Press the clicker's metal strip and let go instantly to make a rapid, two-beat *clickclick* noise.

4. Toss a treat to your dog.

Now repeat the third and fourth steps four more times—only make sure you vary a couple of things each time:

✦ First, each time you click, time it so your dog is doing something different than she was doing the previous time. For example, if she was sitting in front of you, watching you, the last time you clicked, wait until she gets up and starts walking away before you click again. (Hint: Often, if you move, your dog will move, too.)

✦ And second, vary the length of time between the click noise and when you deliver the treat. For example, if it's a 5-second pause the first time, make it a 15-second pause the second time; a two-second pause the third time; and so on.

It's also a good idea not to click when your dog is doing something you don't want her to do. For example, don't click if she happens to jump up at you. Remember, you're giving treats to her—you wouldn't want her to get the wrong idea.

What you'll notice is that your dog will catch on, very quickly, that this clicker business is important. Most people will find that their dogs start responding to the click noise after only a couple of repetitions. If you're not sure, wait until your dog is looking away from you. Then click. Does her head whip around? If so, you've done it. You've established the clicker as a secondary reinforcer.

Capturing Behaviors

Now that you've charged the clicker, you can start using it for training.

Start by picking a behavior you'd like to teach your dog. Your next job is to click the clicker at the moment your dog performs that behavior.

For example, suppose you decide you want to train your dog to shake paws. The basic idea is to click the clicker when your dog puts his paw in your hand.

Now, some dogs offer a front paw spontaneously and often. If this is your dog, you've got it easy. Have your dog sit, crouch down in front of him, and wait. Ignore any other behavior except his offering a paw. Don't say a word; just wait. At some point, because he wants to initiate play, he'll offer a paw. When he does that, click. Then give him a treat.

At first, work on only letting the dog touch his paw to your hand. Later, you can shape the behavior into a true shake. See the next section for tips on shaping.

Other dogs, however, don't offer their paws that much. If this is your dog, you can use luring. Luring is the technique we described when we explained how to teach behaviors like the sit. You use a bit of food to lure your dog into a particular behavior.

To lure a shake-paws behavior, have your dog sit. Crouch down in front of him with a bit of food clenched in your fist, at his chest level. He's apt to put his nose on your hand. Ignore that. Tease him a little bit. Sooner or later, he'll use a front paw to try to make you give up your food. Click. Then open your hand and let him take the treat.

Shaping: When a Behavior Is Only Close

A nice thing about combining reward-based training with a clicker is that you can give your dog feedback even when she isn't doing exactly what you want her to do.

For example, suppose you're luring your dog to shake paws. She doesn't understand, at first, that she's supposed to touch your fist with her paw. So to begin, instead of expecting her to know what you want, watch for her to approximate the behavior. Maybe, for example, when you hold a tidbit out in front of your dog, she starts by nosing your hand. After a while, when you don't give her the treat, she sits back and moves her paw. Maybe she raises it a little off the ground.

Click it!

Now it's time for the next step. The key is that you shouldn't click for that same behavior again. After all, that isn't the final behavior you want, right? Instead, wait until she offers something that's a little bit closer to the final behavior you want. For example, if she only moved her paw last time, wait until she raises it. If she raised it last time, wait until she moves it closer to your hand. If she touched your hand last time, wait until she rests her paw quietly on top of your hand for a couple of seconds. And so on.

Trainers call this shaping. You have a picture, in your mind, of what the final behavior should be. You use your clicker to mold a behavior that is somewhat like the final behavior. Little by little, you guide your dog closer to the final.

The nice thing is, your dog will be happy to work with you on the shaping. Recall that, with operant conditioning, dogs offer behaviors to try to manipulate the environment. As you clicker train to shape behaviors, your dog is actually working it out like a puzzle. What will earn the reward this time? It's a mystery—a mystery your dog will love to solve.

In fact, as she comes to understand the clicker game, she may even start getting amazingly creative. She may learn to quickly begin offering new things—new variations on her behaviors—in the hope that when she does, she'll get that wonderful *click*.

Improving Your Timing

A clicker is a very precise tool for marking behaviors. The problem is that dogs don't always wait for us to click. They often move quickly.

Their behaviors often flow swiftly from one to another. This means it's easy to be late—or early, for that matter—with your click.

And that works against you, because it means you mark the wrong behavior.

For this reason, it's a great idea to work on your timing. Here are some exercises you can do to improve your timing. Do them at a time when your dog is not with you:

✓ Drop a book on the floor. See if you can click just as the book hits.

✓ Toss a tennis ball into the air. See if you can click when the ball hits its highest point.

✓ Watch a TV weather report. See if you can click to coincide with the reporter touching the map.

Adding the Cue

In chapter 7 we explained our approach for adding a cue to a behavior. Cues are words (or other signals, such as hand signals) that are so completely and strongly associated with a particular behavior that when the dog hears that signal, he automatically executes the behavior.

As you work on reward-based training using operant conditioning, you'll reach the point where your dog gets it that you're rewarding a particular behavior, such as his putting his paw in your hand. He'll start offering that behavior—a lot. As soon as he sees you have the clicker in hand, or possibly even a treat, he'll sit down and give you his paw.

At this point, you can start to add the cue.

Think of it as a slight change in the shape of the behavior. Before, the behavior was: *give my human my paw*. Now it's *give my human my paw when I hear "shake."*

Note: We're using the cue *shake* in our example, but you can choose any cue you want for a behavior. Some people use *high five* or *give me five*. But you can also be creative. For example, your cue could be *will you marry me?* or *it's a deal!*

Here's how you add the cue: From now on, every time your dog is about to give you his paw (it's up to you to anticipate this by watching for clues that the behavior is coming), say "shake."

Then click and treat.

After a few repetitions of this, your dog will start shaking when you say your cue. Then stop rewarding him for the shake behavior *unless* you've cued it. Unless, of course, you don't mind if he offers his paw a lot—even when you don't ask him to.

You can also use the Four D's (see chapter 8) to help your dog become fluent in this behavior—or any other behavior, of course.

Behavior Chains

As with all dog training, the better we become at observing our dogs, the better we get at training.

Often this means we have to concentrate on what a dog is actually doing—not what we think she's doing. A great example of this is when we see something called a chained behavior.

Consider the behavior we call the sit. To us, that behavior is a dog, seated. It begins when the dog's rear end hits the floor and ends when she starts to stand up again.

But suppose something like this happens as you teach your dog to sit: First, she realizes you have a treat. She runs up to you. Right about the time you say "sit," she hits you, full force: jumping up and stabbing your thighs enthusiastically with both front paws. Then she quickly drops into a sit and gazes up at you expectantly. Well, she's sitting. So you give her a treat.

Guess what? If you've rewarded this *run over > jump up > sit* sequence more than a couple of times or so, you're not teaching sit. You're teaching a chain of behaviors that begins with your dog running over and stabbing at your thighs with her paws, and only ends with a sit.

Your dog doesn't care. The difference between *sit* and *run > jump up > sit* means nothing to her, the little sweetheart. If this is what she's been rewarded for, she's perfectly happy to repeat it.

You, on the other hand, might not be too crazy about it. Do you really want a dog who thinks that dashing over and throwing herself at you is a good thing?

So what's the moral of the story? First, as you train, pay attention to how your dog approaches the behavior you want. Pay attention to what she does after she finishes the behavior she wants. Does it vary, or is there a pattern?

If you see a pattern, then you need to find a way to break the pattern. With the example given above, your first step is to stop rewarding sits that are preceded by jumping up. Don't make any exceptions, ever.

The second step is to get your dog to learn a different way to approach you and sit for a reward. There are probably dozens of ways to do this. You might try luring her to approach you differently, for example, by holding a treat in your fist, with your arm extended to your side.

Another possibility is to work on shaping an *approach > stand* behavior (have her approach you and then stand in front of you). Then add a sit again when your dog is in front of you and standing still. By rewarding this, you'll build a new, more desirable behavior chain to replace the old one.

Yet another possible approach is to shape your dog to sit before she gets close enough to you to jump up. Try separating her from you with a barrier, such as a baby gate. Call her, and when she gets to the gate, wait for her to sit. When she does, click (or say "yes!" if you're not using a clicker) and treat.

A Few More Tips for Effective Clicker Training

Clicker training is an exciting, rewarding training technique that can give you and your dog hours of fun. And clickers are by no means useful for training tricks alone. As you build your clicker training skills, you'll find it's a great tool for working on training at any level. Clicker-trained dogs today compete in conformation, obedience, agility, and hunting trials.

Here are some additional tips for making clicker training an enjoyable—and successful—part of your training toolbox:

✦ **Keep your training sessions short.** A minute or two on each exercise per session is plenty. Stop the training while the dog is still fully involved and wanting more. Otherwise, you may find that your dog loses focus. The behaviors you're training may start to get sloppy or even break down completely. Remember, the goal of marking operant behaviors is to catch your dog doing things right. Shorter sessions help ensure you can do this. (You can have multiple sessions per day, however.)

✦ **Observe your dog.** Many dogs adore the clicker game. You may find that the second your dog sees you bring out a clicker and treats, he'll start getting excited. But in some cases, dogs respond differently. For example, some dogs are very noise-reactive and may find the click noise frightening. If you need to, review the signs of stress described in chapter 10. Then pay attention to your dog's body language, and modify your training so that he's enjoying himself. For example, if the click noise scares your dog, muffle the clicker with a piece of cotton, keep your hand in your pocket as you click, or substitute a retractable pen, which makes a softer click.

✦ **Find a clicker trainer to help you refine your skills.** Clicker training has become a very popular training technique. So look around: You may find clicker training classes in your community. These can be very helpful for improving your technique. (See the next chapter for tips on picking dog trainers.)

Tricks for Treats

Whether or not you decide clicker training is right for you, it's always fun to teach your dog to do a few special behaviors. After all, what good is outwitting your dog if you can't impress your friends with her clever tricks?

So here are a few ideas to try. We've used the lure-and-reward technique in the descriptions, but you can also use your clicker if you like.

For each of these tricks, remember to add a cue *after* your dog reliably offers the behavior (see Adding the Cue above if you need to review this part of training). Then, once you've added the cue, don't reward your dog for the behavior anymore *unless* you've said the cue.

SIT UP AND BEG

Find a spot that isn't slippery to train this trick.

Ask your dog to sit. Hold a piece of food slightly above her head. Don't hold it too high—if you do, you'll encourage her to jump up and break out of the sit completely.

When she picks up her front feet, give the treat.

Some dogs may be cautious about lifting both feet, so may only lift one paw. That's okay: Give the treat. But then, next time, don't give the treat until your dog has lifted her paw a bit higher, or moved her second paw as well—something that's a little closer to the final sit-up behavior.

You may also find that your dog has to develop the muscles to hold this position. So don't ask for her to hold the position too long at first.

Sometimes it's helpful to practice this trick with your dog's back to the corner of a room, or with you standing behind the dog with your legs as support.

CRAWL

Put your dog in a down. Hold a treat on the floor slightly farther away than he can reach. If he starts to get up, repeat your *down* cue. You can also hold one hand above his shoulders to guide him to stay down. Don't hold him down by force; just put your hand where he will bump it if he starts to get up.

Now, when he makes any forward movement while still in a down position, reward and treat.

Start over, gradually extending how far he has to crawl to get the treat.

Like sit up and beg, this trick may use some muscle the dog hasn't used before, so don't ask him to overdo it at first.

HIGH FIVE

This trick is similar to shake.

Have your dog sit, and hold a treat, hidden in your hand, in front of her nose. She may try to get it with her mouth. Ignore this. Finally, she will get a bit frustrated and paw at your hand. Reward that by giving her the food.

Repeat until she begins lifting her foot as soon as you hold your hand out.

Then use your empty fist as a target. When she paws it, give her the food, but from your pocket or your other hand.

Start changing your hand from a fist into the flat high-five position so that she paws that. Then add the *high five* cue.

GO DOWN, WAY DOWN

You begin teaching this trick from a regular down. The goal is to train your dog to quickly and distinctly place his head flat on the floor between his paws.

Some dogs do this behavior all by themselves. If your dog does, all you need to do is catch him doing it, reward him, and add a cue.

For dogs who don't do this on their own, use a food lure. Put your dog in a down, hold a treat in front of his nose, and move it slightly down. You might need to use a barrier, like the rung of a chair, to get his head in the right position: Put the chair in front of him and then lure his nose under the rung. Experiment to find the right obstacle so that his entire head goes down, not just his nose.

When he eats the treat and then offers another head-down pose, you know he's getting the right idea, and you can start working on keeping his head down for longer periods.

WIND AND UNWIND

For this trick, you teach your dog to "dance" by turning circles in either direction. You may find that one direction seems easier or more natural than the other. Work on this direction first.

To begin, lure your dog partway around in a circle, and offer the treat in a position that will make her complete the circle. After doing this once or twice while holding the treat, do it using the same hand motion but with no treat in your hand. Add the cue *wind* to this motion. Then use the same technique to teach your dog to circle the other way, with the cue *unwind*.

ROLL OVER

To train this behavior, put your dog in a macaroni down: his spine in a C-shape, hips over in a resting position. Begin from a regular or sphinx down, then lure his nose along the floor to his rib cage. As he follows the treat, his hips will roll into a macaroni down.

Once he's comfortable having you do this, simply continue to lure him all the way over: Move your fist up over his head so that, when he follows it with his nose, he rolls onto his back and then over to his other side.

While training any tricks, use the same approach as when training the sit, down, or other behaviors: Work in short sessions of three to five repetitions per session. Take breaks between sessions, and practice three to five sessions per day, six or seven days per week.

THE ADDED BONUS OF TRICKS

Training your dog to do tricks is fun and satisfying in its own right.

But it has added benefits as well. When your dog learns to do tricks on cue, it helps her develop better focus and self-control. Learning and performing tricks is also mentally stimulating for your dog. It gives the two of you an activity that you can do together.

And last but not least, you can use these behaviors to help your dog pay attention to you in distracting situations. For example, suppose you take your dog to the vet. You sit together in the waiting room, which is crowded, and your dog is becoming anxious and reactive about the other animals she sees and smells.

Now is a great time to do some tricks. Ask her to do several of her favorite trick behaviors. Give her treats when she performs them successfully. You'll find this keeps her focused on something besides the other pets in the room—or the upcoming exam.

And that means more peace of mind for you.

Chapter 17

OUTWITTING DOG TRAINERS (AND YOU THOUGHT THIS BOOK WOULDN'T HELP YOU OUTWIT OTHER PEOPLE)

Properly trained, a man can be a dog's best friend.
    —Corey Ford, *Cold Noses and Warm Hearts*

Okay, we know: there's already been a chapter that covered outwitting kids. But now we're ready to tackle a *really* serious challenge: outwitting grown-ups. Specifically, grown-ups who would like you to pay them to show you how to train your dog.

The problem is that not all dog trainers are equal. Some trainers base their techniques, as much as they can, on science. They adapt and improve their techniques as research on dog behavior advances. Unfortunately, other trainers do things simply because that's the way they were taught. If a dog doesn't respond well to their techniques, they'll blame the dog—or you.

To make things even more interesting, there's the question of using positive vs. punishment-based training. Positive training has become popular over the last few years. More and more trainers, therefore, claim their training is based on rewards, not punishment. But before you accept, at face value, what a trainer says about how she trains, observe a class.

What You See Is What You'll Get

Here's a checklist to help you evaluate a training class you're considering:

1. A good instructor will have a variety of techniques, most of them based on rewarding appropriate behavior. Are the majority of the exercises in the class taught by reinforcing good behavior or by punishing inappropriate behavior?

2. Are the people getting individual attention and coaching or is the instructor simply calling out general directions? How many students are enrolled at one time? If there are more than five students per instructor, consider taking your business elsewhere.

3. Are the instructor's directions clear to you? Do the people and dogs seem to be catching on with ease? If either the people or the dogs seem confused, that's a warning sign.

4. Is there reasonable control of the class? It should be clear to you right away *who* the instructor is and what is happening in the class. However, don't confuse lack of class control with enthusiasm and animation. A good class can have both.

5. Can the instructor tell you the goals for the class and the steps that will be taken to attain the objectives? Are the exercises being taught useful for your lifestyle or consistent with your expectations?

6. Does the instructor manage the dogs so that each has adequate space? In chapter 11 we introduced the concept of critical distance: an imaginary line around a dog, which, if crossed by something the dog finds threatening, can cause the dog to exhibit anxious, defensive, or aggressive behaviors. Savvy instructors will keep an eye on the dogs in their classes and intervene before dogs enter each other's critical distances.

Old Theory Isn't Always Good Theory

You should also watch for signs that indicate the instructor still relies on theory that has been discredited. One example is the use of the so-called alpha roll. Years ago, people had the idea that forcing a dog over onto her back would show her that you were dominant. This was based, as it turns out, on a misinterpretation of wolf pack behavior. Wolves, and dogs, do sometimes roll over *by themselves* to communicate to an individual of higher status. But wolves don't alpha roll each other. And neither do dogs.

Another example is scruff shaking: grabbing a dog by the neck fur and shaking the dog.

More than one dog has been taught to be aggressive or fear aggressive by the misuse of alpha rolls and similar techniques, such as scruff shaking. It's a tragic outcome of a popular but wrongheaded 20th-century dog training "technique"—and sadly, it's still in use among some trainers.

So don't fall into the trap of engaging a dog training instructor who thinks you need to use alpha rolls, scruff shakes, or other types of forced intimidation to show you are "dominant."

Puppy Classes

Enrolling puppies in specialized training classes—often called puppy kindergarten—is a great way to get a jump start on training, while providing valuable socialization. In fact, as we discussed in chapter 3, the experiences a dog has in early puppyhood influence her for the rest of her life.

Unfortunately, this can work both ways. If a puppy is exposed to positive experiences, it will help her grow into a more confident, relaxed dog. But if she's exposed to experiences that frighten or overwhelm her, the opposite could happen.

So take special care when you evaluate puppy classes. As with any class, the key is to observe before you commit. Here are some things to look for:

1. There should be a very tight window as to age grouping. Young puppies, regardless of size, can be set back by the brashness of

an older pup. So look for a class that carefully limits puppies by age (for example, only admitting puppies who are under 16 weeks old).

2. Families should be welcome, but the class should not turn into a wild free-for-all party. The instructor should make sure that any children in attendance are carefully supervised, or the pups could learn the wrong things about kids.

3. Free play among small groups of carefully selected puppies is beneficial to their social skills. However, if free play will be allowed among the puppies, very tight age groupings are critically important. In addition, the instructor must take all the puppies' ages, sizes, and personalities into consideration before allowing free play. Make sure, for example, that the instructor doesn't let more assertive, confident dogs push around or frighten the quieter ones. This type of experience works against the best interest of all the puppies. Smaller playgroups (four or five puppies at a time, maximum) are generally a better idea than putting lots of puppies together at once.

4. Positive, reward-based training is as important for puppies as for adult dogs—if not more so. Stay away from puppy classes that emphasize compulsion or punishment-based training.

Stand Up for What You Believe

In many cases it's human nature for people to defer to experts. A dog trainer is a professional. What she says carries authority.

But dog trainers, like everybody else, are fallible. They can make mistakes. They can be flat-out wrong.

So sometimes, you have to trust your gut instinct. Your training class should be the highlight of your week—a fun night out with your best friend. If it isn't, don't assume it's your fault, or your dog's. It's more likely that the class isn't a good fit for you. If you don't like what's going on in the class, don't participate in it.

Quitting a training class may mean you forfeit some money. Nobody likes to do that. But ask yourself: What's it worth to you to protect your dog from experiences that may affect him negatively for the rest of his life?

Assume the same attitude if your instructor passes a judgment on your dog that makes you feel uncomfortable. For example, trainers have been known to claim dogs are "vicious," "have aggression problems," or are even "untrainable" when the problem is the instructor, not the dog.

So Where'd You Go to School?

Some dog trainers have learned their craft strictly through on-the-job training. Others have participated in "how to be a dog trainer" courses and seminars. Some have completed certification programs. And some have earned advanced college degrees.

Does this mean that you should reject a trainer just because he doesn't have a master's degree in behavioral science? The answer is: It depends.

Suppose you're looking for a basic obedience class. You have a dog who doesn't have any particular training issues or behavior-related challenges. If this is the case, the most important criteria are how the instructor runs the class and the techniques he uses.

But if you need something a little more intensive, you may want to look for someone with a bit more background. For example, if your dog is aggressive toward other dogs, you're better off finding a canine behavior specialist.

Here's an overview of some of the certifications and degrees that you may encounter as you evaluate trainers. This is not an endorsement of these programs or degrees. We list them here only to give you an idea of what kinds of background instructors in your community may have.

Certified Pet Dog Trainer

This is a certification awarded by the Certification Council for Pet Dog Trainers (CCPDT). Requirements include 300 hours of training experience and the passing of a written exam that covers theory, instruction skills, husbandry, ethology, and equipment.

IACP Professional Dog Training Instructor

This is a certification awarded by the International Association of Canine Professionals (IACP). Requirements include membership in the IACP, 250 hours of hands-on training experience, and the IACP's evaluation of a videotape of the instructor giving private dog training lessons.

Applied Animal Behaviorist

This certification—and a similar, less rigorous certification, Associate Applied Animal Behaviorist—is awarded by the Animal Behavior Society. Requirements include an advanced degree in a biological or behavioral science with an emphasis in animal behavior, as well as professional experience in applied animal behavior, among others.

College Degrees

Sometimes instructors have attended college to study fields that provide a background for dog training, such as ethology (the study of animal behavior), behavioral science, or comparative psychology.

Some DVM (doctorate of veterinary medicine) programs also provide veterinarians with background in dog behavior and training. Numerous private schools offer dog training instruction as well.

Another question you can ask about an instructor is whether he is a member of a professional training organization. Examples include the National Association of Dog Obedience Instructors and the Association of Pet Dog Trainers. However, be aware that the criteria for joining some organizations are pretty minimal. In some cases, all somebody needs to join is to come up with money for a membership fee.

What membership does mean is that the instructor has access to that organization's training literature and seminars. But it doesn't necessarily mean that the organization is vouching for the trainer.

These organizations can, however, help you find instructors. Contact them for a list of members in your community. (Check the appendix for contact information.)

You can also ask other dog owners in your community about area trainers. Make sure you ask for information on training philosophy as well as results.

Do You Need a Behaviorist?

Most dog training and even most dog behavior issues can be managed with some combination of common sense, education—like reading this book—and the help of a training instructor.

But once in a while people run into problems with their dogs that require more sophisticated intervention. Here are some examples of issues that may require the help of a behavioral consultant:

+ Your dog growls, snaps, or gives you a stony stare when you touch him, stand over him, try to get him off a resting place, or get near his food or toys.

+ Your dog lunges at or chases, nips, or bites other people or animals.

+ Your dog seems unduly afraid of anything in the environment.

+ Anytime you feel stumped or overwhelmed by your dog's behavior.

When you select a behavior consultant, look for one who:

+ **Uses mostly reward-based training methods.**

+ **Sees your dog in person.** A phone-only consultation is not an effective way of evaluating your dog.

+ **Works with you and your dog.** Avoid trainers who ask you to board your dog with them to train—you need to learn how to work with your dog, and that won't happen if you aren't there.

✦ **Doesn't misrepresent credentials.**

✦ **Gives no guarantees.** Every dog is unique. Nobody can promise, in advance, that your dog can be completely cured of a problem or issue in a certain amount of time. An ethical behaviorist
acknowledges this and will focus more on how she will approach the problem.

To find a behavioral consultant, check the Internet and your phone
book, or contact a professional organization such as Animal Behavior
Associates, Inc., the College of Veterinary Behaviorists, or the American
Veterinary Society of Animal Behavior.

Your veterinarian or local Humane Society may also be able to refer
you to a behavioral consultant. As with trainers, you can learn about behavioral consultants by talking to other dog owners, too.

Professional trainers have seen lots of dogs—in action. They can
spot quirks in your dog's temperament and learning ability that a less experienced person would overlook.

Training classes can also give your dog a chance to practice obedience behaviors around other dogs—a highly distracting environment.
And many trainers can also steer you toward specialized classes, if
you're interested, including dog sports like agility and fly ball.

So take a look at what training opportunities are available in your
community. It's a great way to have fun with your dog.

Appendix

Terry Ryan

For more information on Terry's seminars and training classes, contact:

Legacy Canine
P.O. Box 3909
Sequim, WA 98302
360-683-1522
Terry@LegacyCanine.com
www.legacycanine.com

Dogs and Dog Breeds

American Kennel Club (AKC)
260 Madison Avenue
New York, NY 10016
212-696-8200
www.akc.org.

Further Reading

After You Get Your Puppy by Ian Dunbar. James and Kenneth Publishers, 2001.

Calming Signals: Visit the Turid Rugaas Web site at http://www.canis.no/rugaas/.

Click for Joy! Questions and Answers from Clicker Trainers and Their Dogs by Melissa C. Alexander and Robert Bailey. Sunshine Books, 2003.

Dogs: A Startling New Understanding of Canine Origin, Behavior and Evolution by Raymond Coppinger and Lorna Coppinger. Scribner, 2001.

Don't Shoot the Dog! The New Art of Teaching and Training by Karen Pryor. Bantam Books, 1999.

Excel-Erated Learning: Explaining in Plain English How Dogs Learn and How Best to Teach Them by Pamela J. Reid. James and Kenneth Publishers, 1996.

The Study of Instinct by Nikolaas Tinbergen. Oxford University Press (paperback reprint edition), 1991.

FOR PROFESSIONAL TRAINERS

Coaching People to Train Their Dogs: A Manual for Pet Dog Class Instruction by Terry Ryan. Legacy Canine Behavior and Training, Inc., 2005.

Head Collars

If you would like to try a training tool to help teach your dog to walk nicely on a leash, we recommend the Gentle Leader brand head collar, by Premier, 406 Branchway Road, Richmond, VA 23236. Phone 1-888-640-8840 (804-379-4702 in the Richmond, Virginia, area) or visit www.gentleleader.com. Gentle Leader head collars are also sold in many local pet supply stores and Internet-based pet supply stores.

Professional Dog Training and Canine Behaviorist Organizations

Animal Behavior Associates, Inc.
4994 South Independence Way
Littleton, CO 80123
303-932-9095
info@AnimalBehaviorAssociates.com

Association of Pet Dog Trainers (APDT)
5096 Sand Road SE
Iowa City, IA 52240-8217
1-800-PET-DOGS
information@apdt.com
www.apdt.com

National Association of Dog Obedience Instructors (NADOI)
PMB 369
729 Grapevine Highway
Hurst, TX 76054-2085
http://www.nadoi.org

INDEX

A

age, 9
aggression, 191–206
American Kennel Club (AKC), 4–5
animal shelters, 6, 8, 9, 41
anxiety, 166–68
appeasement, 204
attention, 25–26, 88–89, 158
Australian Cattle Dogs, 6
avoidance, 203–4

B

babies, 221–24
barking, 155
    anxiety and fear, 166–68
    causes of, 158–62
    densensitization, 168–70
    other people's dogs and, 231–32
    stress reduction, 170–71
    training for, 162–66
begging, 101
behavior, 99–100
    aggression, 191–206
    calm behavior, 103–6, 163–64
    distance, 114–16
    down, 110–11
    expectations, 100–102
    leash, 121–22, 124
    management, 102
    other people's dogs, 229–40
    resource guarding, 114
    self-control, 116–17
    sit, 106–10
    stay, 111–12
behaviorists, 265–66
bite inhibition, 29
biting, 18, 29, 100, 187–89
boredom, 66, 67–69, 160
breeds
    quirks of, 6
    temperament and, 4–9
bullying, 34–35

C

calm behavior, 103–6, 163-64
calming signals, 202–3
cause and effect, 53–54
certifications, 263–65
chew toys, 12, 70–72
chewing, 2, 61–62, 73–74

causes of, 66–69
directing behavior, 69–70
positive chewing, 72–73
puppies and, 62–66
toys, 71–72
children, 14, 207–9, 227
babies, 221–24
behavior of, 210–11
lessons for, 213–17
management and, 211–13
manners and, 217–18
resource guarding and, 209–10
school-aged, 224–26
socialization and, 219–21
supervision, 208–9
toddlers, 224
choke collars, 127–26
clicker training, 244–57
collars, 12, 127–26, 129
come, 92–94
commands
come, 92–94
down, 110–11
heel, 130–35
sit, 106–10
stay, 111–12
vs. cues, 108
communication, 196–203
control harnesses, 128
crates, 12, 45–47
older dogs, 49
puppies, 47–48
soiling of, 49–50

D
defensive aggression, 194–95
defensive barking, 159–60, 166–68
developmental stages, 26–29, 35–36
diet, 10–11

dishes, 11
distance, 112–16
dominance, 193
door manners, 82–84
down, 110–11

E
electric fences, 79–81
enthusiasm, 160
environment, 113, 163
excited urination, 56
exercise, 163
extinction bursts, 164–65

F
fear, 192–93
feeding, 39
fences, 78–81
fighting, 191–206
food, 10–11, 89–90, 101, 162–63
Foraging game, 39
Fox Terriers, 4–5
furniture, 2, 3

G
games, 37–39, 225–26
getting a dog, 1–3
choices, 3–9
supplies, 9–12
timing, 13
training, 13–14
Give and Take game, 38–39
greetings, 14, 100
grooming, 6
guard dogs, 174–75

H
Hand-feeding game, 39
handling, 30–31

harnesses, 128
head collars, 129
health
    aggression and, 194–95
    barking and, 162–63
    separation anxiety and, 152
heel, 130–35
Hide-and-Seek, 39
housetraining, 2, 8, 41–42
    accidents, 55–56
    cleaning up, 57–58
    crates and, 45–50
    excited urination, 56
    habits, 43–45
    rewards and, 51–55
    strategy, 42–43, 54
    submissive urination, 57
    tethering, 50

I
instincts, 17–19
intimidation, 21–22

K
Keep Away, 37

L
language, xii, 29-30
laws, 237–38
learning, 20–21
leash manners, 14, 119–20
    dog's perspective, 124–25
    loose leash, 125–26
    tools for, 127–29
    walking nicely, 121–22, 124
leashes, 12, 82, 120–21,
        238–40
lifestyle, 3
loose dogs, 233–34, 236–37

M
management, 44–45
manners, 99–100
    calm behavior and, 103–6
    children and, 217–18
    commands, 106–13
    door, 83–84
    expectations, 100–102
    leash, 119–35
    management of, 102
    other people's dogs, 235–36
    resource guarding, 114
    self-control, 116–17
    space and, 114–16
mischief, 144

N
neutering, 78–79
Newfoundlands, 5

O
offensive barking, 159
overfeeding, 11
ownership, 1–15

P
pack-facilitated aggression, 195
play time, 37–38
possessiveness, 193
predatory behavior, 195–96, 216–17
problem solving, xii, 18-19
prong collars, 126–28
protectiveness, 194
Pulis, 5
puppies, 25–26
    bite inhibition, 29
    chewing and, 62–66
    communication skills, 29–30
    developmental stages, 26–29, 35–36

housetraining, 47–48
leash walking, 129–30
other dogs and, 34–35
socialization, 30–33
training and, 36–39
veterinary visits, 33–34
puppy mills, 8–9

Q
quiet time, 101

R
reactions, 175–78
recall, 76–77, 85–87
    attention and, 88–89
    collars and, 90–91
    come cue, 92–94
    do's and don'ts, 96–97
    instincts and, 94–95
    practice, 95–96
redirected aggression, 195
relaxation, 101
rescue organizations, 5
resource guarding, 100, 114, 209–10
rewards, 21–22, 113
    chewing and, 72–73
    heel command and, 133–35
    hierarchy of, 122–24
    housetraining and, 51–55
    separation anxiety and, 150–51
    walking, 126–27

S
self-control, 116–17
self-rewarding behavior, 67–69
separation anxiety, 137–38, 153–54
    barking and, 161–62
    causes of, 151–53
    desensitization, 148–50

evaluation of, 138–39, 142–44
management of, 146–48
prevention of, 139–40
rewards and, 150–51
signs of, 145–46
training, 140–42
sit, 106–10
size, 5–6
slip collars, 128
social facilitation, 195
socialization, 29–30, 173–74
    biting and, 187–89
    children and, 207–27
    desensitization, 178–83
    dog's reactions, 175–78
    experiences, 32–33
    handling exercises, 30–31
    other dogs, 34–35, 191–206
    rewards and, 184–85
    training, 186–87
    veterinary visits, 33–34, 185–86
stay, 111–12
strangers, 7–8
stress, 66, 67–69
submission, 204
submissive urination, 57
supplies, 9–12

T
taste deterrents, 65, 68
temperament, 4–9, 23, 102
territorial aggression, 194
tethering, 50, 81–82
threatening behavior, 204–5
tie-outs, 81–82
timing, 13
toileting, 232–33
toys, 12, 70–72
training, 13–14

advanced, 241–43
aggression and, 198, 205–6
children and, 218–19
clicker, 244–57
Four D's, The, 112–13
future consequences, 20–21
instincts and, 17–19
other people's dogs, 229–40
prevention, 22–23, 25–26
puppies, 36–39
rewards *vs.* intimidation,
    21–22
trainers, 259–66
treats and, 19–20
training classes, 259–66
treats, 11, 19–20
tricks, 253–57

V

veterinarians, 33–34, 185–86

W

walking, 119–20
    barking and, 163
    behavior, 121–22, 124
    dog's perspective, 124–25
    heel command, 130–35
    leash types, 120–21
    loose leash and, 125–26
    puppies and, 129–30
    rewards, 126–27
    tools for leash training, 127–29
Welsh Corgis, 6

Y

yard time, 75–76
    fences, 78–81
    leashes, 82
    open doors, 82–84
    recall and, 76–77, 85–97
    tethering, 81–82